DOCTOR WHO
THE TWELFTH DOCTOR

TIME TRIALS VOL 1
THE TERROR BENEATH

"George Mann made it feel as though Peter Capaldi was running around the pages of this story! The art by Mariano Laclaustra was excellent throughout, as was the coloring by Carlos Cabrera."
NERDLY

"Exciting, fast-moving, funny and mysterious."
GEEK MOM

"Absolutely delightful."
THE GEEK GIRL PROJECT

"If you're a fan of Capaldi's Doctor, you should absolutely check this out!"
THE FANDOM POST

"Surprisingly fun!"
GAME 4 ME

"Perfect, enjoyable and intriguing!"
MCM BUZZ

"A smart, funny romp through the world of comic books. Absolutely recommended."
SCI FI PULSE

"Gives me the same sort of feeling I get settling in to watch an episode..."
WE THE NERDY

"If you're a fan of the show, you'll be a fan of this comic. And if you aren't a fan of the show, this comic may make you into one!"
KABOOOOOM

"The Twelfth Doctor's comic adventures are something insanely special!"
WARPED FACTOR

"Titan's Twelfth Doctor Who comics are everything that's good about comic books."
FANBOY NATION

TITAN COMICS

SENIOR COMICS EDITOR
Andrew James

COLLECTION EDITOR
Jessica Burton

ASSISTANT EDITORS
Amoona Saohin, Lauren Bowes
& Lauren McPhee

COLLECTION DESIGNER
Andrew Leung

TITAN COMICS EDITORIAL
Tom Williams, Jonathan Stevenson

PRODUCTION ASSISTANT
Natalie Bolger

PRODUCTION SUPERVISOR
Maria Pearson

PRODUCTION CONTROLLER
Peter James

**SENIOR PRODUCTION
CONTROLLER**
Jackie Flook

ART DIRECTOR
Oz Browne

SENIOR SALES MANAGER
Steve Tothill

PRESS OFFICER
Will O'Mullane

COMICS BRAND MANAGER
Chris Thompson

ADS & MARKETING ASSISTANT
Tom Miller

**DIRECT SALES &
MARKETING MANAGER**
Ricky Claydon

COMMERCIAL MANAGER
Michelle Fairlamb

HEAD OF RIGHTS
Jenny Boyce

PUBLISHING MANAGER
Darryl Tothill

PUBLISHING DIRECTOR
Chris Teather

OPERATIONS DIRECTOR
Leigh Baulch

EXECUTIVE DIRECTOR
Vivian Cheung

PUBLISHER
Nick Landau

Special thanks to Steven Moffat, Brian Minchin, Mandy Thwaites,
Matt Nicholls, James Dudley, Edward Russell, Derek Ritchie,
Scott Handcock, Kirsty Mullan, Kate Bush, Julia Nocciolino and
Ed Casey for their invaluable assistance.

BBC WORLDWIDE

**DIRECTOR OF
EDITORIAL GOVERNANCE**
Nicholas Brett

HEAD OF UK PUBLISHING
Chris Kerwin

**DIRECTOR OF CONSUMER
PRODUCTS AND PUBLISHING**
Andrew Moultrie

PUBLISHER
Mandy Thwaites

PUBLISHING CO-ORDINATOR
Eva Abramik

**For rights information
contact Jenny Boyce**
jenny.boyce@titanemail.com

**DOCTOR WHO: THE TWELFTH DOCTOR
TIME TRIALS VOL 1: THE TERROR BENEATH**
HB ISBN: 9781785860829 | SB ISBN: 9781785860836
Published by Titan Comics, a division of
Titan Publishing Group, Ltd. 144 Southwark Street, London, SE1 0UP.

A CIP catalogue record for this title is available from the British Library.
First edition: September 2017

10 9 8 7 6 5 4 3 2 1

Printed in China.

Titan Comics does not read or accept unsolicited
DOCTOR WHO submissions of ideas, stories or artwork.

BBC

DOCTOR WHO

THE TWELFTH DOCTOR

TIME TRIALS VOL 1
THE TERROR BENEATH

**WRITERS: GEORGE MANN &
JAMES PEATY**

**ARTISTS: MARIANO LACLAUSTRA
& WARREN PLEECE**

WITH FER CENTURION

**COLORISTS: CARLOS CABRERA,
HERNÁN CABRERA & HI-FI**

LETTERS: RICHARD STARKINGS AND
COMICRAFT'S JIMMY BETANCOURT

Titan
COMICS

BBC

BBC

DOCTOR WHO

THE TWELFTH DOCTOR

THE DOCTOR

Last of the Time Lords of Gallifrey. Never cruel or cowardly, he champions the oppressed across time and space. Even without a regular companion to show off to, the Doctor still manages to find adventure – and danger – wherever he goes!

HATTIE

A punk space-bassist rockstar, Hattie first met the Doctor on the futuristic space colony of the Twist, and proved herself to be a worthy co-adventurer! How has traveling with the Doctor influenced her musical career? The Doctor is going to check in and see how things are going...!

THE TARDIS

'Time and Relative Dimension in Space'. Bigger on the inside, this unassuming blue box is your ticket to unforgettable adventure! The Doctor likes to think he's in control, but more often than not, the TARDIS takes him where and when he needs to be...

PREVIOUSLY...

The Doctor is traveling on his own, making new friends – and enemies! – across time and space.

Now he's returning to the Twist, a giant human space colony in the far future, where the Doctor recently helped the humans and the native Foxkin learn to live in harmony. Last time he was there, he inspired bassist Hattie to greater musical heights – but how has she fared in the time since the Doctor saw her last?

When you've finished reading the collection, please email your thoughts to doctorwhocomic@titanemail.com

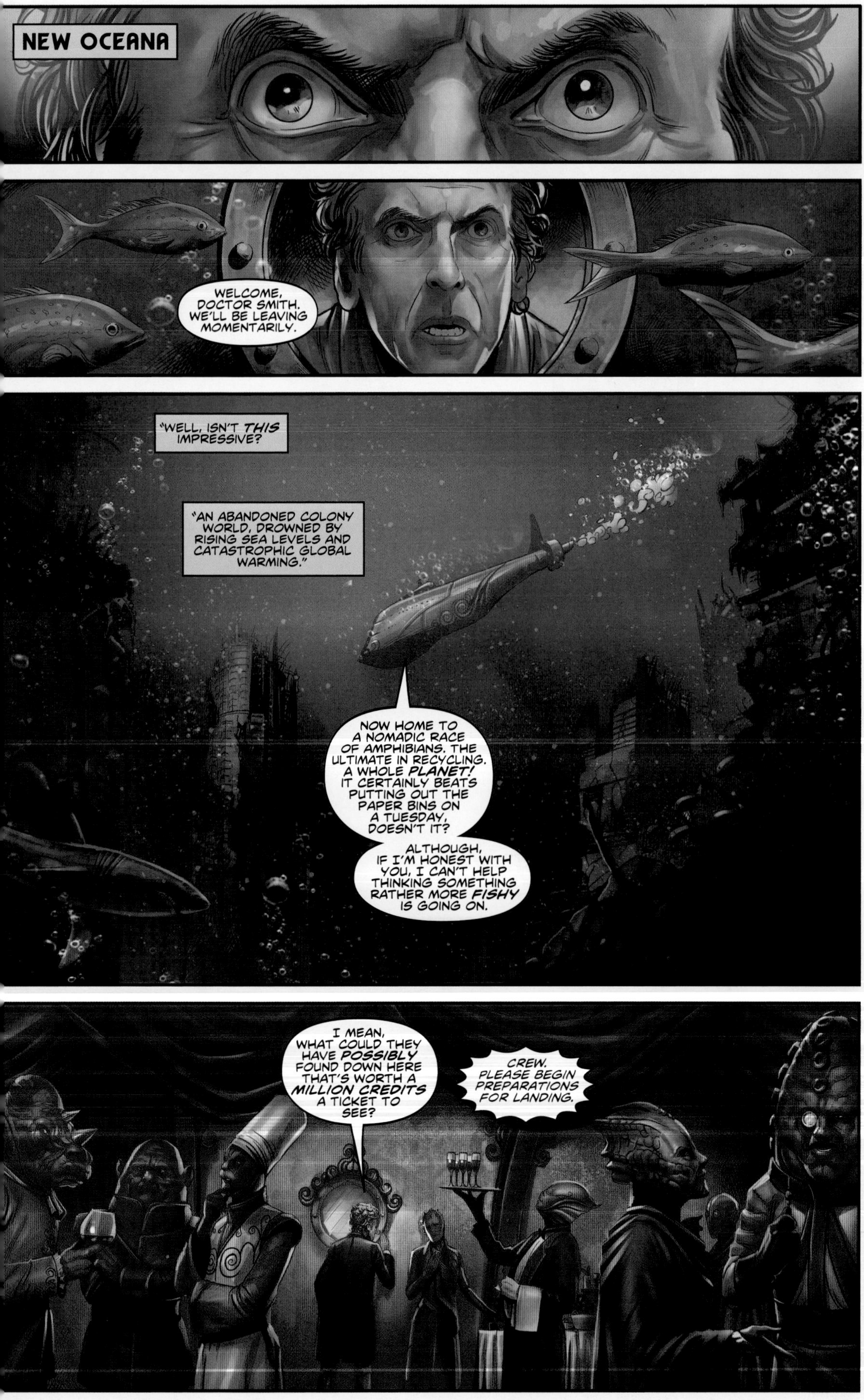
NEW OCEANA
WELCOME, DOCTOR SMITH. WE'LL BE LEAVING MOMENTARILY.
"WELL, ISN'T THIS IMPRESSIVE?
"AN ABANDONED COLONY WORLD, DROWNED BY RISING SEA LEVELS AND CATASTROPHIC GLOBAL WARMING."
NOW HOME TO A NOMADIC RACE OF AMPHIBIANS. THE ULTIMATE IN RECYCLING. A WHOLE PLANET! IT CERTAINLY BEATS PUTTING OUT THE PAPER BINS ON A TUESDAY, DOESN'T IT?
ALTHOUGH, IF I'M HONEST WITH YOU, I CAN'T HELP THINKING SOMETHING RATHER MORE FISHY IS GOING ON.
I MEAN, WHAT COULD THEY HAVE POSSIBLY FOUND DOWN HERE THAT'S WORTH A MILLION CREDITS A TICKET TO SEE?
CREW. PLEASE BEGIN PREPARATIONS FOR LANDING.

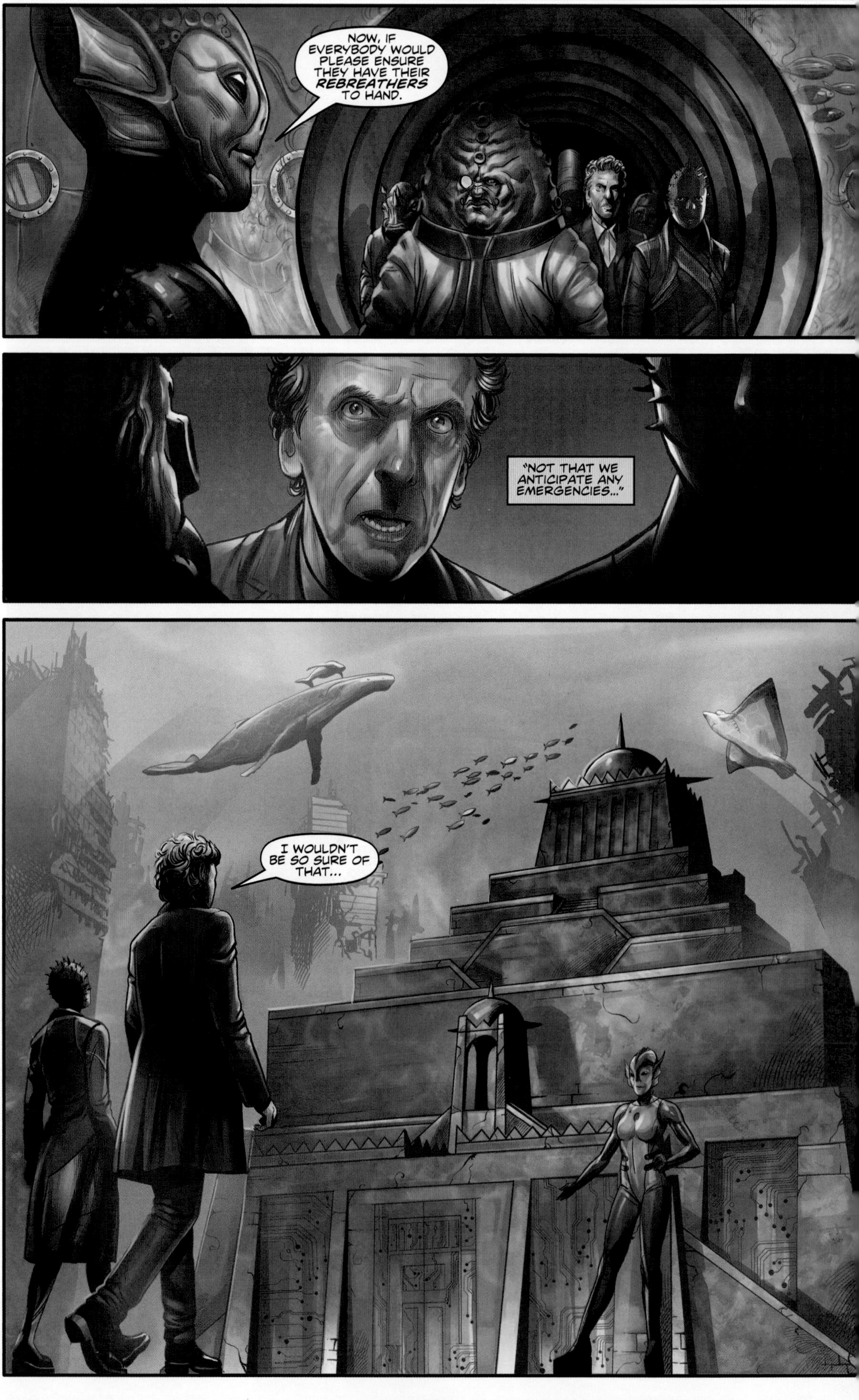

NOW, IF EVERYBODY WOULD PLEASE ENSURE THEY HAVE THEIR *REBREATHERS* TO HAND.
"NOT THAT WE ANTICIPATE ANY EMERGENCIES..."
I WOULDN'T BE SO SURE OF THAT...

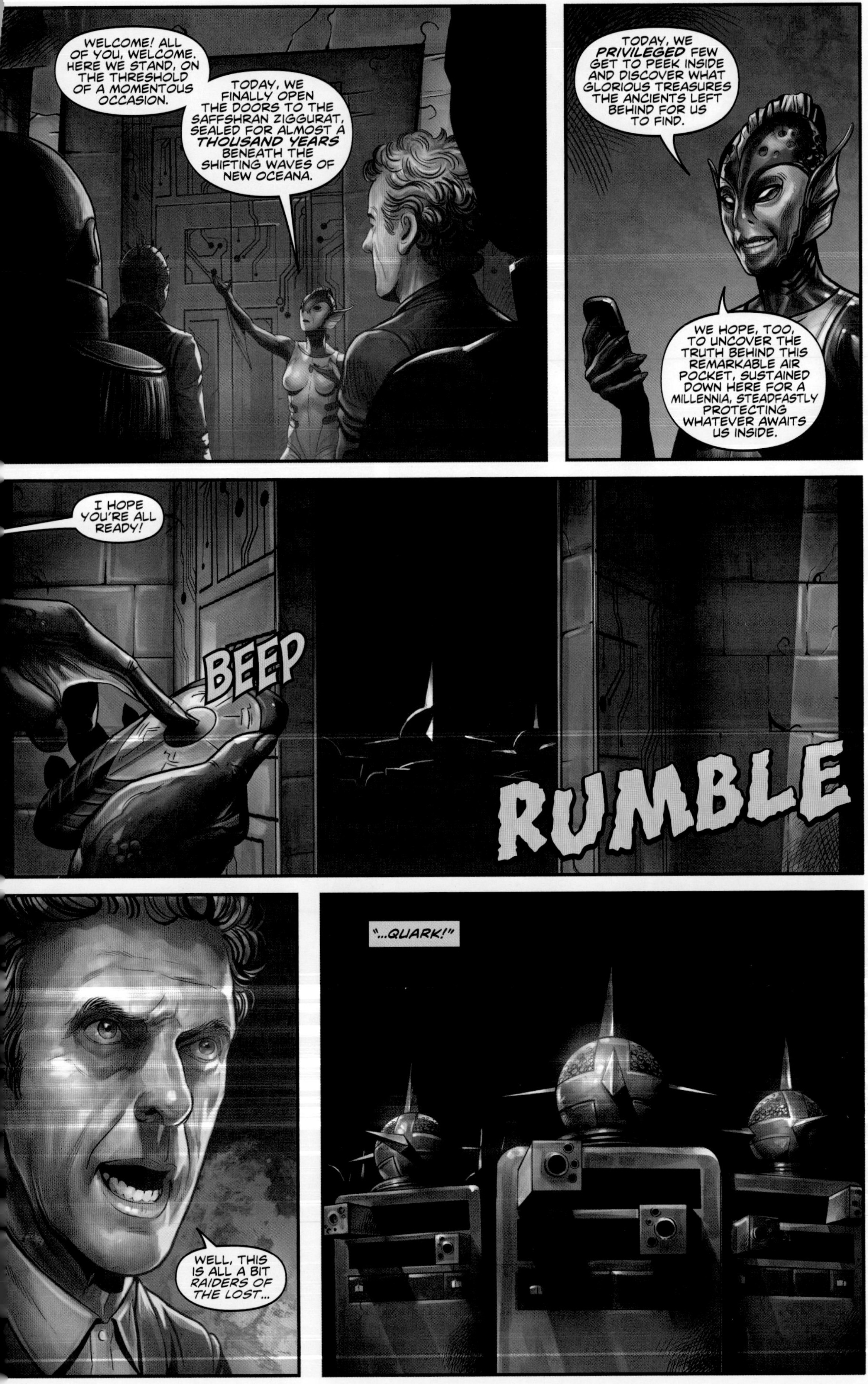
WELCOME! ALL OF YOU, WELCOME. HERE WE STAND, ON THE THRESHOLD OF A MOMENTOUS OCCASION.
TODAY, WE FINALLY OPEN THE DOORS TO THE SAFFSHRAN ZIGGURAT, SEALED FOR ALMOST A THOUSAND YEARS BENEATH THE SHIFTING WAVES OF NEW OCEANA.
TODAY, WE PRIVILEGED FEW GET TO PEEK INSIDE AND DISCOVER WHAT GLORIOUS TREASURES THE ANCIENTS LEFT BEHIND FOR US TO FIND.
WE HOPE, TOO, TO UNCOVER THE TRUTH BEHIND THIS REMARKABLE AIR POCKET, SUSTAINED DOWN HERE FOR A MILLENNIA, STEADFASTLY PROTECTING WHATEVER AWAITS US INSIDE.
I HOPE YOU'RE ALL READY!
BEEP
RUMBLE
WELL, THIS IS ALL A BIT RAIDERS OF THE LOST...
"...QUARK!"

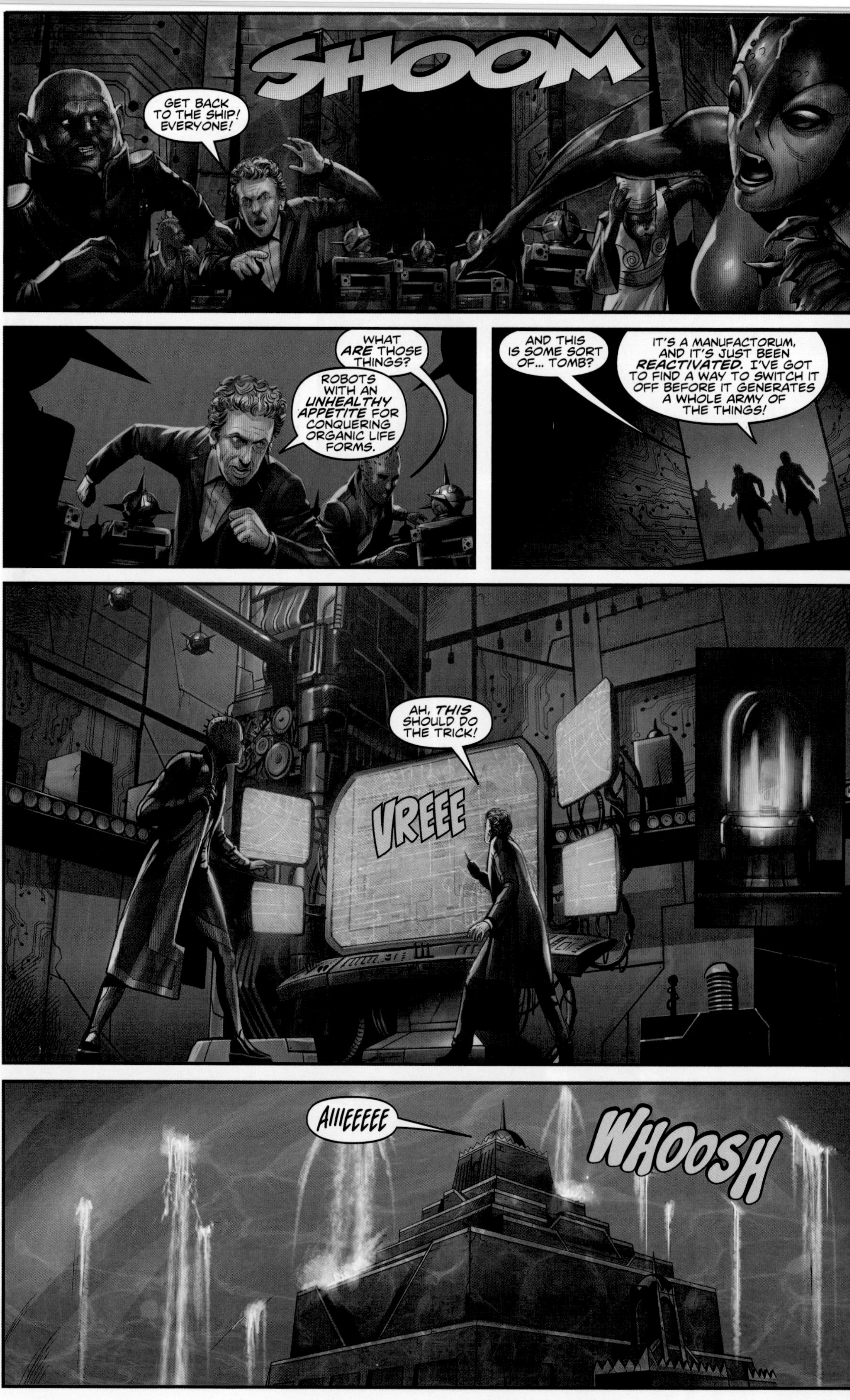
SHOOM
GET BACK TO THE SHIP! EVERYONE!
WHAT ARE THOSE THINGS?
ROBOTS WITH AN UNHEALTHY APPETITE FOR CONQUERING ORGANIC LIFE FORMS.
AND THIS IS SOME SORT OF... TOMB?
IT'S A MANUFACTORUM, AND IT'S JUST BEEN REACTIVATED. I'VE GOT TO FIND A WAY TO SWITCH IT OFF BEFORE IT GENERATES A WHOLE ARMY OF THE THINGS!
AH, THIS SHOULD DO THE TRICK!
VREEE
AIIIEEEEE
WHOOSH

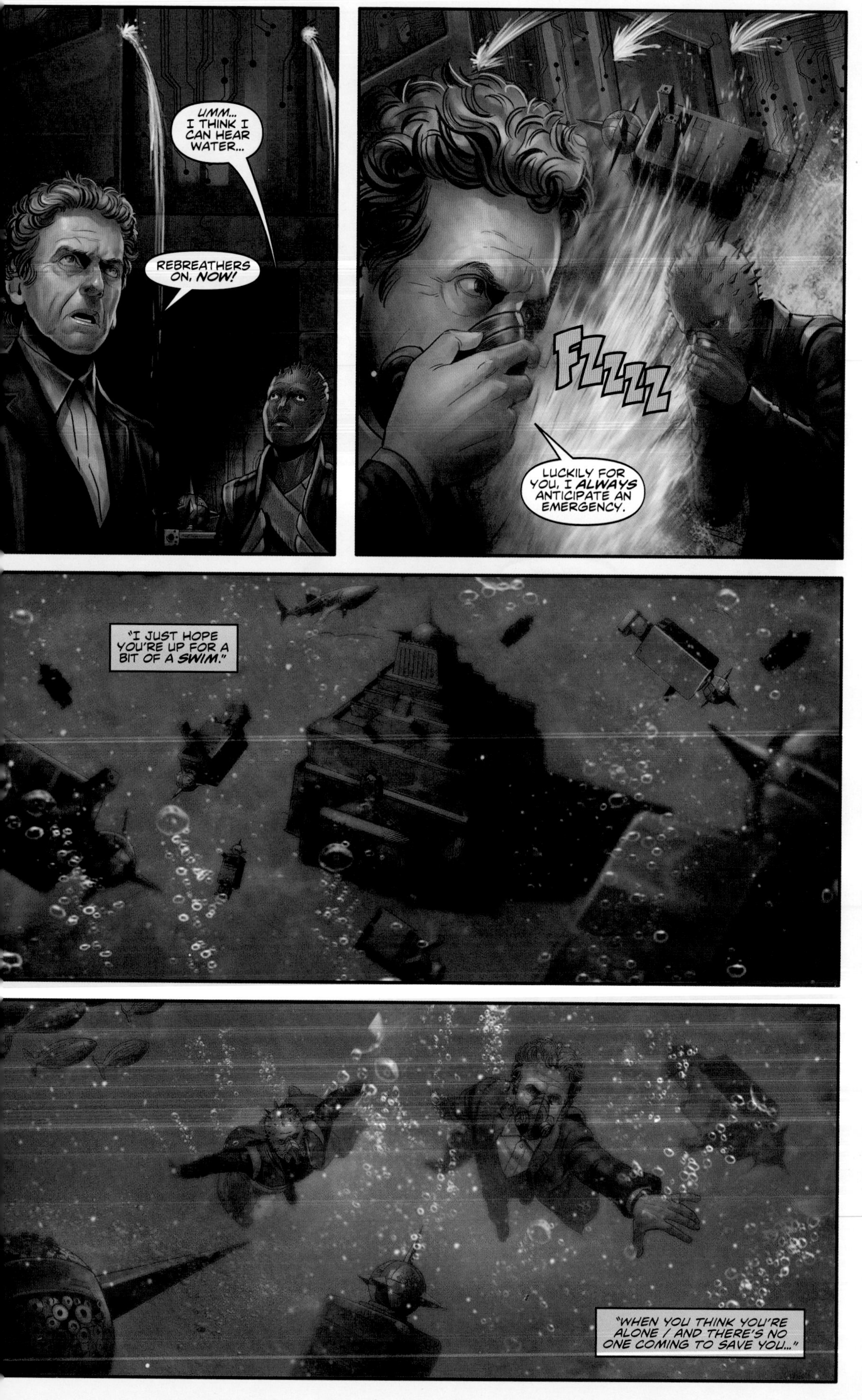
UMM... I THINK I CAN HEAR WATER...
REBREATHERS ON, *NOW!*
FZZZZ
LUCKILY FOR YOU, I *ALWAYS* ANTICIPATE AN EMERGENCY.
"I JUST HOPE YOU'RE UP FOR A BIT OF A *SWIM*."
"WHEN YOU THINK YOU'RE ALONE / AND THERE'S NO ONE COMING TO SAVE YOU..."

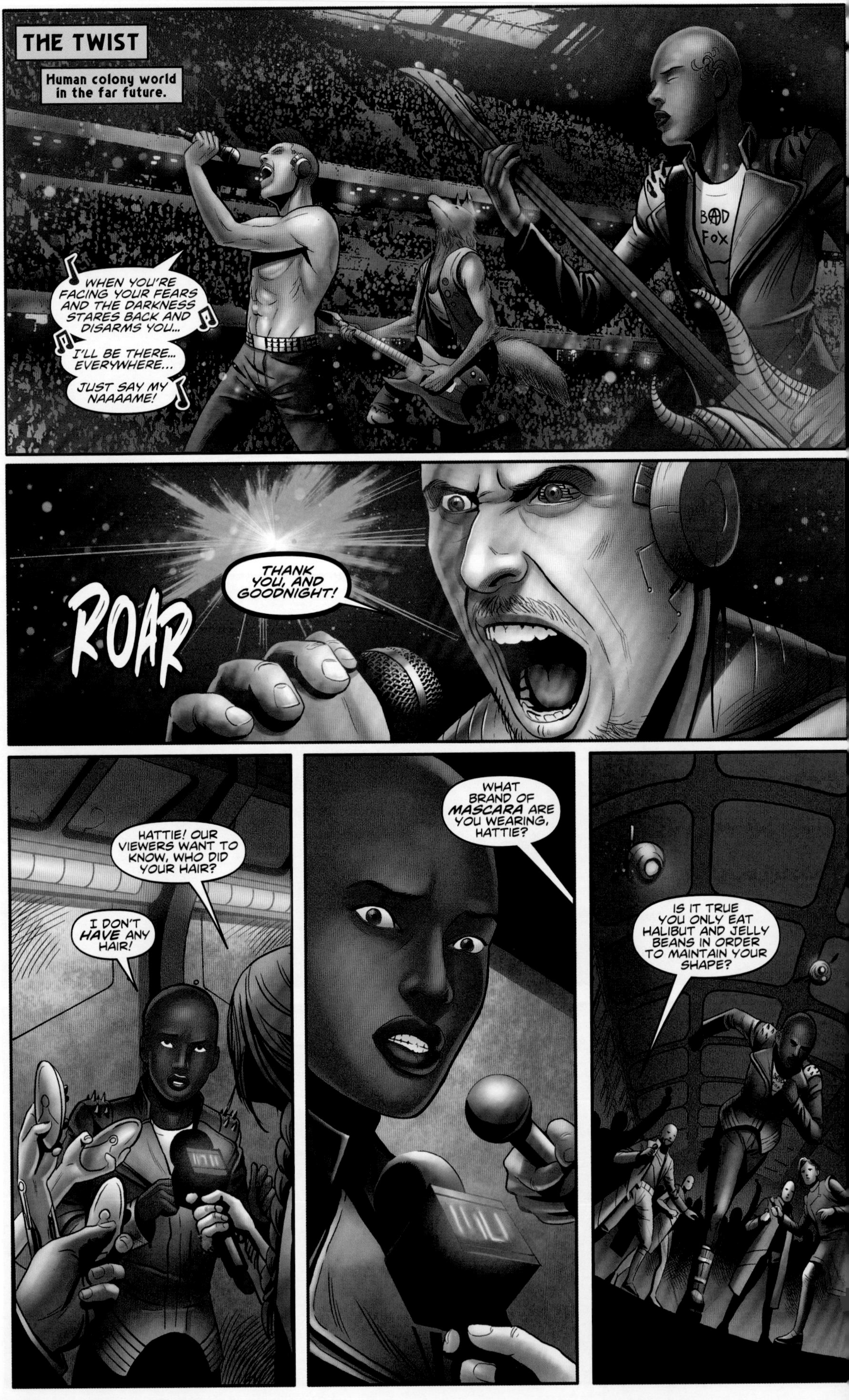
THE TWIST
Human colony world in the far future.
WHEN YOU'RE FACING YOUR FEARS AND THE DARKNESS STARES BACK AND DISARMS YOU...
I'LL BE THERE... EVERYWHERE...
JUST SAY MY NAAAAME!
BAD FOX
ROAR
THANK YOU, AND GOODNIGHT!
HATTIE! OUR VIEWERS WANT TO KNOW, WHO DID YOUR HAIR?
I DON'T HAVE ANY HAIR!
WHAT BRAND OF MASCARA ARE YOU WEARING, HATTIE?
IS IT TRUE YOU ONLY EAT HALIBUT AND JELLY BEANS IN ORDER TO MAINTAIN YOUR SHAPE?

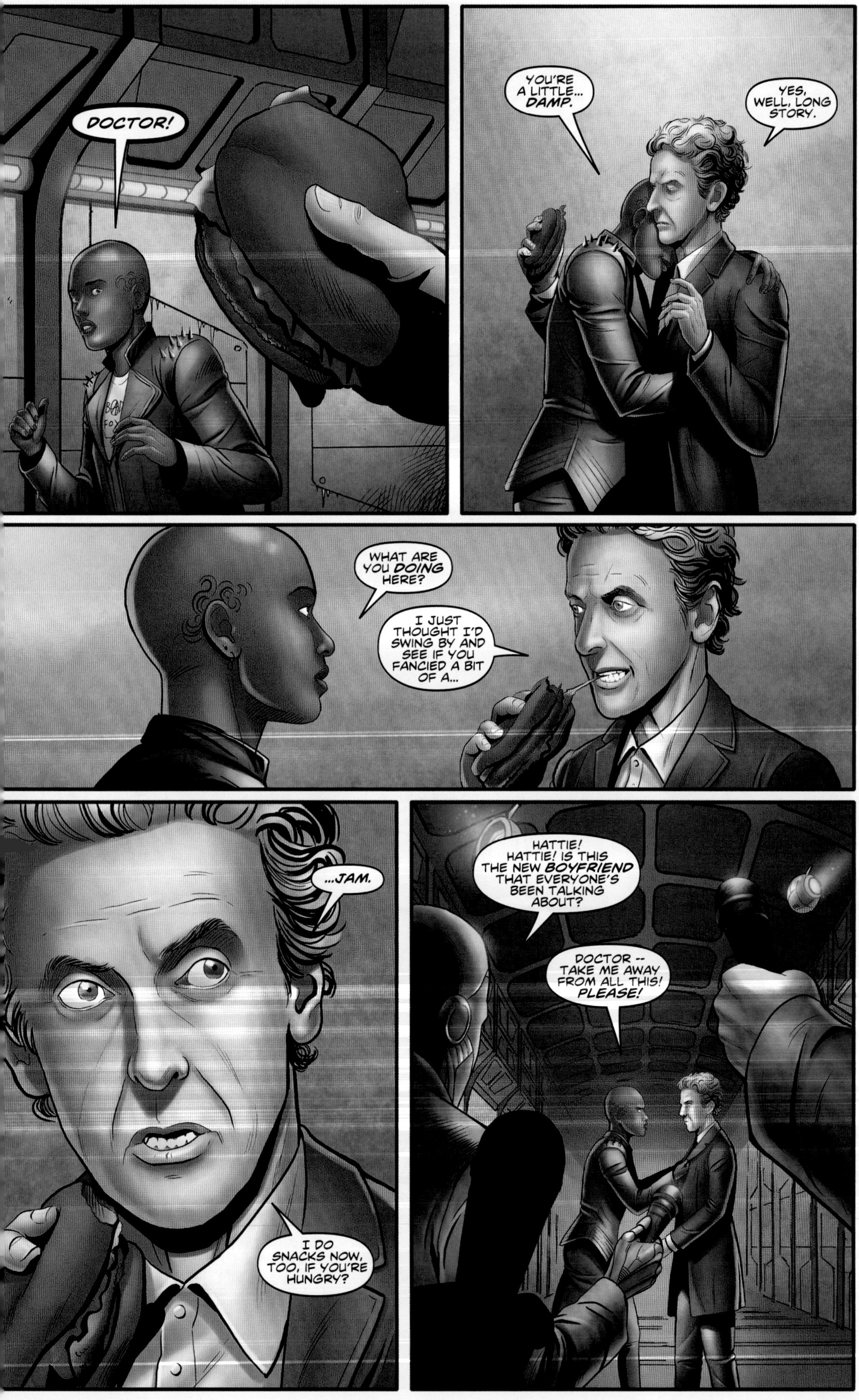
DOCTOR!
YOU'RE A LITTLE... DAMP.
YES, WELL, LONG STORY.
WHAT ARE YOU DOING HERE?
I JUST THOUGHT I'D SWING BY AND SEE IF YOU FANCIED A BIT OF A...
...JAM.
I DO SNACKS NOW, TOO, IF YOU'RE HUNGRY?
HATTIE! HATTIE! IS THIS THE NEW BOYFRIEND THAT EVERYONE'S BEEN TALKING ABOUT?
DOCTOR -- TAKE ME AWAY FROM ALL THIS! PLEASE!

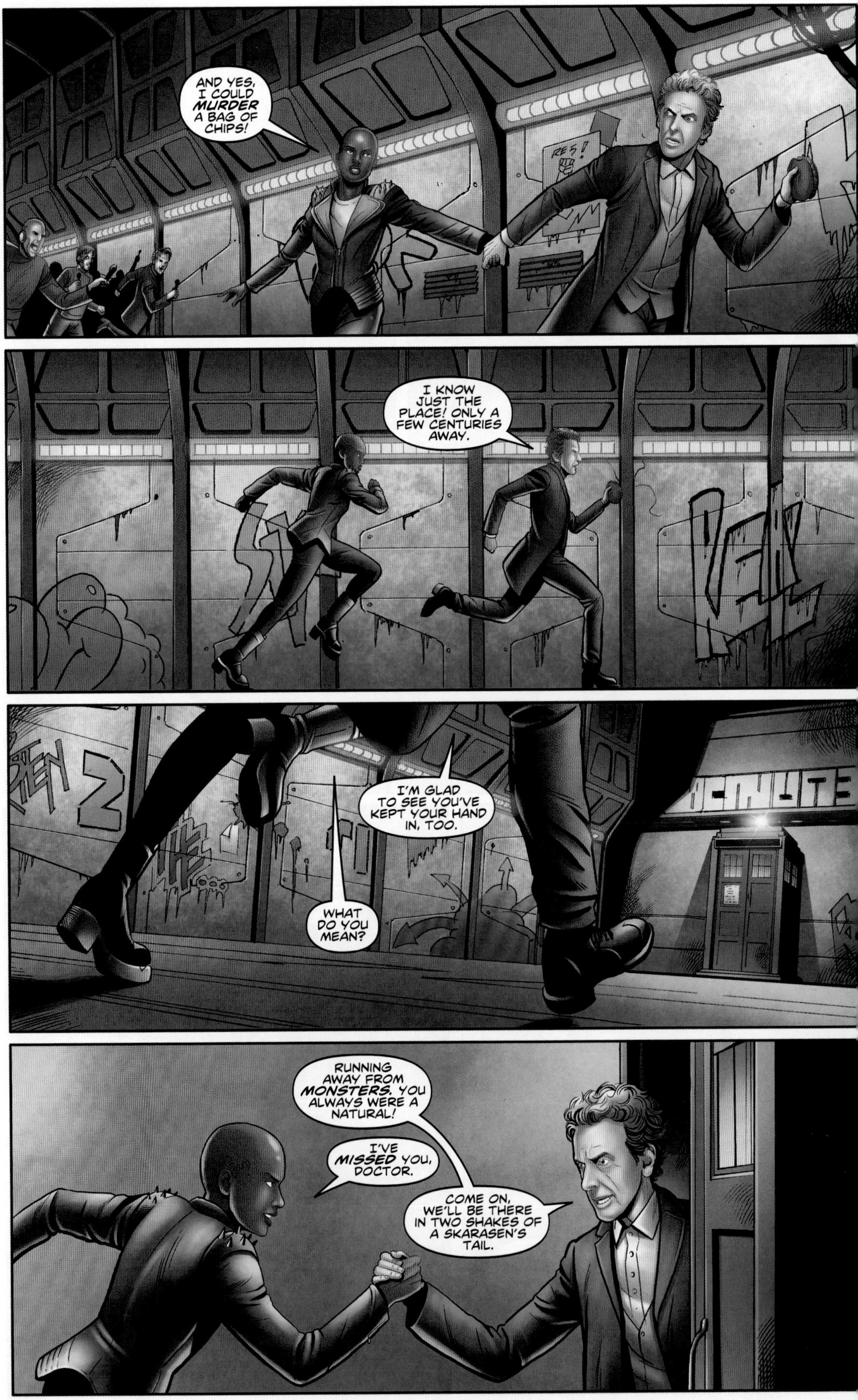
AND YES, I COULD MURDER A BAG OF CHIPS!
I KNOW JUST THE PLACE! ONLY A FEW CENTURIES AWAY.
I'M GLAD TO SEE YOU'VE KEPT YOUR HAND IN, TOO.
WHAT DO YOU MEAN?
RUNNING AWAY FROM MONSTERS. YOU ALWAYS WERE A NATURAL!
I'VE MISSED YOU, DOCTOR.
COME ON, WE'LL BE THERE IN TWO SHAKES OF A SKARASEN'S TAIL.

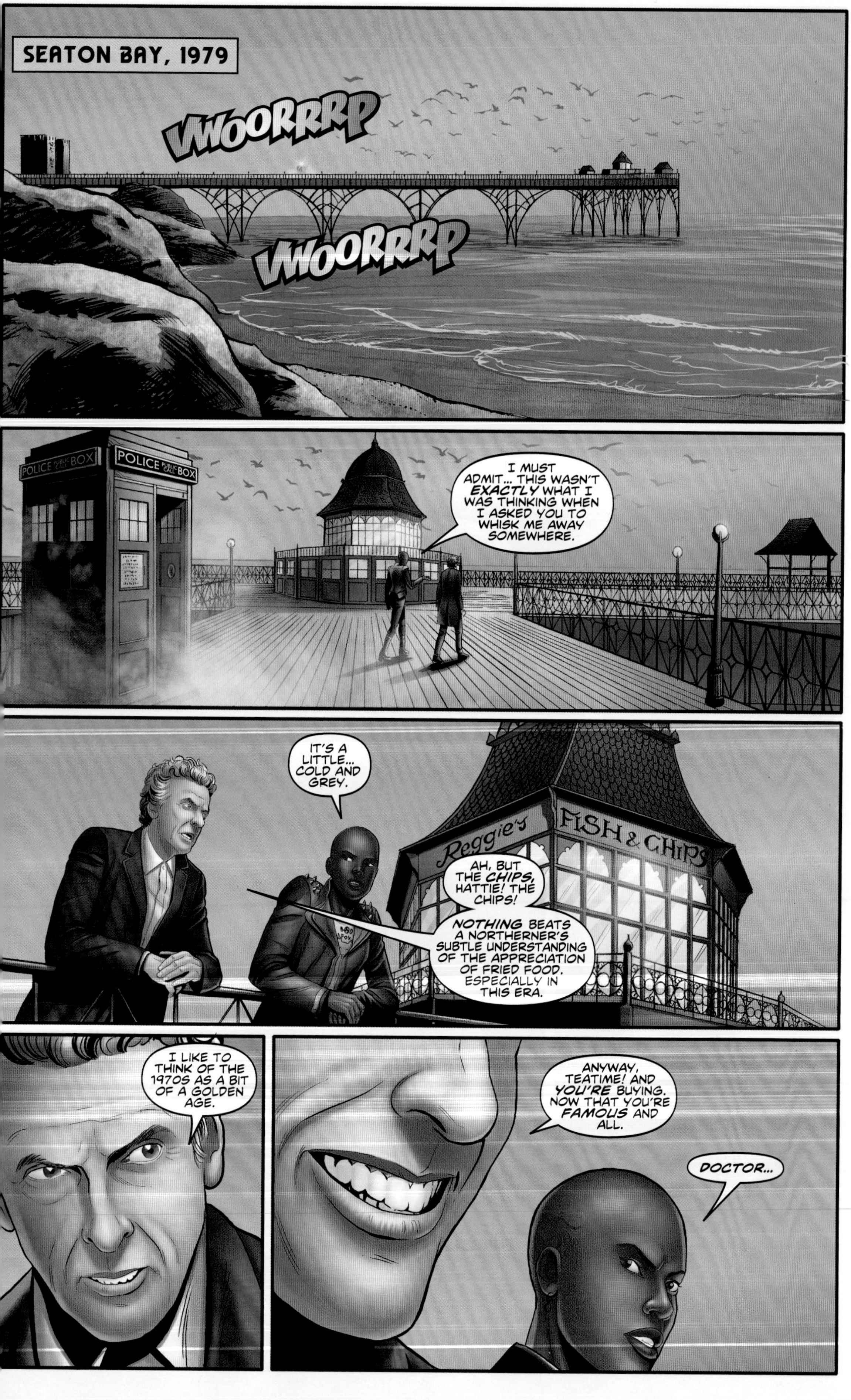
SEATON BAY, 1979
VWOORRRP
VWOORRRP
POLICE PUBLIC CALL BOX
I MUST ADMIT... THIS WASN'T EXACTLY WHAT I WAS THINKING WHEN I ASKED YOU TO WHISK ME AWAY SOMEWHERE.
IT'S A LITTLE... COLD AND GREY.
Reggie's FISH & CHIPS
AH, BUT THE CHIPS, HATTIE! THE CHIPS!
NOTHING BEATS A NORTHERNER'S SUBTLE UNDERSTANDING OF THE APPRECIATION OF FRIED FOOD. ESPECIALLY IN THIS ERA.
I LIKE TO THINK OF THE 1970S AS A BIT OF A GOLDEN AGE.
ANYWAY, TEATIME! AND YOU'RE BUYING. NOW THAT YOU'RE FAMOUS AND ALL.
DOCTOR...

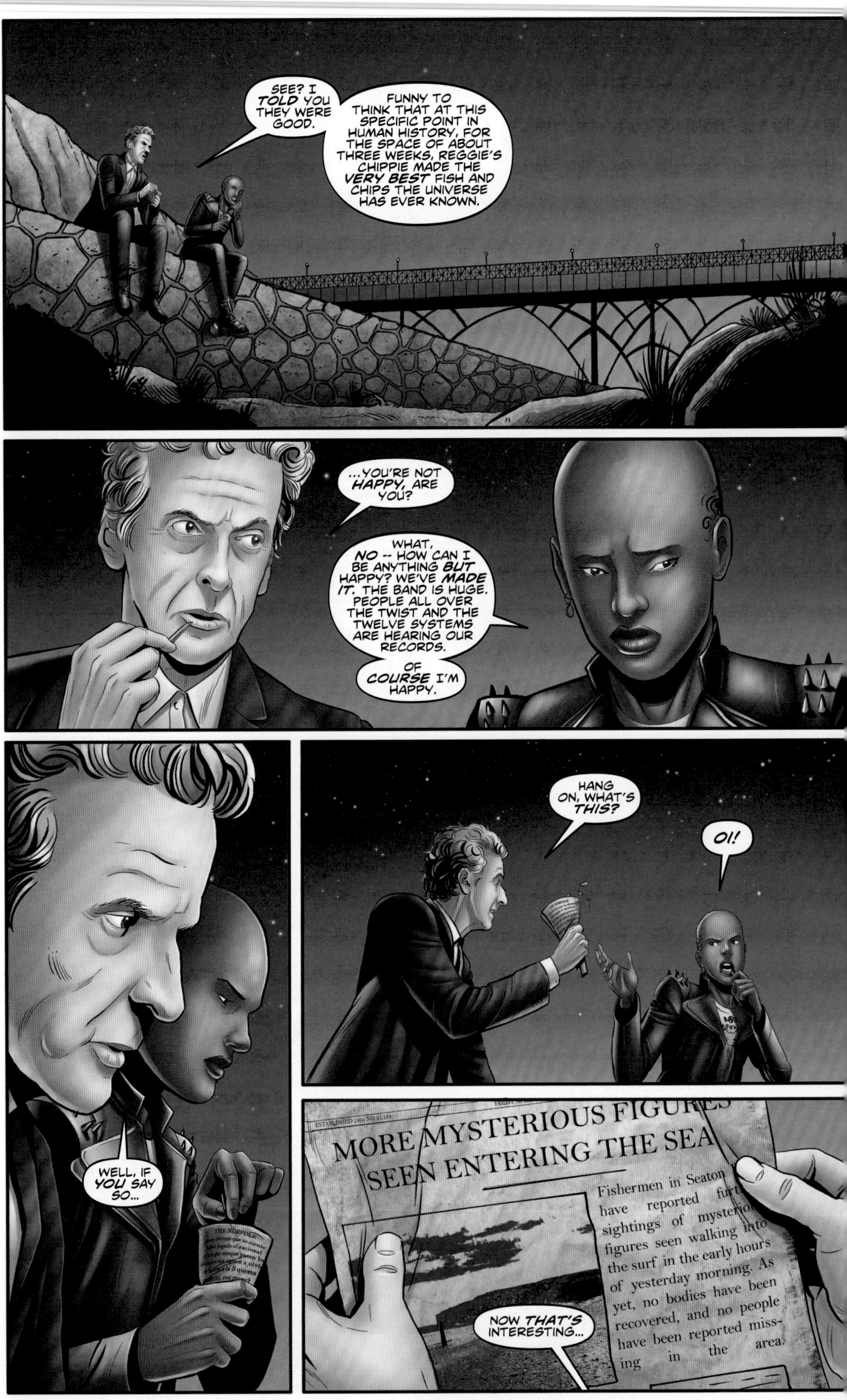
SEE? I TOLD YOU THEY WERE GOOD.
FUNNY TO THINK THAT AT THIS SPECIFIC POINT IN HUMAN HISTORY, FOR THE SPACE OF ABOUT THREE WEEKS, REGGIE'S CHIPPIE MADE THE VERY BEST FISH AND CHIPS THE UNIVERSE HAS EVER KNOWN.
...YOU'RE NOT HAPPY, ARE YOU?
WHAT, NO -- HOW CAN I BE ANYTHING BUT HAPPY? WE'VE MADE IT. THE BAND IS HUGE. PEOPLE ALL OVER THE TWIST AND THE TWELVE SYSTEMS ARE HEARING OUR RECORDS.
OF COURSE I'M HAPPY.
WELL, IF YOU SAY SO...
HANG ON, WHAT'S THIS?
OI!
MORE MYSTERIOUS FIGURES
SEEN ENTERING THE SEA
Fishermen in Seaton
have reported furt
sightings of mysterio
figures seen walking into
the surf in the early hours
of yesterday morning. As
yet, no bodies have been
recovered, and no people
have been reported miss-
ing in the area.
NOW THAT'S INTERESTING...

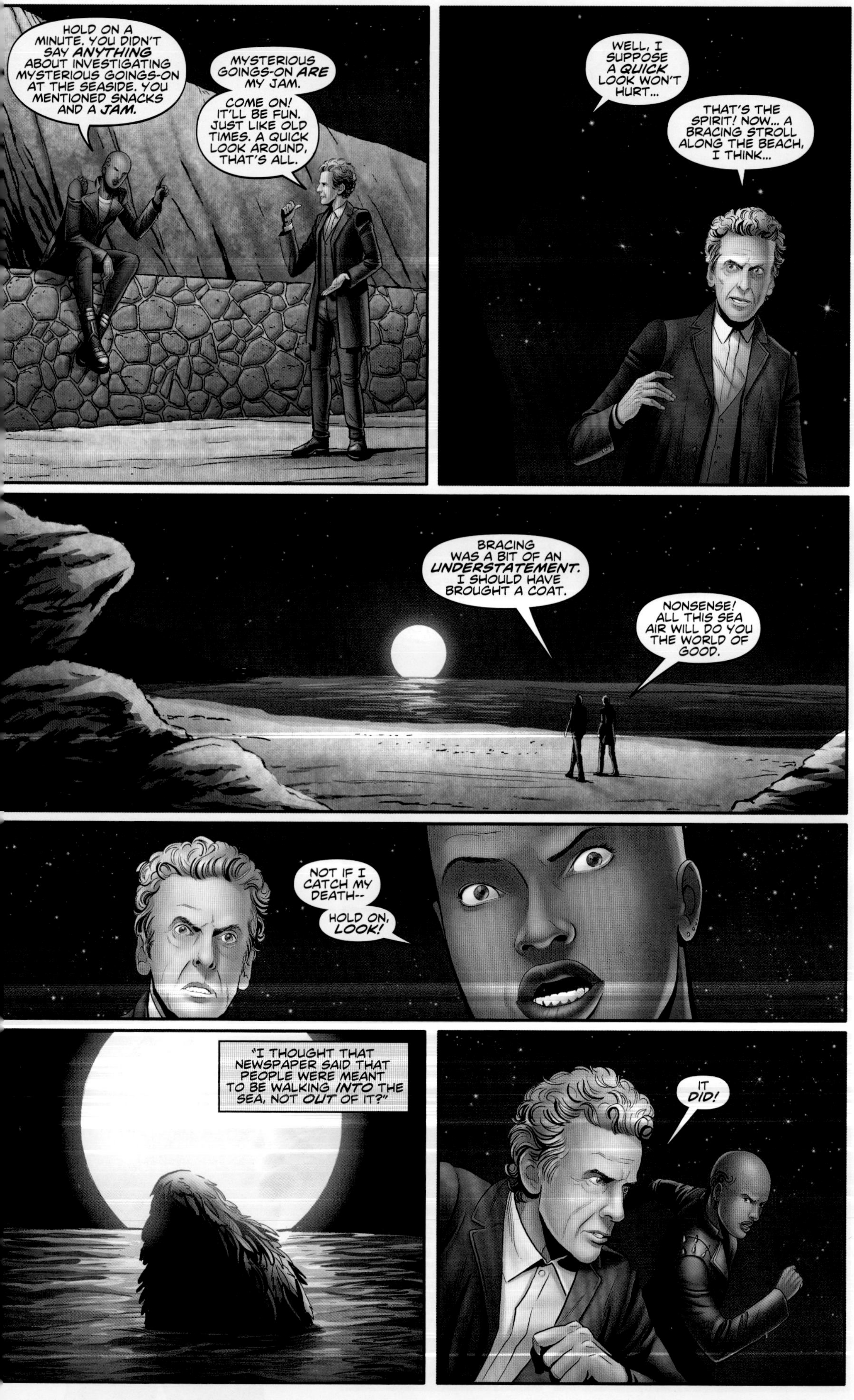
HOLD ON A MINUTE. YOU DIDN'T SAY ANYTHING ABOUT INVESTIGATING MYSTERIOUS GOINGS-ON AT THE SEASIDE. YOU MENTIONED SNACKS AND A JAM.
MYSTERIOUS GOINGS-ON ARE MY JAM.
COME ON! IT'LL BE FUN. JUST LIKE OLD TIMES. A QUICK LOOK AROUND, THAT'S ALL.
WELL, I SUPPOSE A QUICK LOOK WON'T HURT...
THAT'S THE SPIRIT! NOW... A BRACING STROLL ALONG THE BEACH, I THINK...
BRACING WAS A BIT OF AN UNDERSTATEMENT. I SHOULD HAVE BROUGHT A COAT.
NONSENSE! ALL THIS SEA AIR WILL DO YOU THE WORLD OF GOOD.
NOT IF I CATCH MY DEATH--
HOLD ON, LOOK!
"I THOUGHT THAT NEWSPAPER SAID THAT PEOPLE WERE MEANT TO BE WALKING INTO THE SEA, NOT OUT OF IT?"
IT DID!

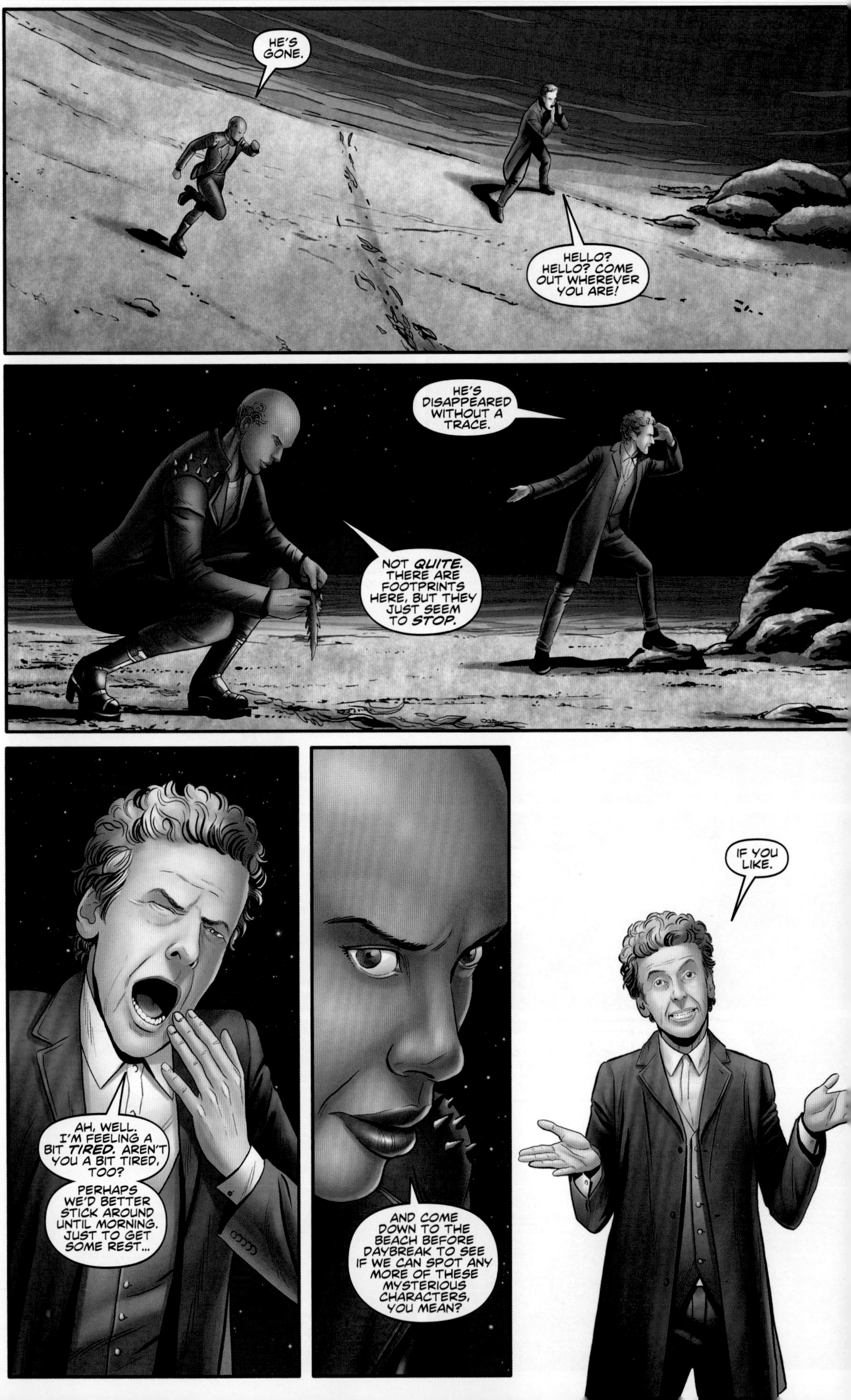
HE'S GONE.
HELLO? HELLO? COME OUT WHEREVER YOU ARE!
HE'S DISAPPEARED WITHOUT A TRACE.
NOT *QUITE.* THERE ARE FOOTPRINTS HERE, BUT THEY JUST SEEM TO *STOP.*
AH, WELL. I'M FEELING A BIT *TIRED.* AREN'T YOU A BIT TIRED, TOO?
PERHAPS WE'D BETTER STICK AROUND UNTIL MORNING. JUST TO GET SOME REST...
AND COME DOWN TO THE BEACH BEFORE DAYBREAK TO SEE IF WE CAN SPOT ANY MORE OF THESE MYSTERIOUS CHARACTERS, YOU MEAN?
IF YOU LIKE.

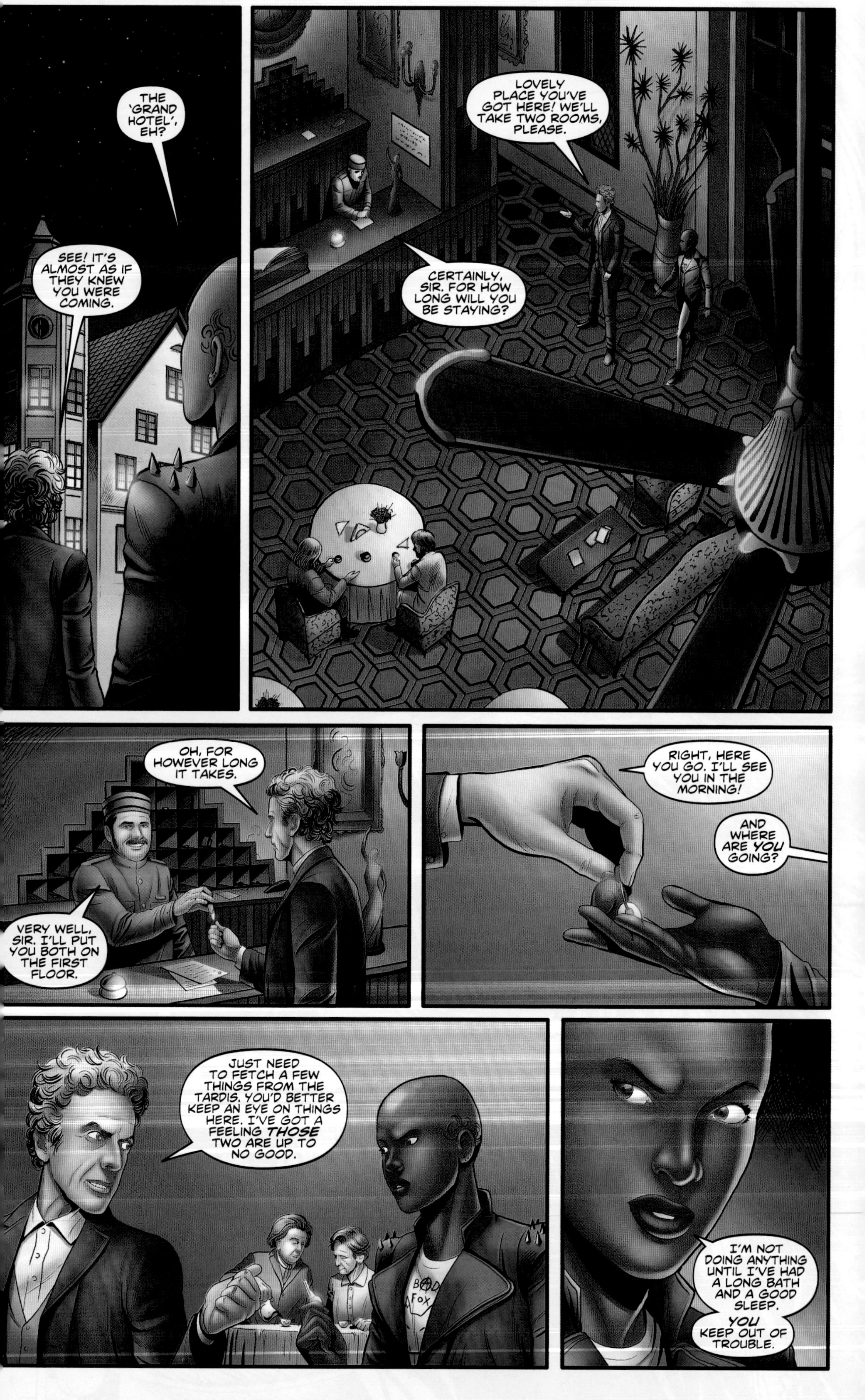
THE 'GRAND HOTEL', EH?
SEE! IT'S ALMOST AS IF THEY KNEW YOU WERE COMING.
LOVELY PLACE YOU'VE GOT HERE! WE'LL TAKE TWO ROOMS, PLEASE.
CERTAINLY, SIR. FOR HOW LONG WILL YOU BE STAYING?
OH, FOR HOWEVER LONG IT TAKES.
VERY WELL, SIR. I'LL PUT YOU BOTH ON THE FIRST FLOOR.
RIGHT, HERE YOU GO. I'LL SEE YOU IN THE MORNING!
AND WHERE ARE YOU GOING?
JUST NEED TO FETCH A FEW THINGS FROM THE TARDIS. YOU'D BETTER KEEP AN EYE ON THINGS HERE. I'VE GOT A FEELING THOSE TWO ARE UP TO NO GOOD.
I'M NOT DOING ANYTHING UNTIL I'VE HAD A LONG BATH AND A GOOD SLEEP. YOU KEEP OUT OF TROUBLE.

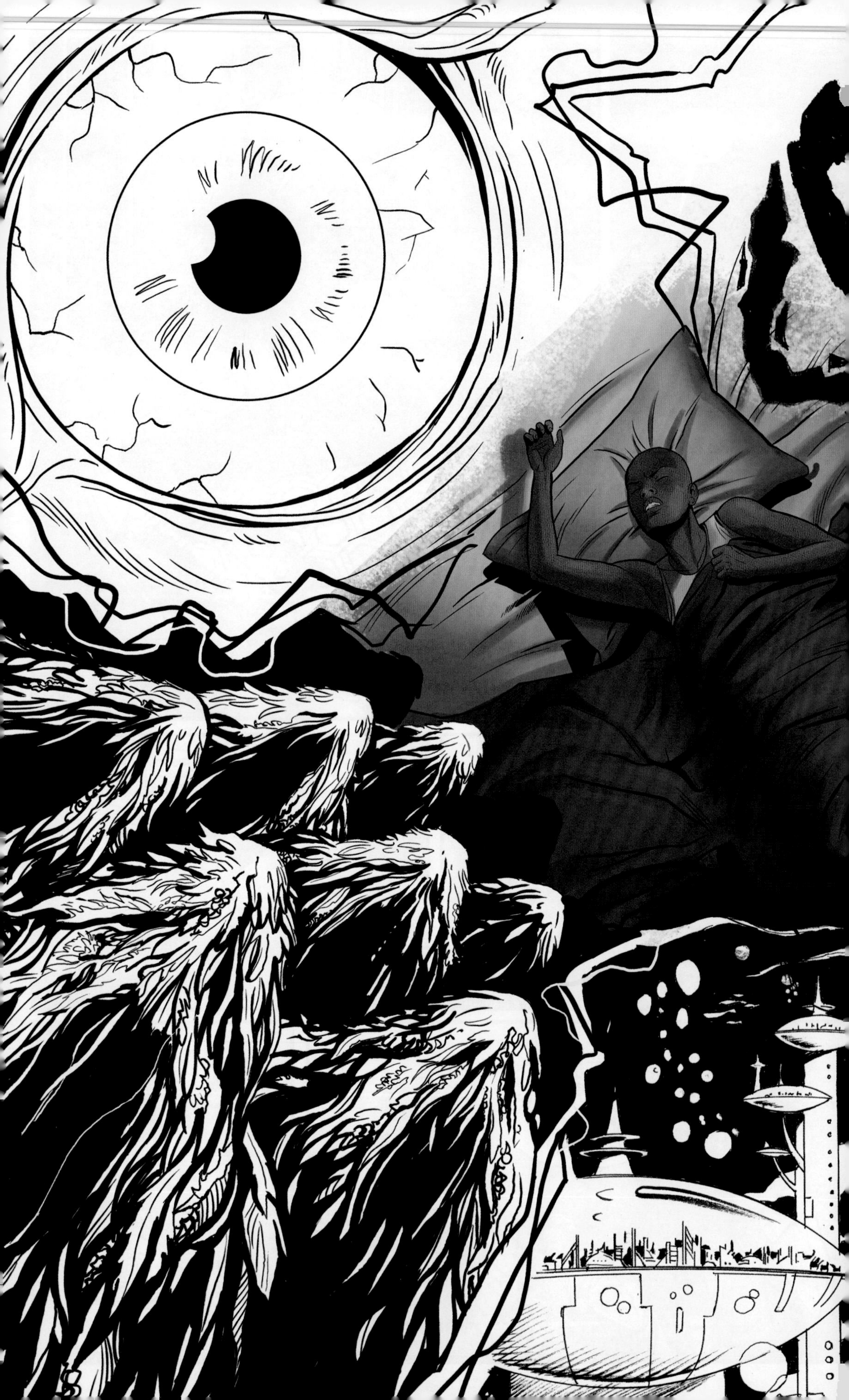

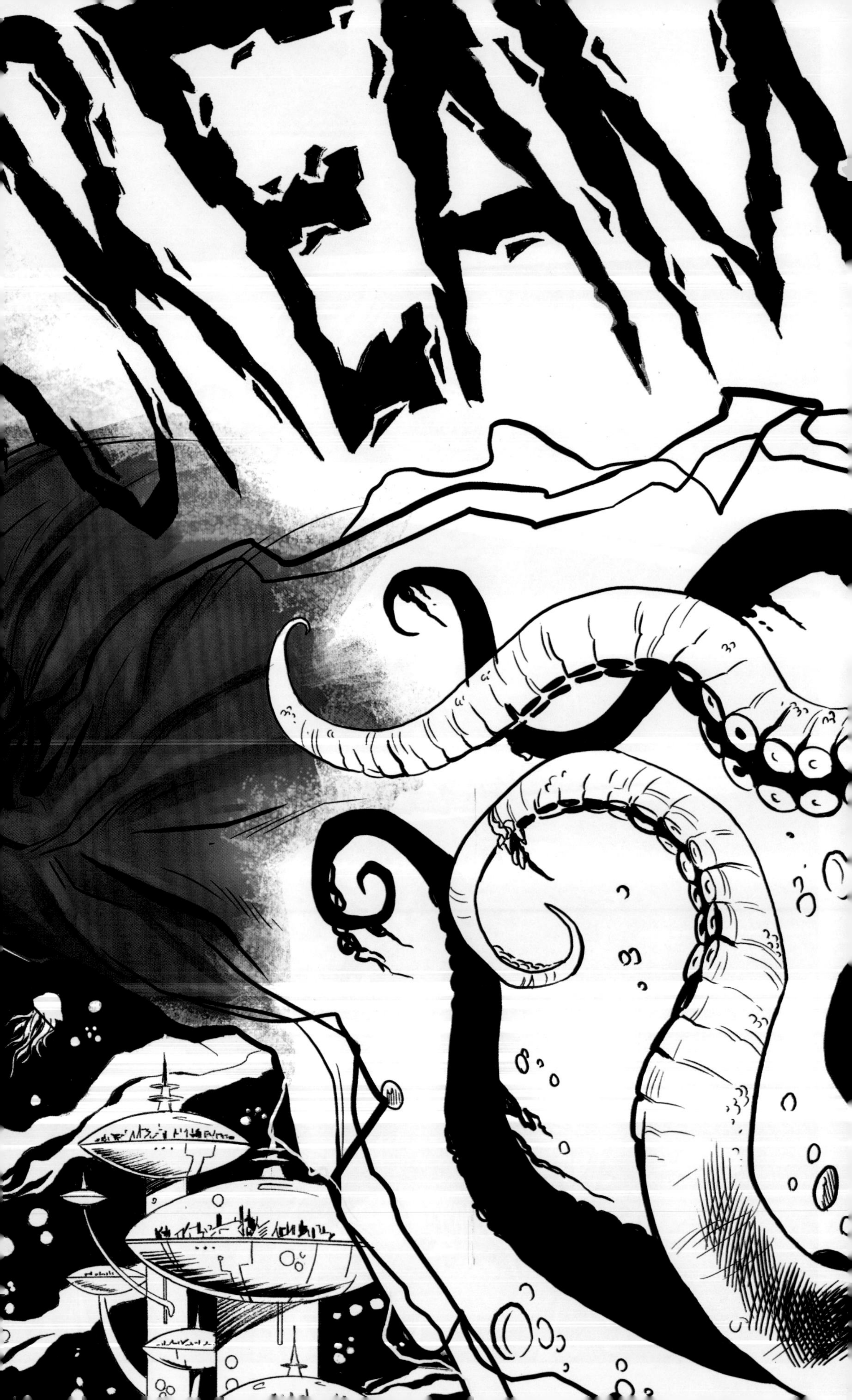

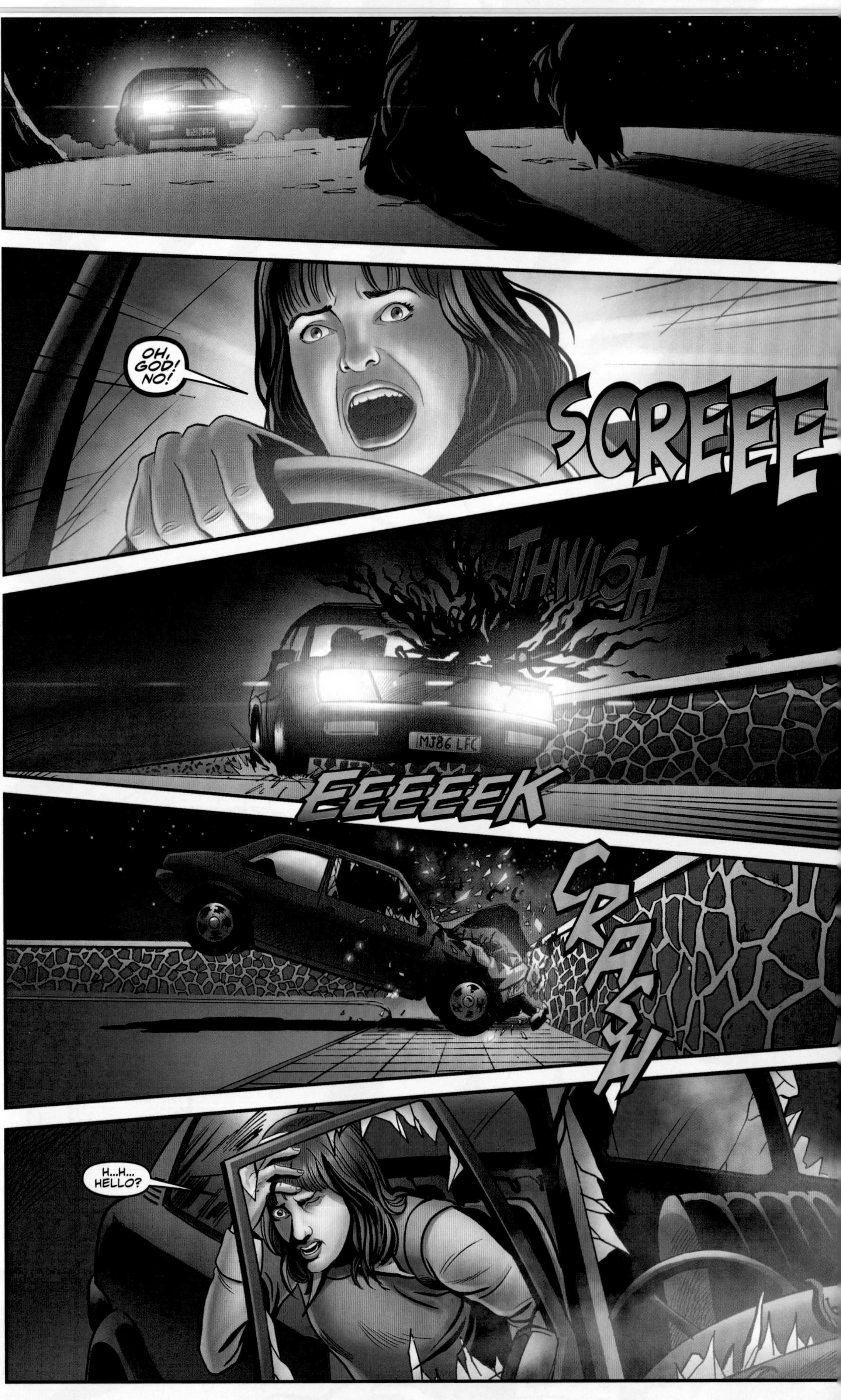
OH, GOD! NO!
SCREEE
THWISH
MJ86 LFC
EEEEEK
CRASH
H...H... HELLO?

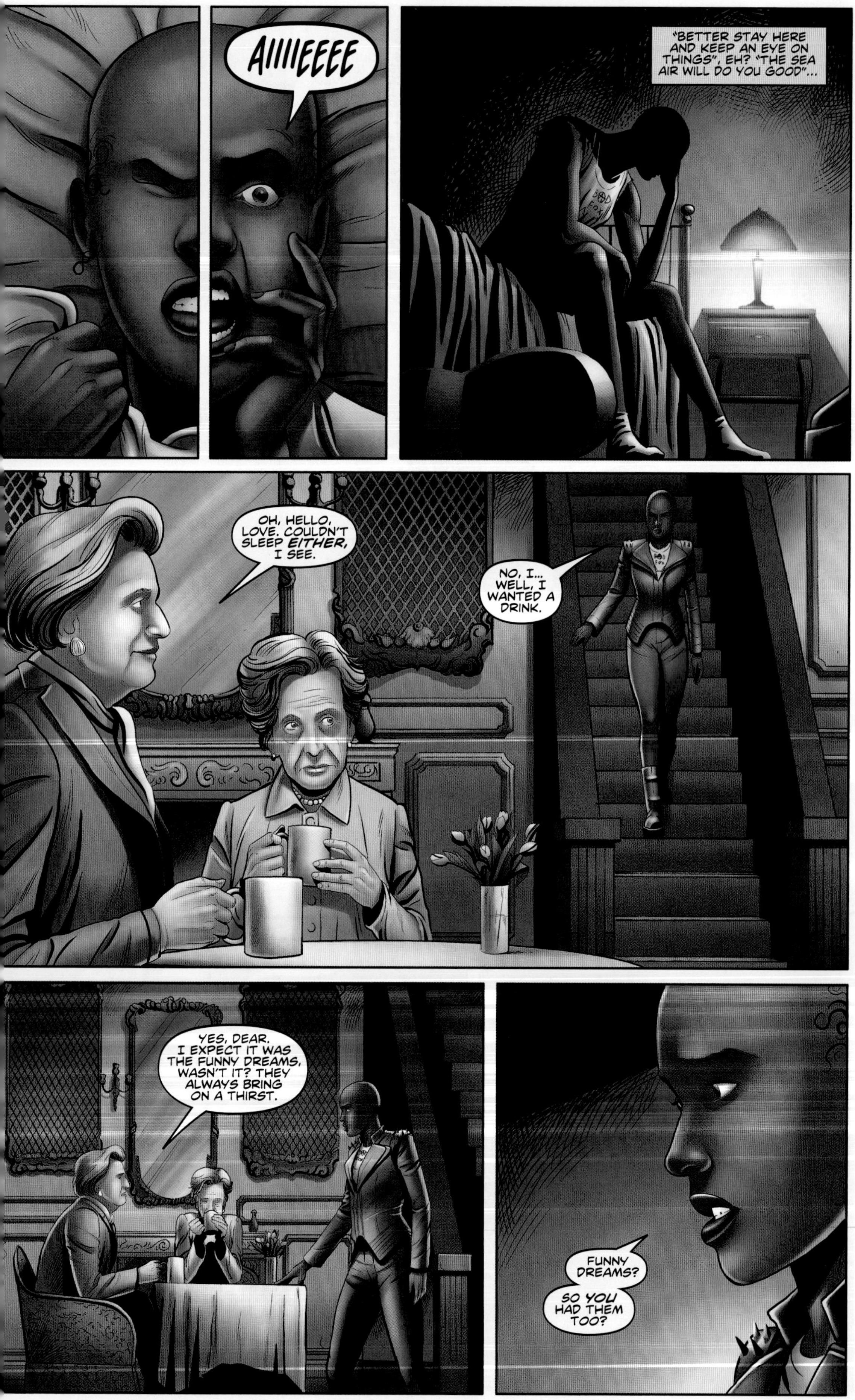
AIIIIEEEE
"BETTER STAY HERE AND KEEP AN EYE ON THINGS", EH? "THE SEA AIR WILL DO YOU GOOD"...
OH, HELLO, LOVE. COULDN'T SLEEP EITHER, I SEE.
NO, I... WELL, I WANTED A DRINK.
YES, DEAR. I EXPECT IT WAS THE FUNNY DREAMS, WASN'T IT? THEY ALWAYS BRING ON A THIRST.
FUNNY DREAMS?
SO YOU HAD THEM TOO?

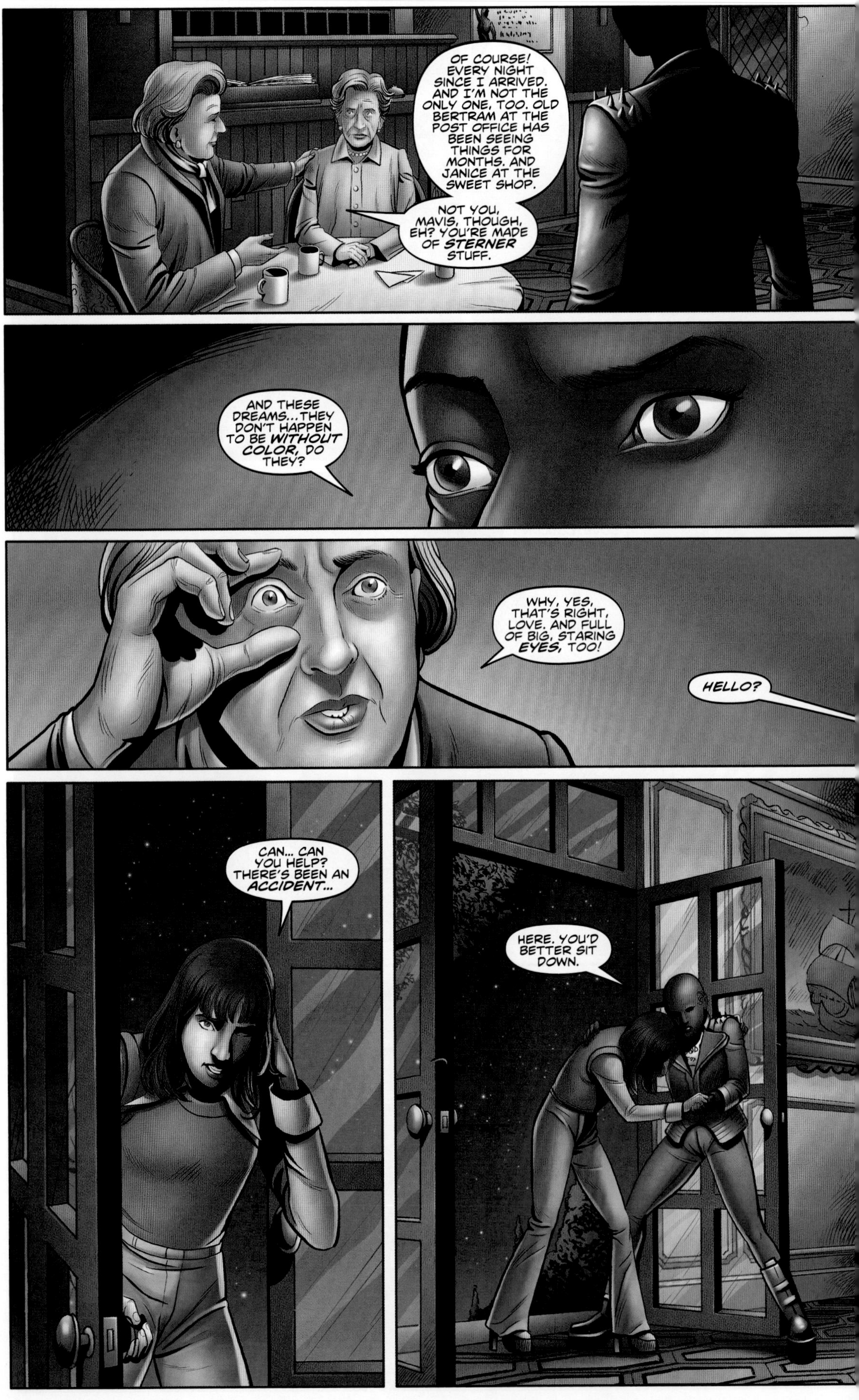
OF COURSE! EVERY NIGHT SINCE I ARRIVED. AND I'M NOT THE ONLY ONE, TOO. OLD BERTRAM AT THE POST OFFICE HAS BEEN SEEING THINGS FOR MONTHS. AND JANICE AT THE SWEET SHOP.
NOT YOU, MAVIS, THOUGH, EH? YOU'RE MADE OF STERNER STUFF.
AND THESE DREAMS... THEY DON'T HAPPEN TO BE WITHOUT COLOR, DO THEY?
WHY, YES, THAT'S RIGHT, LOVE. AND FULL OF BIG, STARING EYES, TOO!
HELLO?
CAN... CAN YOU HELP? THERE'S BEEN AN ACCIDENT...
HERE. YOU'D BETTER SIT DOWN.

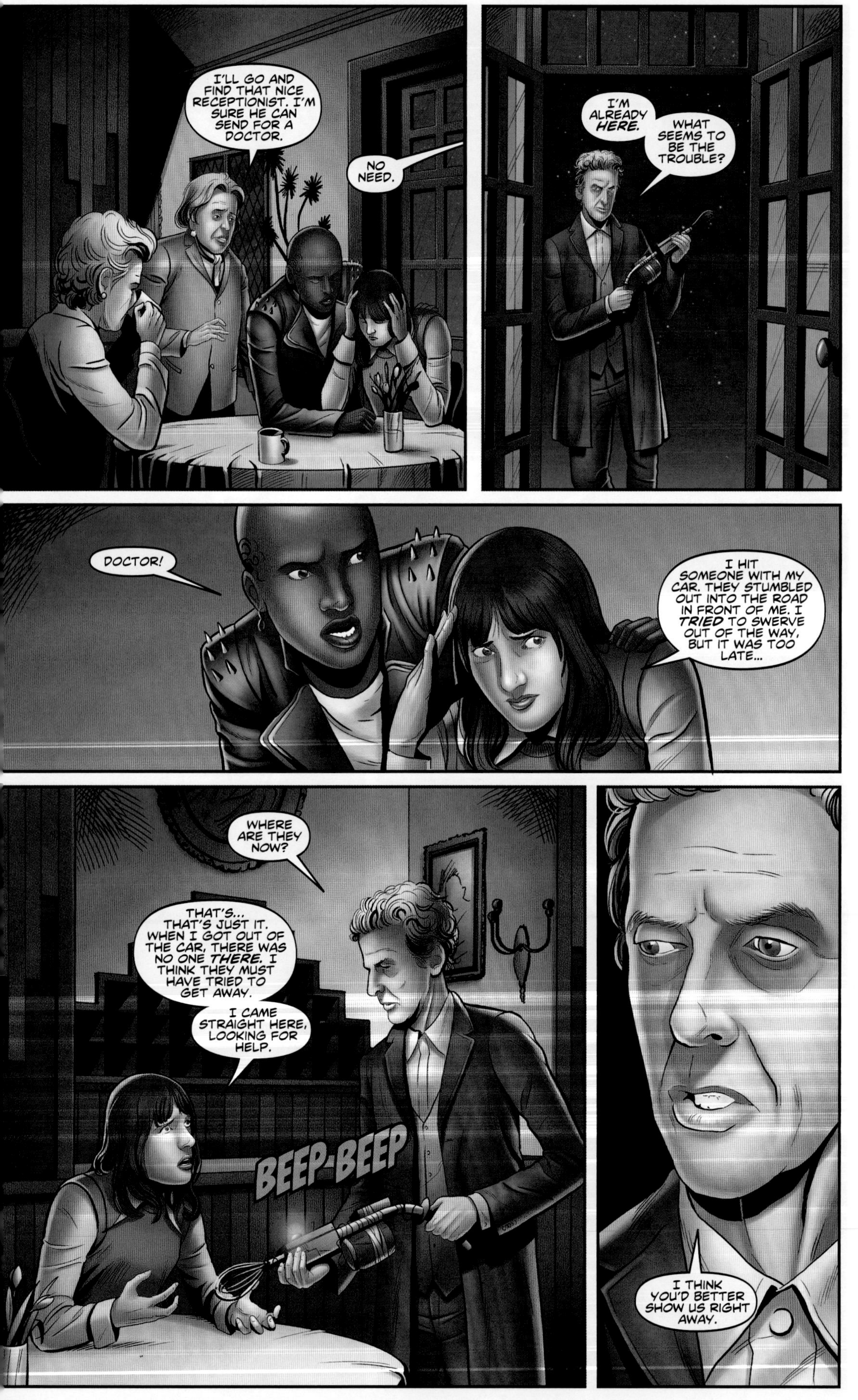
I'LL GO AND FIND THAT NICE RECEPTIONIST. I'M SURE HE CAN SEND FOR A DOCTOR.
NO NEED.
I'M ALREADY HERE.
WHAT SEEMS TO BE THE TROUBLE?
DOCTOR!
I HIT SOMEONE WITH MY CAR. THEY STUMBLED OUT INTO THE ROAD IN FRONT OF ME. I TRIED TO SWERVE OUT OF THE WAY, BUT IT WAS TOO LATE...
WHERE ARE THEY NOW?
THAT'S... THAT'S JUST IT. WHEN I GOT OUT OF THE CAR, THERE WAS NO ONE THERE. I THINK THEY MUST HAVE TRIED TO GET AWAY.
I CAME STRAIGHT HERE, LOOKING FOR HELP.
BEEP-BEEP
I THINK YOU'D BETTER SHOW US RIGHT AWAY.

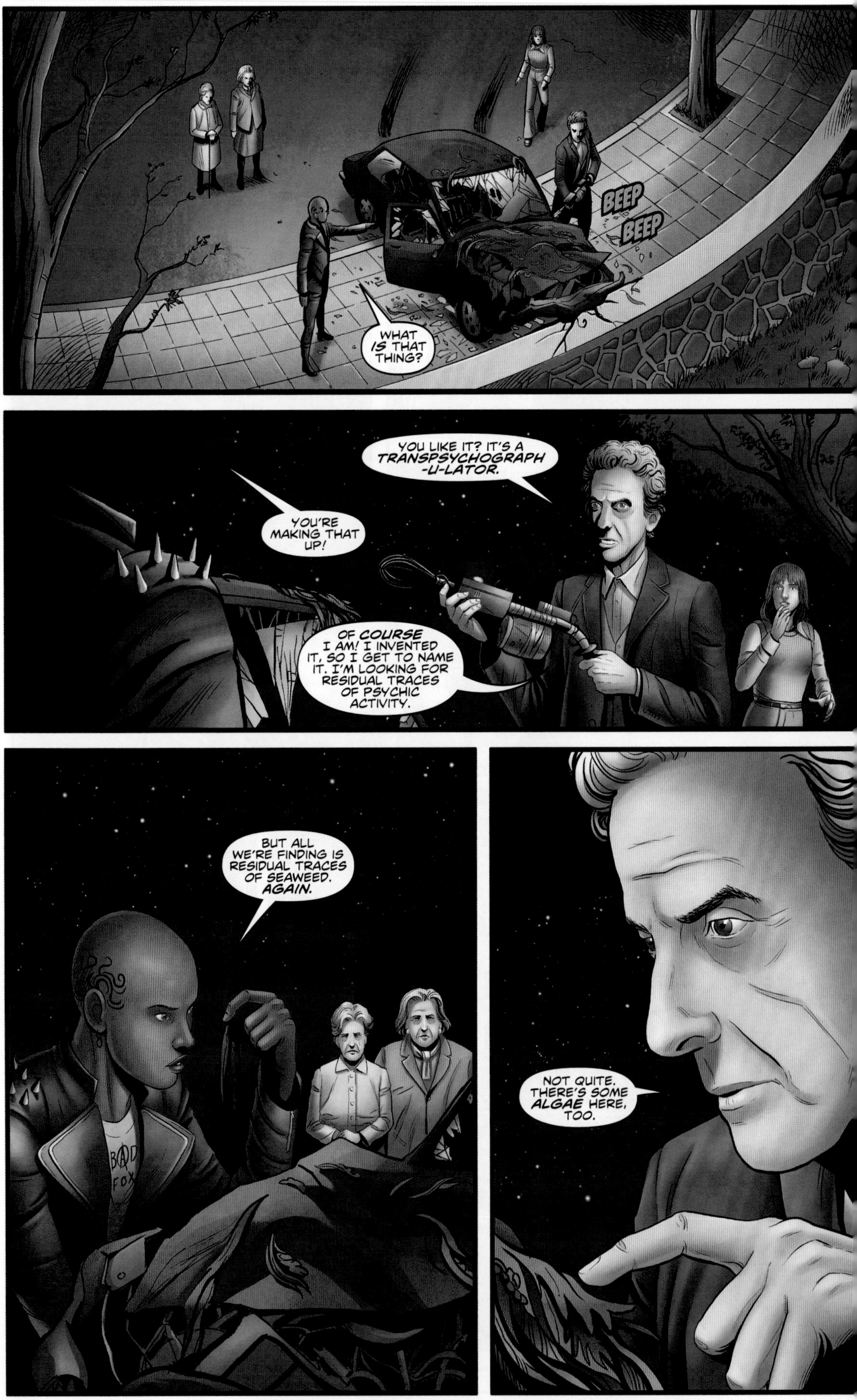
BEEP
BEEP
WHAT IS THAT THING?
YOU LIKE IT? IT'S A TRANSPSYCHOGRAPH-U-LATOR.
YOU'RE MAKING THAT UP!
OF COURSE I AM! I INVENTED IT, SO I GET TO NAME IT. I'M LOOKING FOR RESIDUAL TRACES OF PSYCHIC ACTIVITY.
BUT ALL WE'RE FINDING IS RESIDUAL TRACES OF SEAWEED. AGAIN.
NOT QUITE. THERE'S SOME ALGAE HERE, TOO.

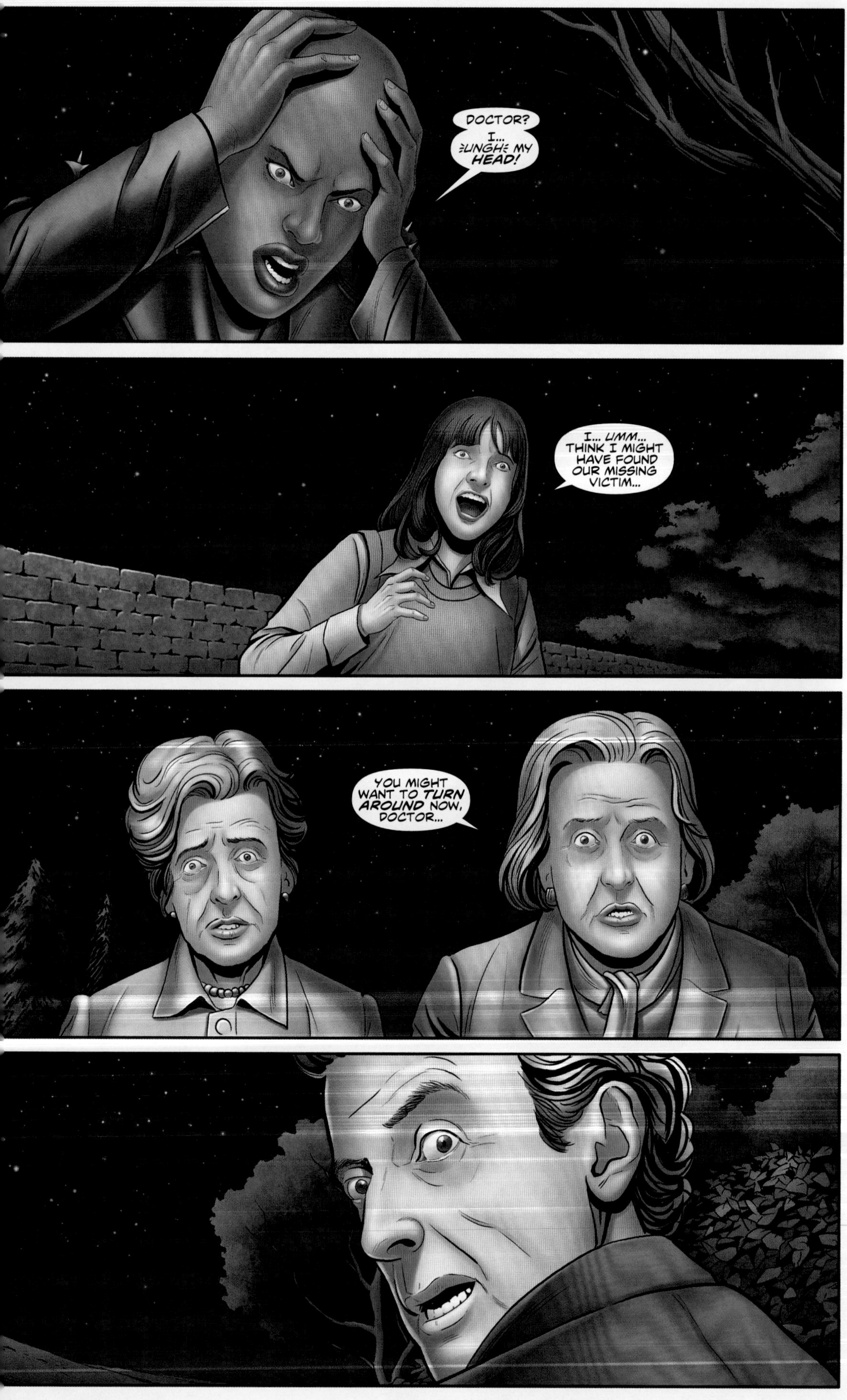
DOCTOR? I... UNGH MY HEAD!
I... UMM... THINK I MIGHT HAVE FOUND OUR MISSING VICTIM...
YOU MIGHT WANT TO TURN AROUND NOW, DOCTOR...

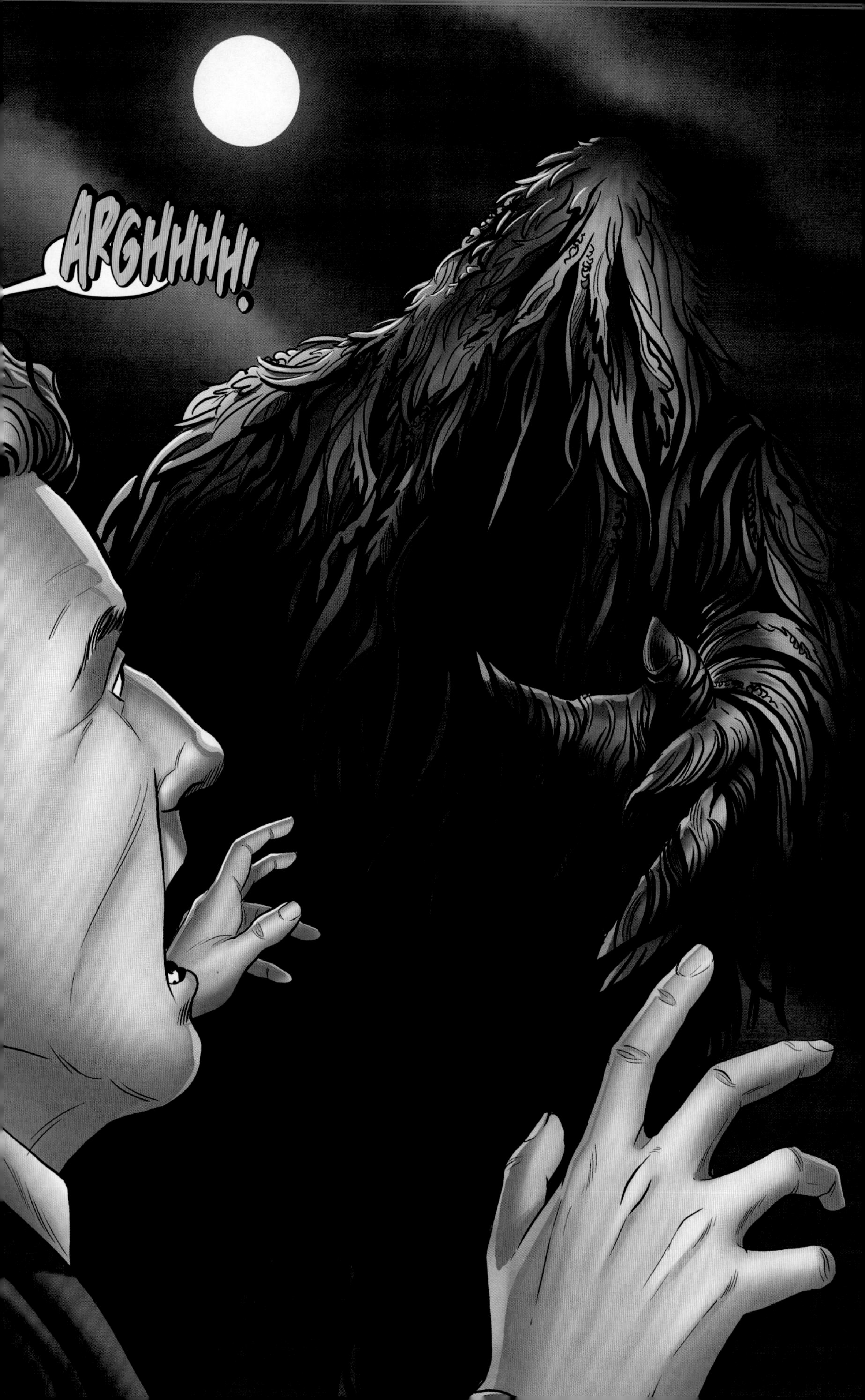
ARGHHHH!

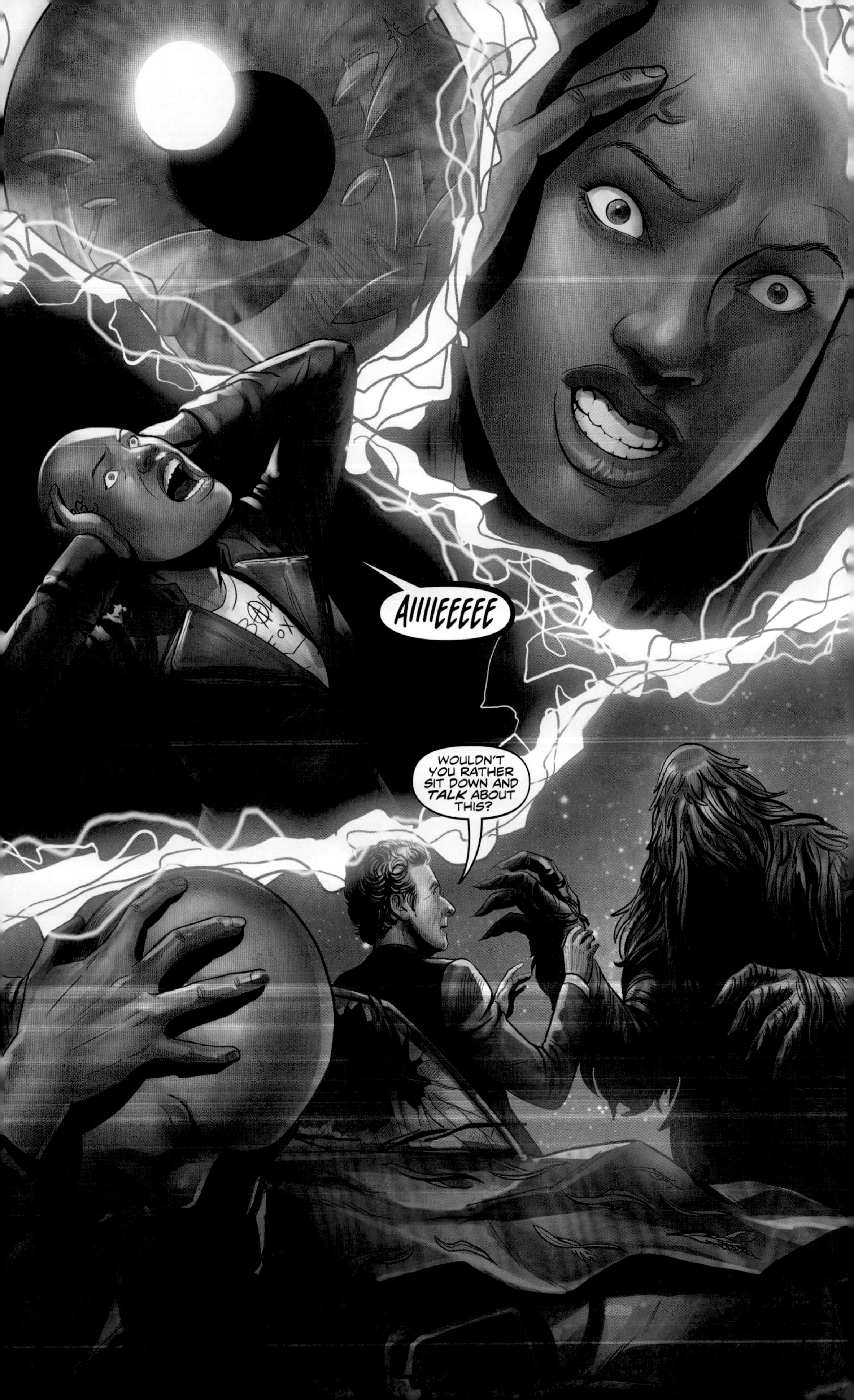
AIIIIEEEEE
WOULDN'T YOU RATHER SIT DOWN AND TALK ABOUT THIS?

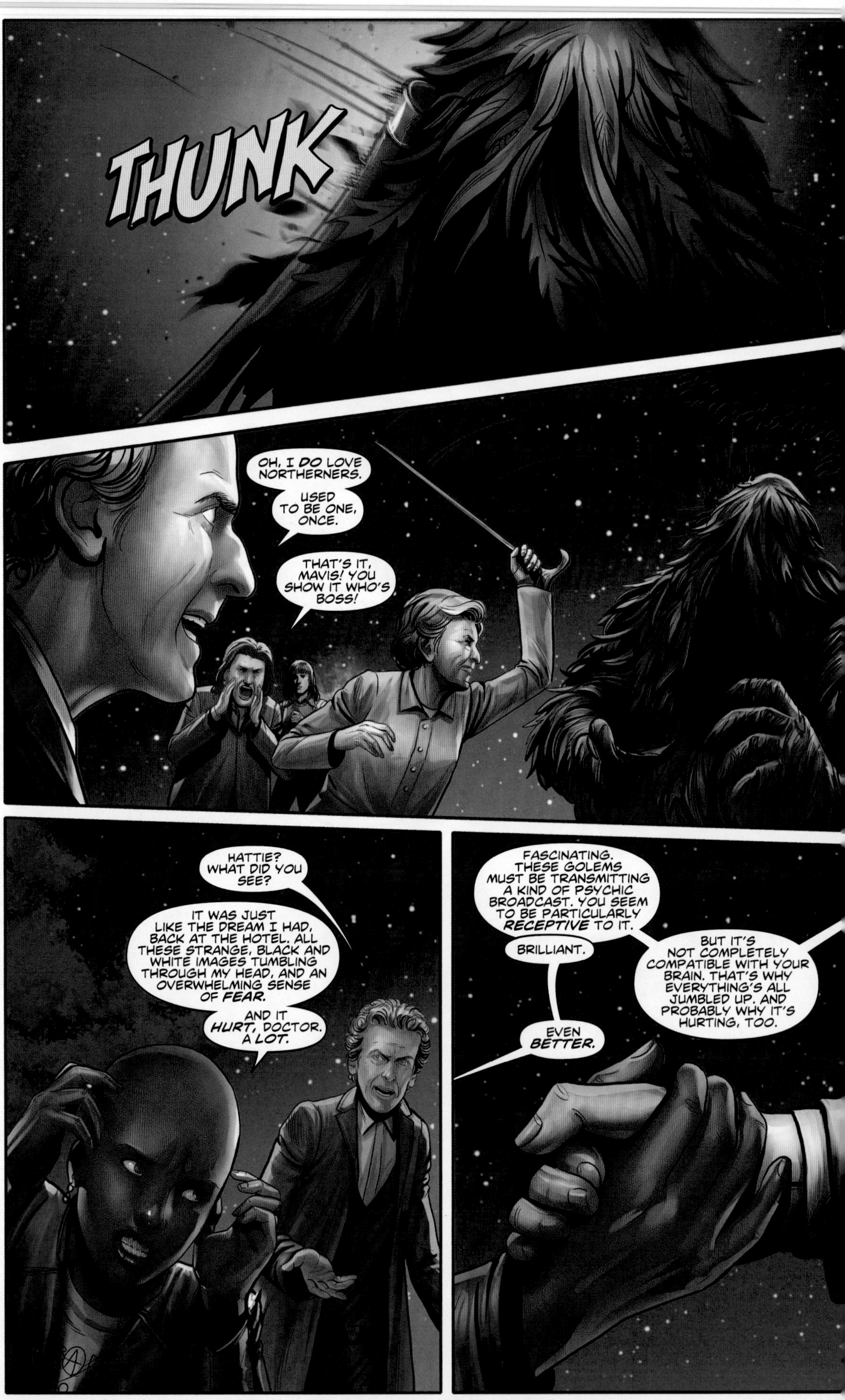
THUNK
OH, I DO LOVE NORTHERNERS.
USED TO BE ONE, ONCE.
THAT'S IT, MAVIS! YOU SHOW IT WHO'S BOSS!
HATTIE? WHAT DID YOU SEE?
IT WAS JUST LIKE THE DREAM I HAD, BACK AT THE HOTEL. ALL THESE STRANGE, BLACK AND WHITE IMAGES TUMBLING THROUGH MY HEAD, AND AN OVERWHELMING SENSE OF FEAR.
AND IT HURT, DOCTOR. A LOT.
FASCINATING. THESE GOLEMS MUST BE TRANSMITTING A KIND OF PSYCHIC BROADCAST. YOU SEEM TO BE PARTICULARLY RECEPTIVE TO IT.
BRILLIANT.
EVEN BETTER.
BUT IT'S NOT COMPLETELY COMPATIBLE WITH YOUR BRAIN. THAT'S WHY EVERYTHING'S ALL JUMBLED UP. AND PROBABLY WHY IT'S HURTING, TOO.

THERE'S MORE OF THEM HEADED THIS WAY. AND I DON'T THINK MAVIS IS GOING TO BE ABLE TO HOLD THEM ALL OFF WITH HER CANE.

I RECKON SHE'D GIVE THEM A RUN FOR THEIR MONEY.

BUT LET'S GET BACK TO THE HOTEL. QUICK AS YOU LIKE.

HURRY UP! THERE ARE LOADS OF THE BLIGHTERS.

WHAT ARE YOU TRYING TO TELL US, EH? WHAT ARE YOU UP TO?

COME ON, DOCTOR...

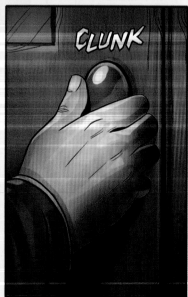

CLUNK

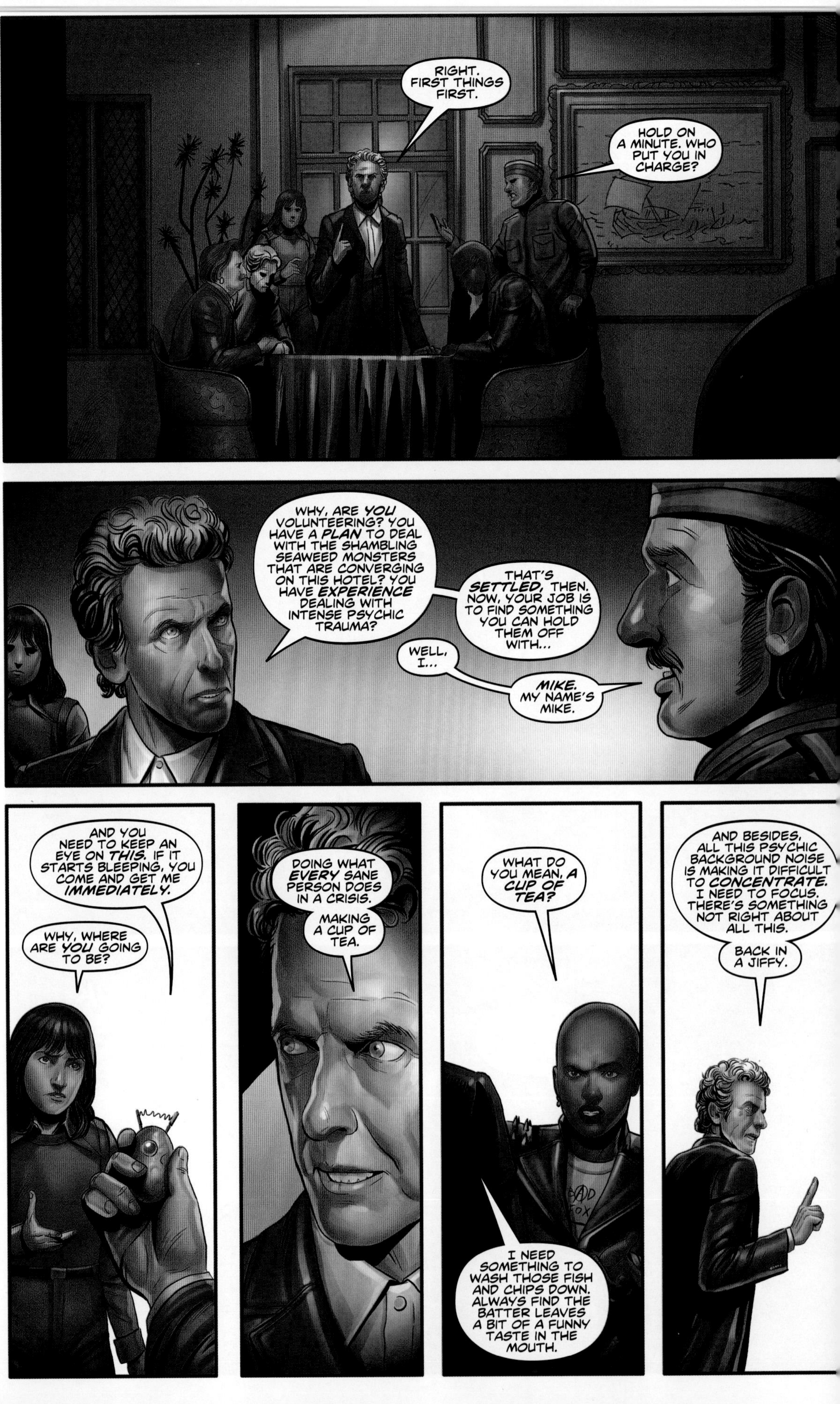
RIGHT. FIRST THINGS FIRST.
HOLD ON A MINUTE. WHO PUT YOU IN CHARGE?
WHY, ARE YOU VOLUNTEERING? YOU HAVE A PLAN TO DEAL WITH THE SHAMBLING SEAWEED MONSTERS THAT ARE CONVERGING ON THIS HOTEL? YOU HAVE EXPERIENCE DEALING WITH INTENSE PSYCHIC TRAUMA?
WELL, I...
THAT'S SETTLED, THEN. NOW, YOUR JOB IS TO FIND SOMETHING YOU CAN HOLD THEM OFF WITH...
MIKE. MY NAME'S MIKE.
AND YOU NEED TO KEEP AN EYE ON THIS. IF IT STARTS BLEEPING, YOU COME AND GET ME IMMEDIATELY.
WHY, WHERE ARE YOU GOING TO BE?
DOING WHAT EVERY SANE PERSON DOES IN A CRISIS.
MAKING A CUP OF TEA.
WHAT DO YOU MEAN, A CUP OF TEA?
I NEED SOMETHING TO WASH THOSE FISH AND CHIPS DOWN. ALWAYS FIND THE BATTER LEAVES A BIT OF A FUNNY TASTE IN THE MOUTH.
AND BESIDES, ALL THIS PSYCHIC BACKGROUND NOISE IS MAKING IT DIFFICULT TO CONCENTRATE. I NEED TO FOCUS. THERE'S SOMETHING NOT RIGHT ABOUT ALL THIS.
BACK IN A JIFFY.

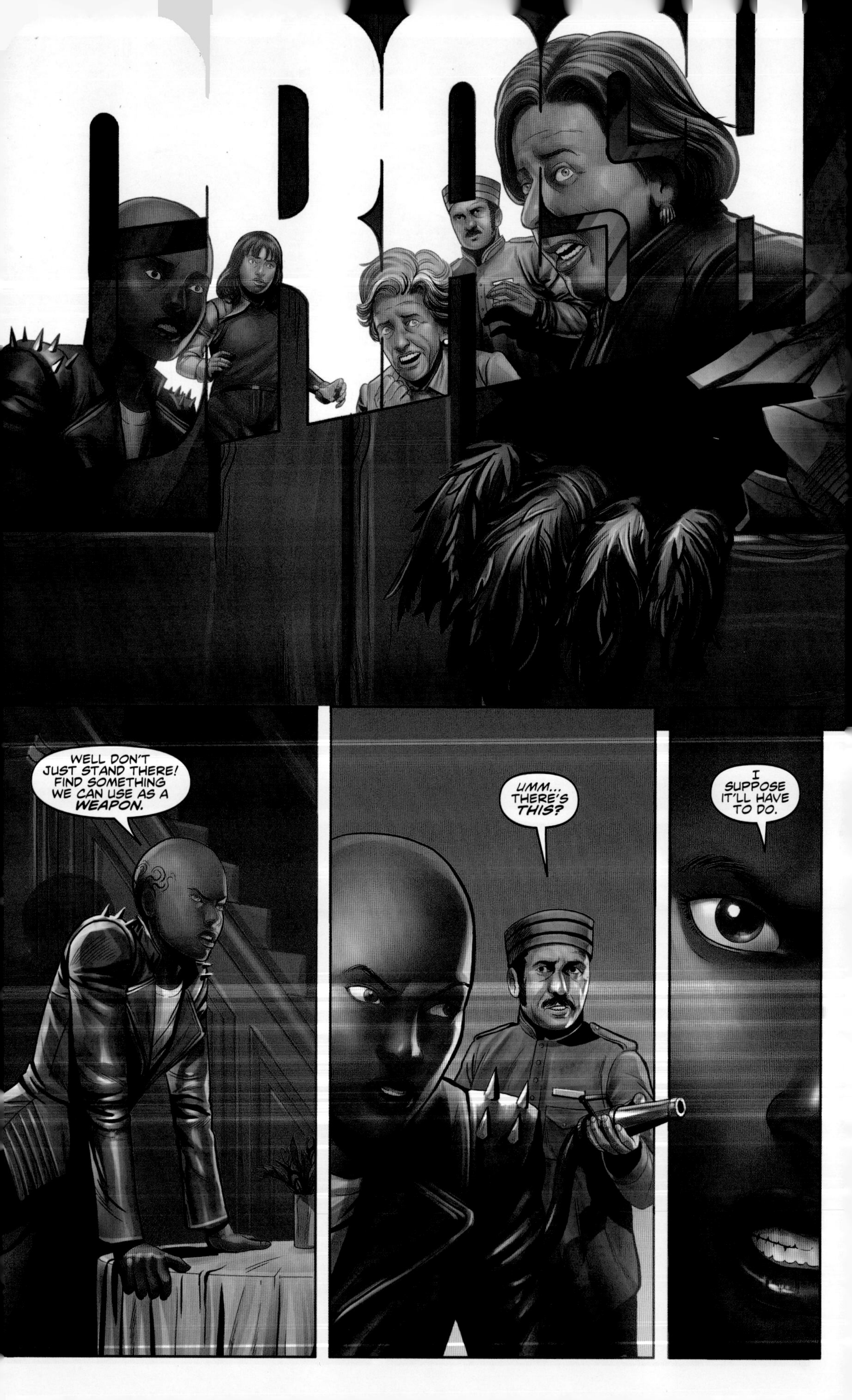
WELL DON'T JUST STAND THERE! FIND SOMETHING WE CAN USE AS A WEAPON.
UMM... THERE'S THIS?
I SUPPOSE IT'LL HAVE TO DO.

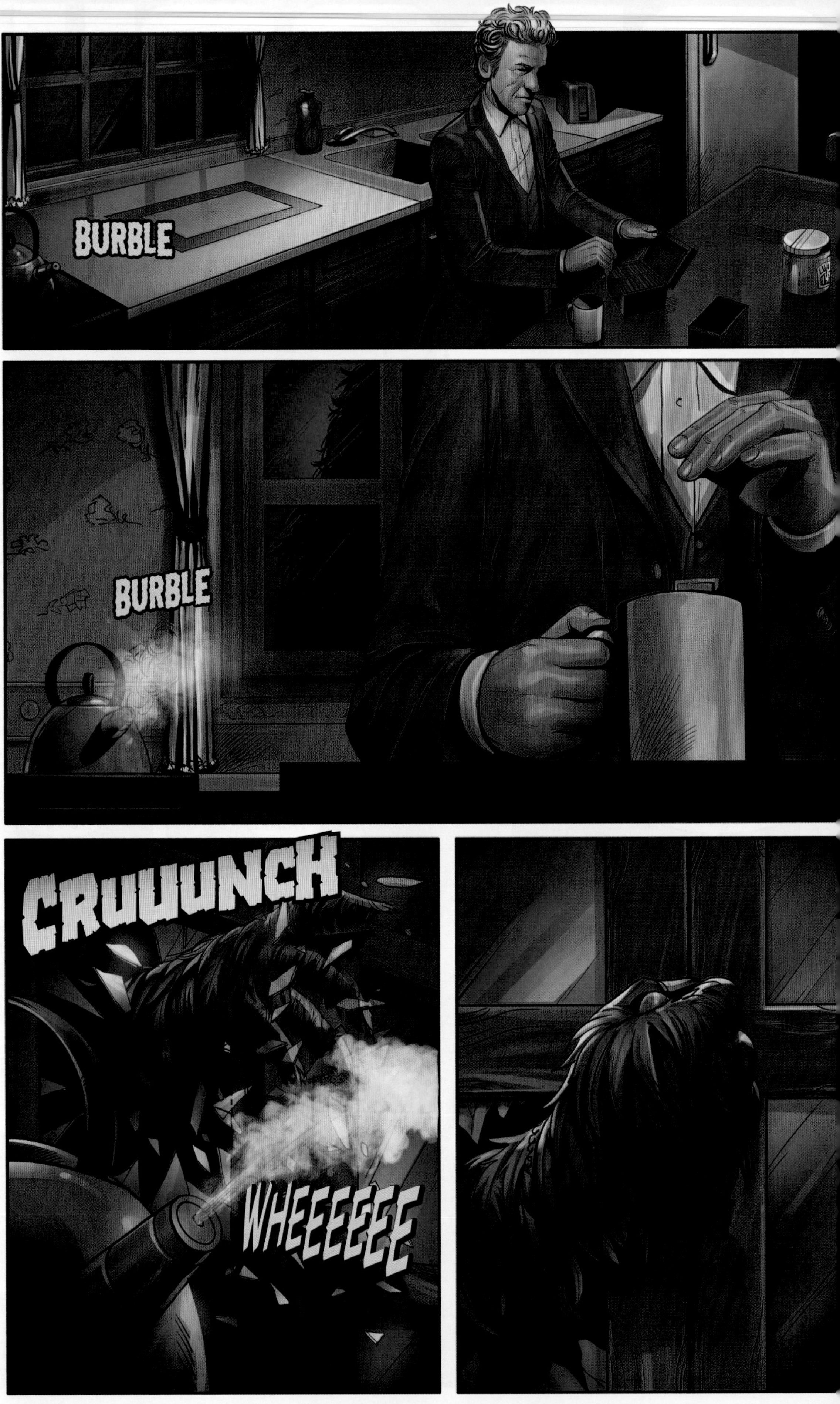
BURBLE
BURBLE
CRUUUNCH
WHEEEEEE

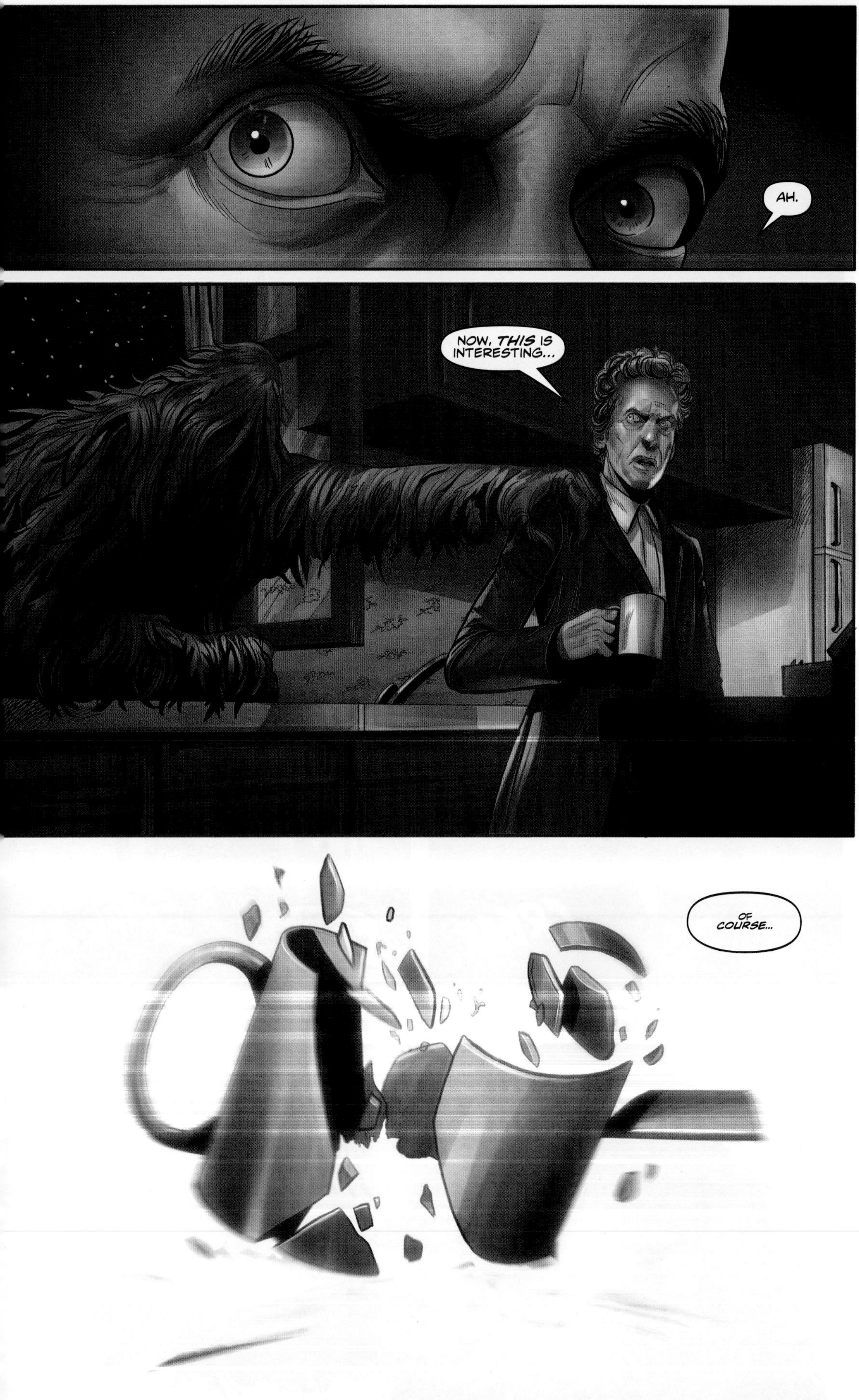
AH.
NOW, THIS IS INTERESTING...
OF COURSE...

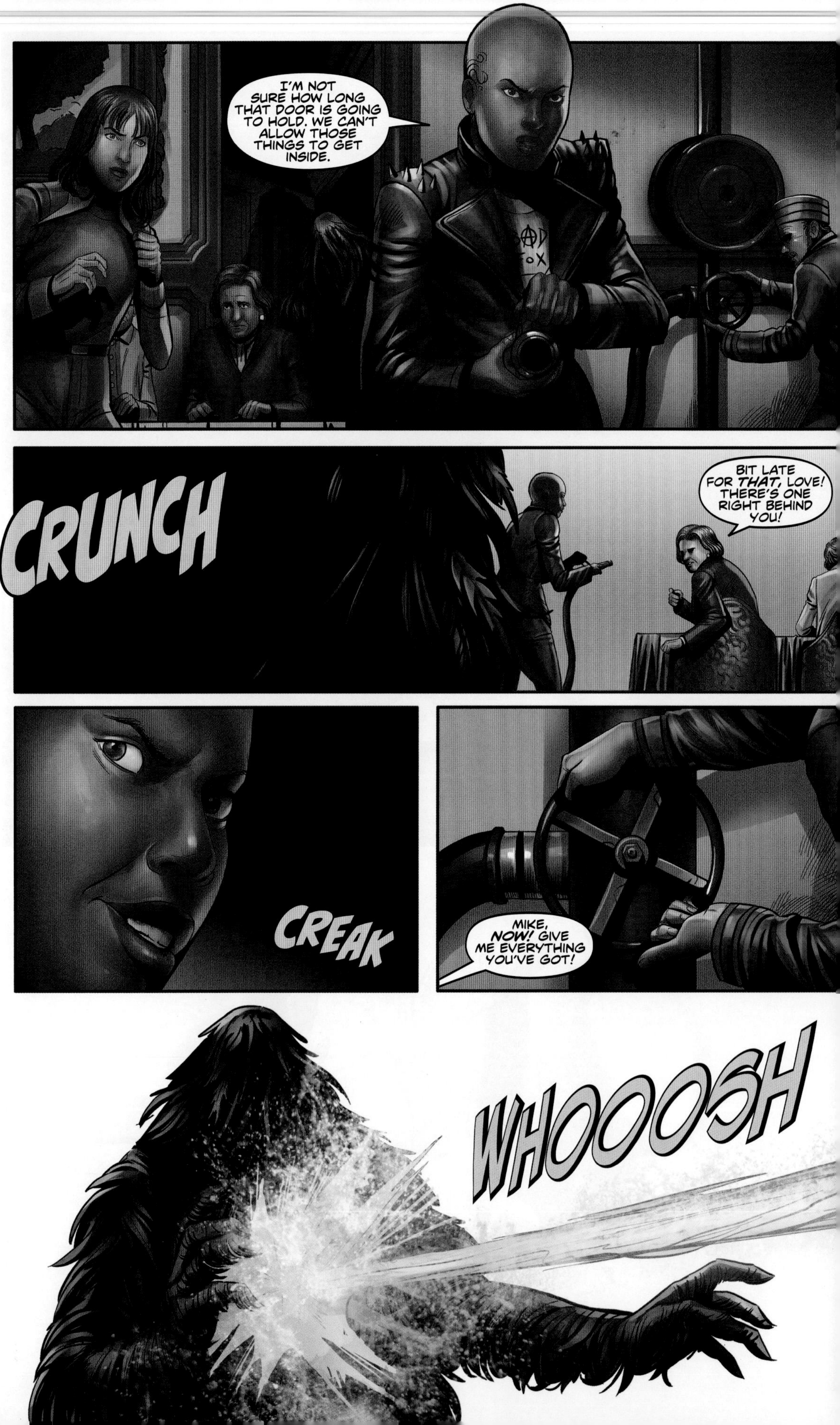

I'M NOT SURE HOW LONG THAT DOOR IS GOING TO HOLD. WE CAN'T ALLOW THOSE THINGS TO GET INSIDE.
CRUNCH
BIT LATE FOR *THAT,* LOVE! THERE'S ONE RIGHT BEHIND YOU!
CREAK
MIKE, **NOW!** GIVE ME EVERYTHING YOU'VE GOT!
WHOOOSH

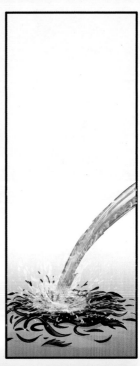

WELL, *THAT* WORKED BETTER THAN I EXPECTED.

IT CAME FROM THE DIRECTION OF THE KITCHEN.

THE DOCTOR!

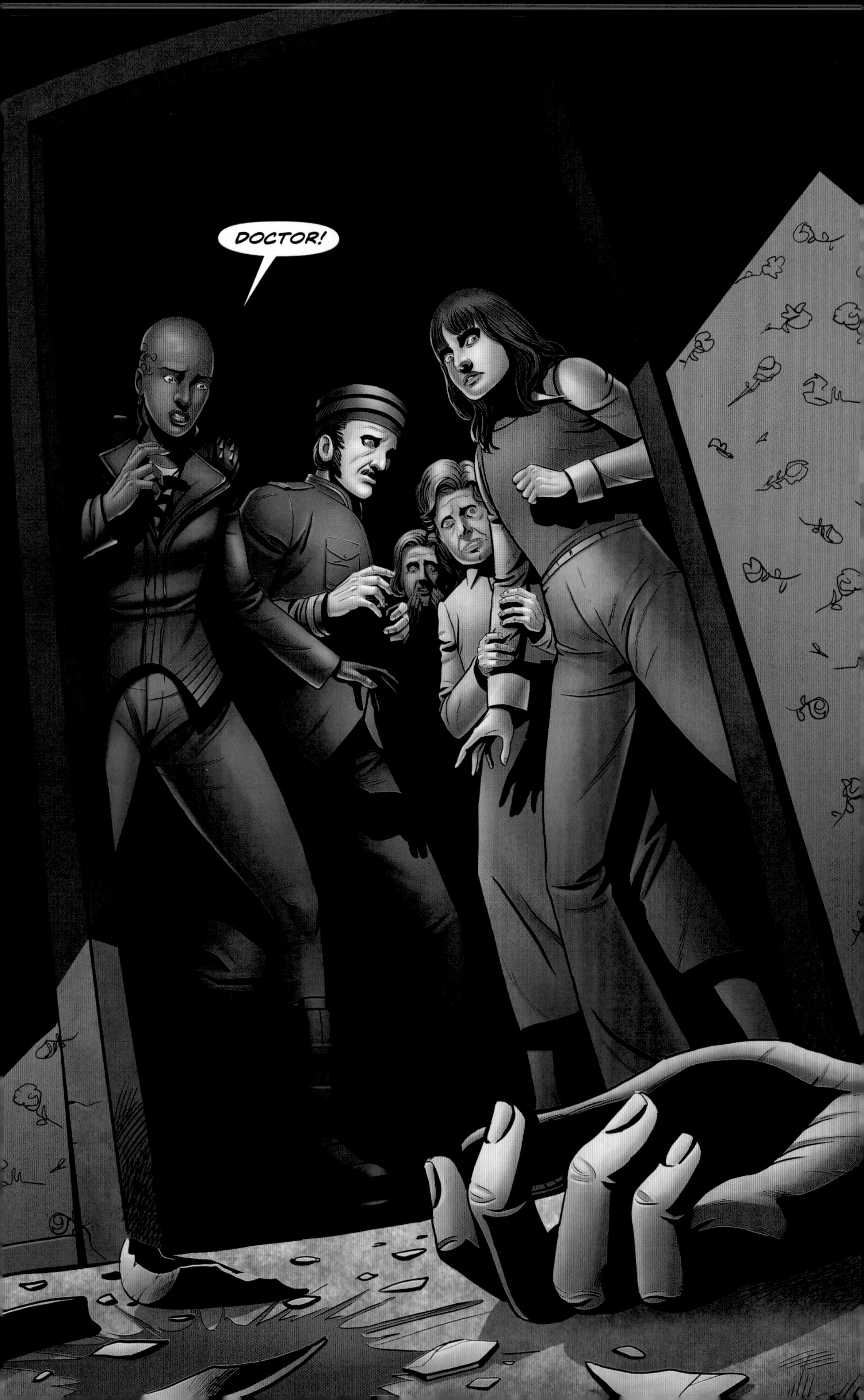
DOCTOR!

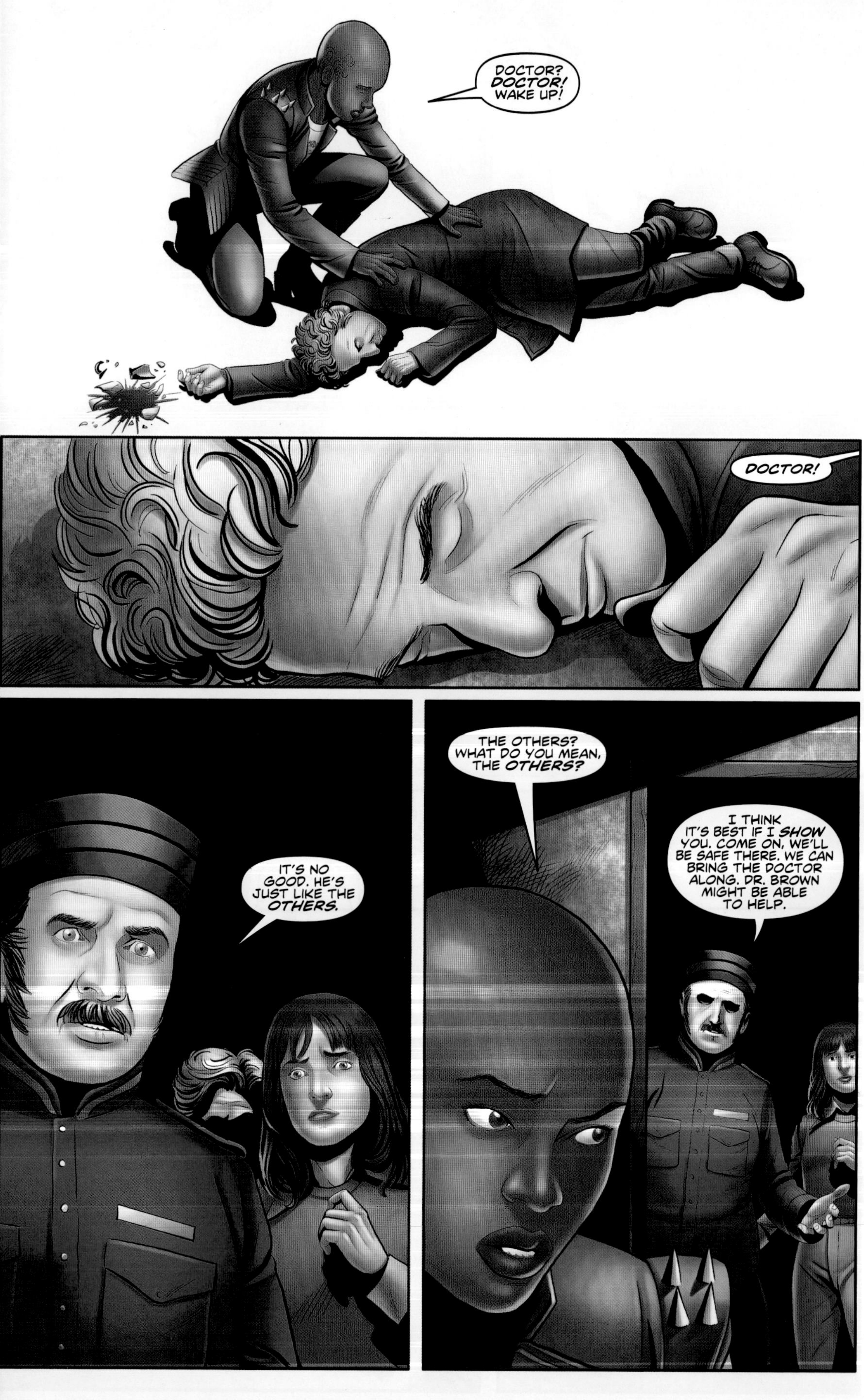

DOCTOR? DOCTOR! WAKE UP!
DOCTOR!
IT'S NO GOOD. HE'S JUST LIKE THE OTHERS.
THE OTHERS? WHAT DO YOU MEAN, THE OTHERS?
I THINK IT'S BEST IF I SHOW YOU. COME ON, WE'LL BE SAFE THERE. WE CAN BRING THE DOCTOR ALONG. DR. BROWN MIGHT BE ABLE TO HELP.

MIKE? WHAT THE DEVIL IS GOING ON?

YES, MIKE. I THINK THAT'S A *VERY* GOOD QUESTION.

DR. BROWN... ARE THE PATIENTS OKAY?

NO CHANGE. ALTHOUGH I SEE YOU HAVE *ANOTHER* ONE FOR ME.

NO, I THINK *YOU'D* BETTER EXPLAIN WHAT'S GOING ON HERE. WHAT'S HAPPENED TO THESE PEOPLE, AND WHY ARE THEY IN THESE BEDS?

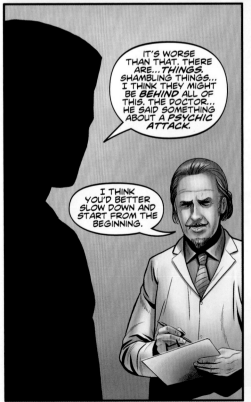

IT'S WORSE THAN THAT. THERE ARE... *THINGS.* SHAMBLING THINGS... I THINK THEY MIGHT BE *BEHIND* ALL OF THIS. THE DOCTOR... HE SAID SOMETHING ABOUT A *PSYCHIC ATTACK.*

I THINK YOU'D BETTER SLOW DOWN AND START FROM THE BEGINNING.

HAVEN'T YOU BEEN READING THE NEWSPAPERS? WATCHING THE *NEWS?*

I'M FROM OUT OF TOWN.

THIS IS OVERSPILL FROM THE LOCAL HOSPITAL. THESE PEOPLE ARE ALL SUFFERING FROM THE *SAME CONDITION.* THERE'S BEEN A RECENT SPATE OF ILLNESS IN THE AREA -- PEOPLE FALLING INTO *COMAS.* WE DON'T HAVE ENOUGH BEDS ON THE WARDS, SO THE HOTEL IS HELPING OUT.

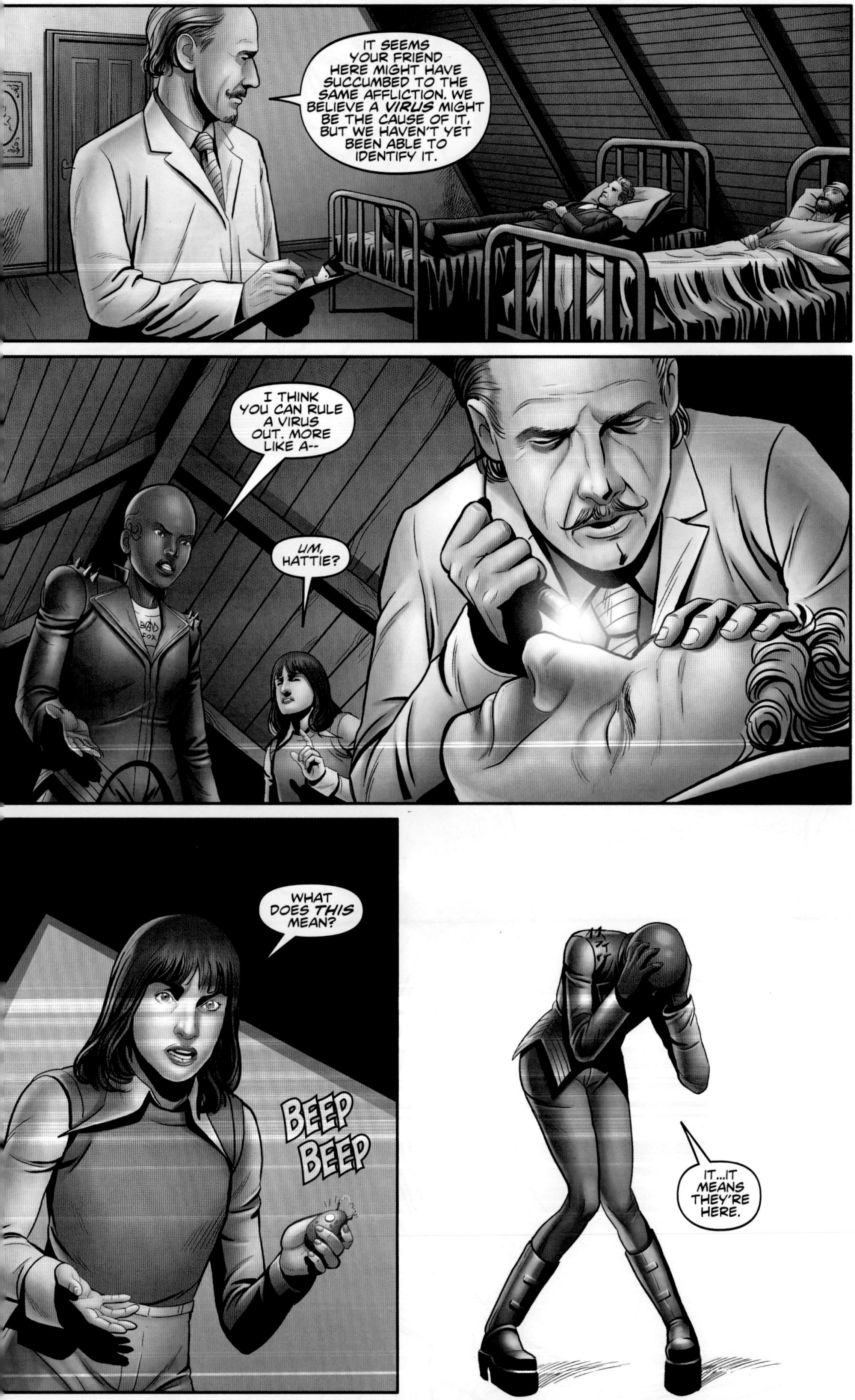
IT SEEMS YOUR FRIEND HERE MIGHT HAVE SUCCUMBED TO THE SAME AFFLICTION. WE BELIEVE A VIRUS MIGHT BE THE CAUSE OF IT, BUT WE HAVEN'T YET BEEN ABLE TO IDENTIFY IT.
I THINK YOU CAN RULE A VIRUS OUT. MORE LIKE A--
UM, HATTIE?
WHAT DOES THIS MEAN?
BEEP BEEP
IT...IT MEANS THEY'RE HERE.

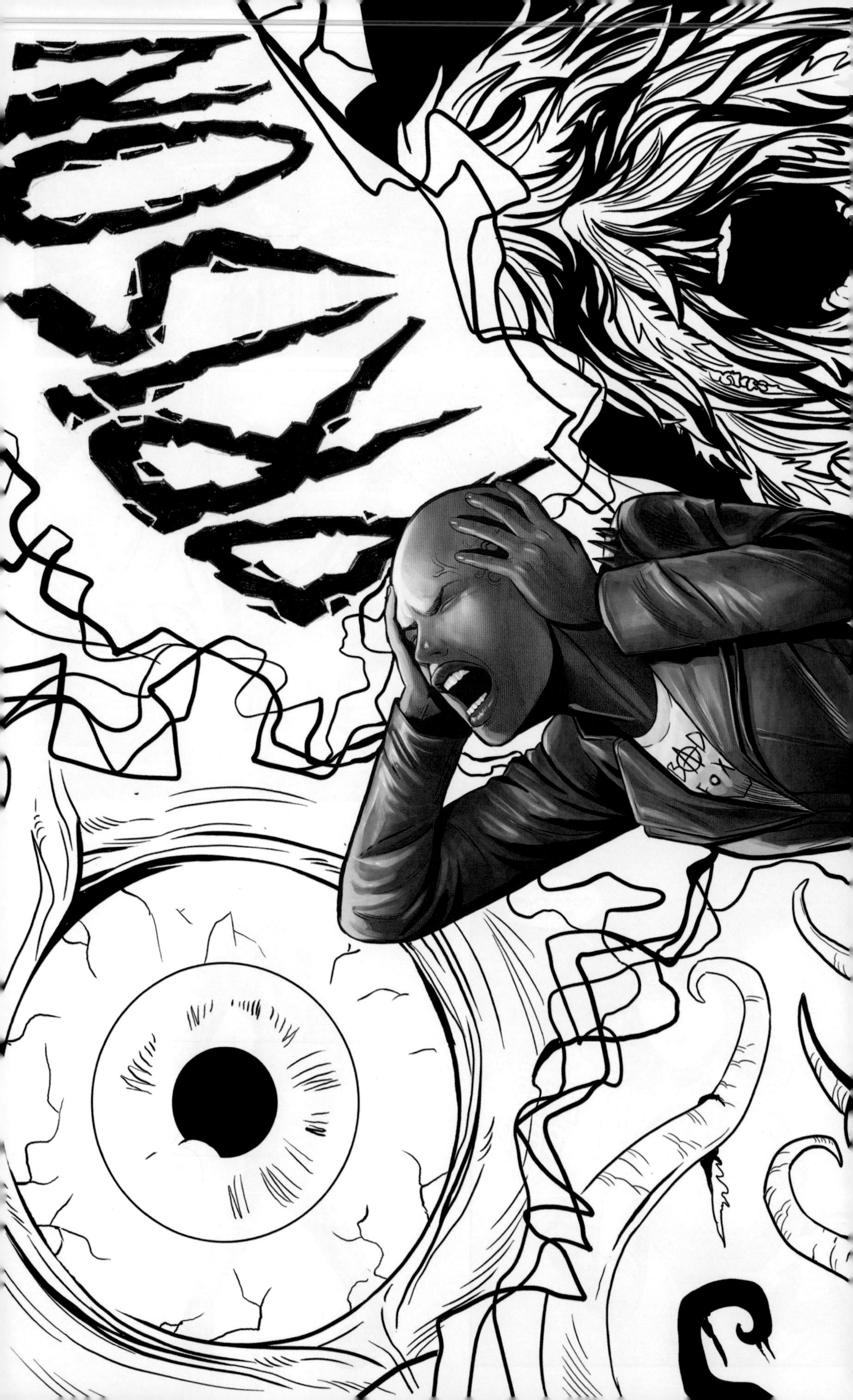

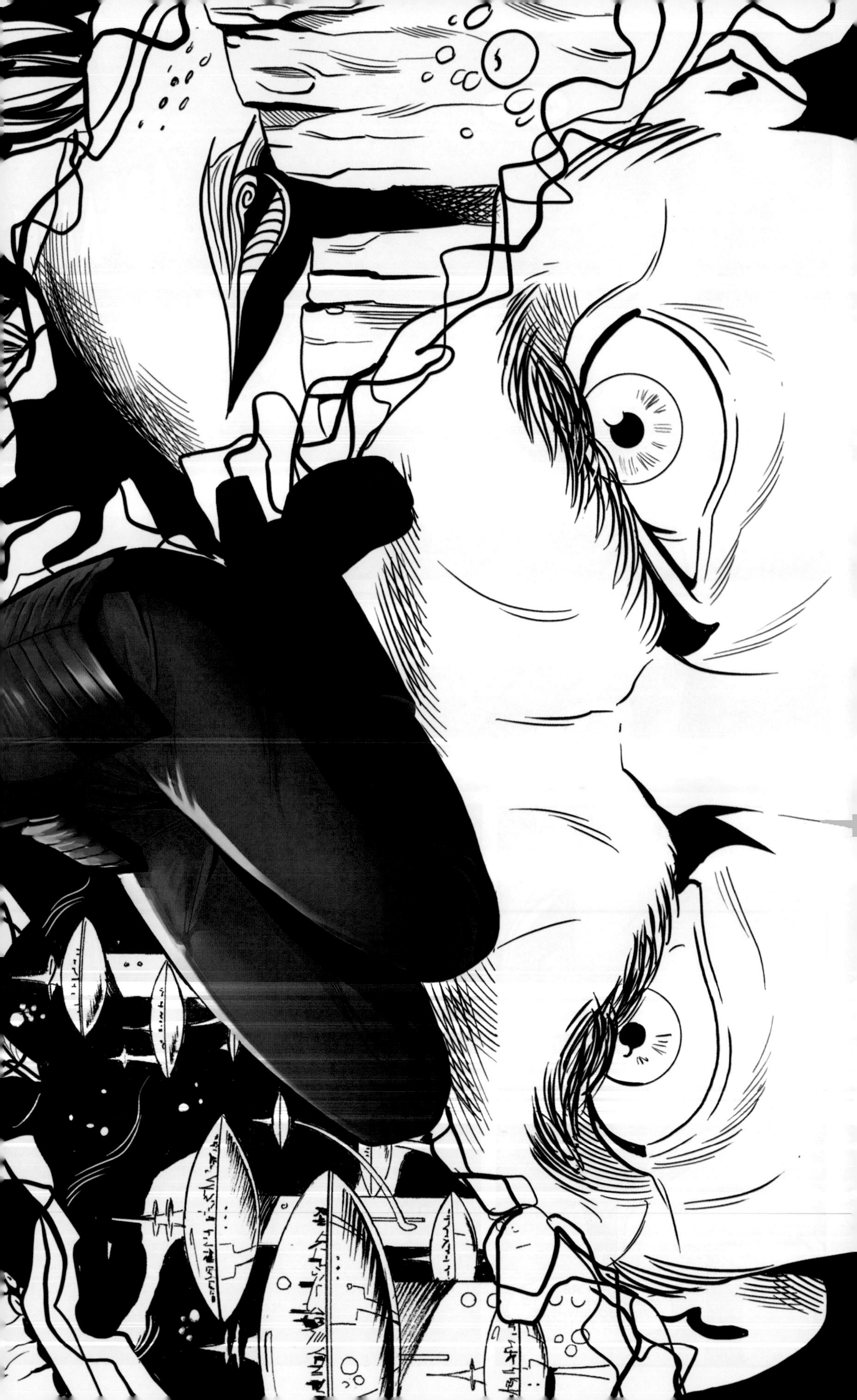

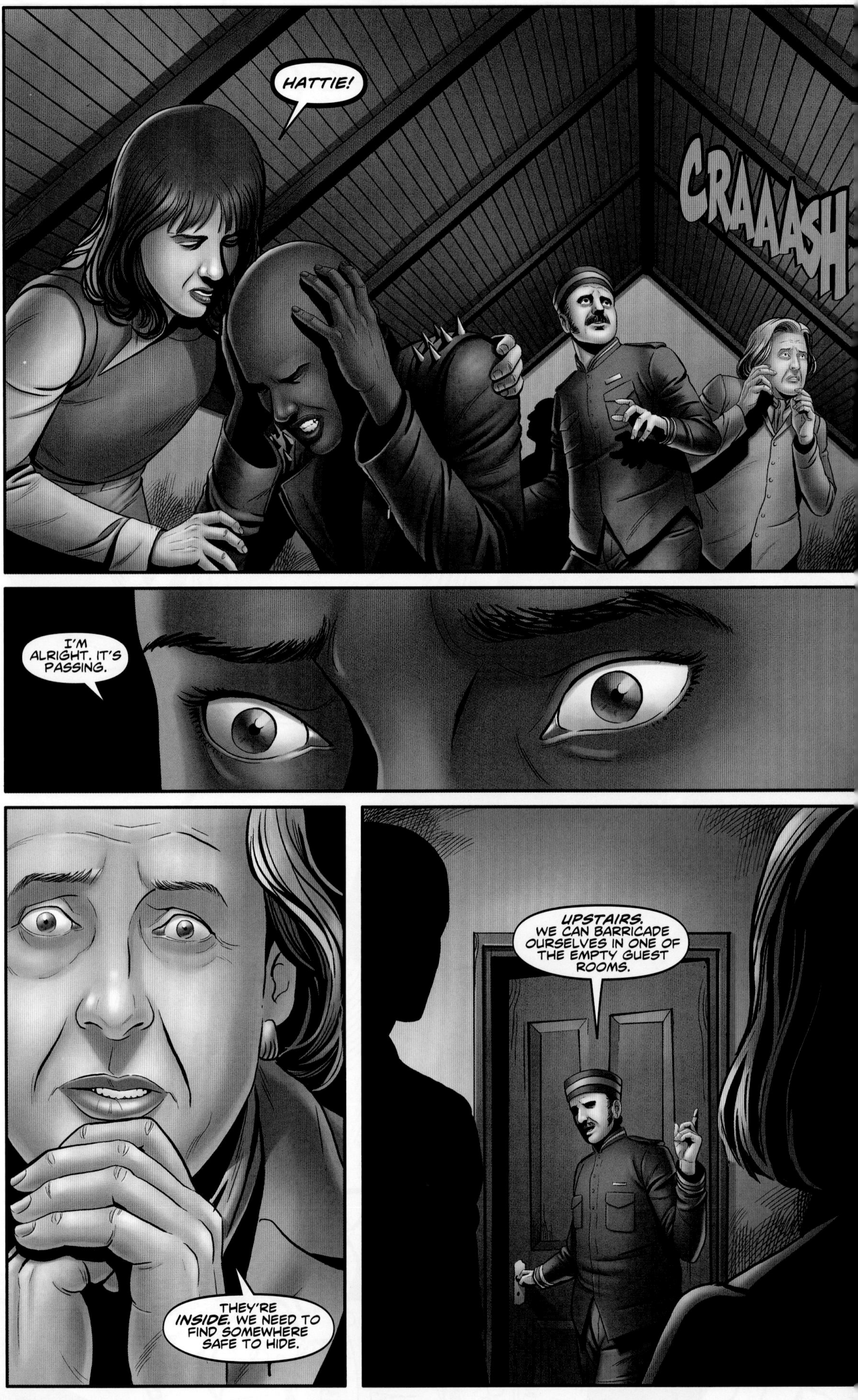
HATTIE!
CRAAASH
I'M ALRIGHT. IT'S PASSING.
THEY'RE *INSIDE.* WE NEED TO FIND SOMEWHERE SAFE TO HIDE.
UPSTAIRS. WE CAN BARRICADE OURSELVES IN ONE OF THE EMPTY GUEST ROOMS.

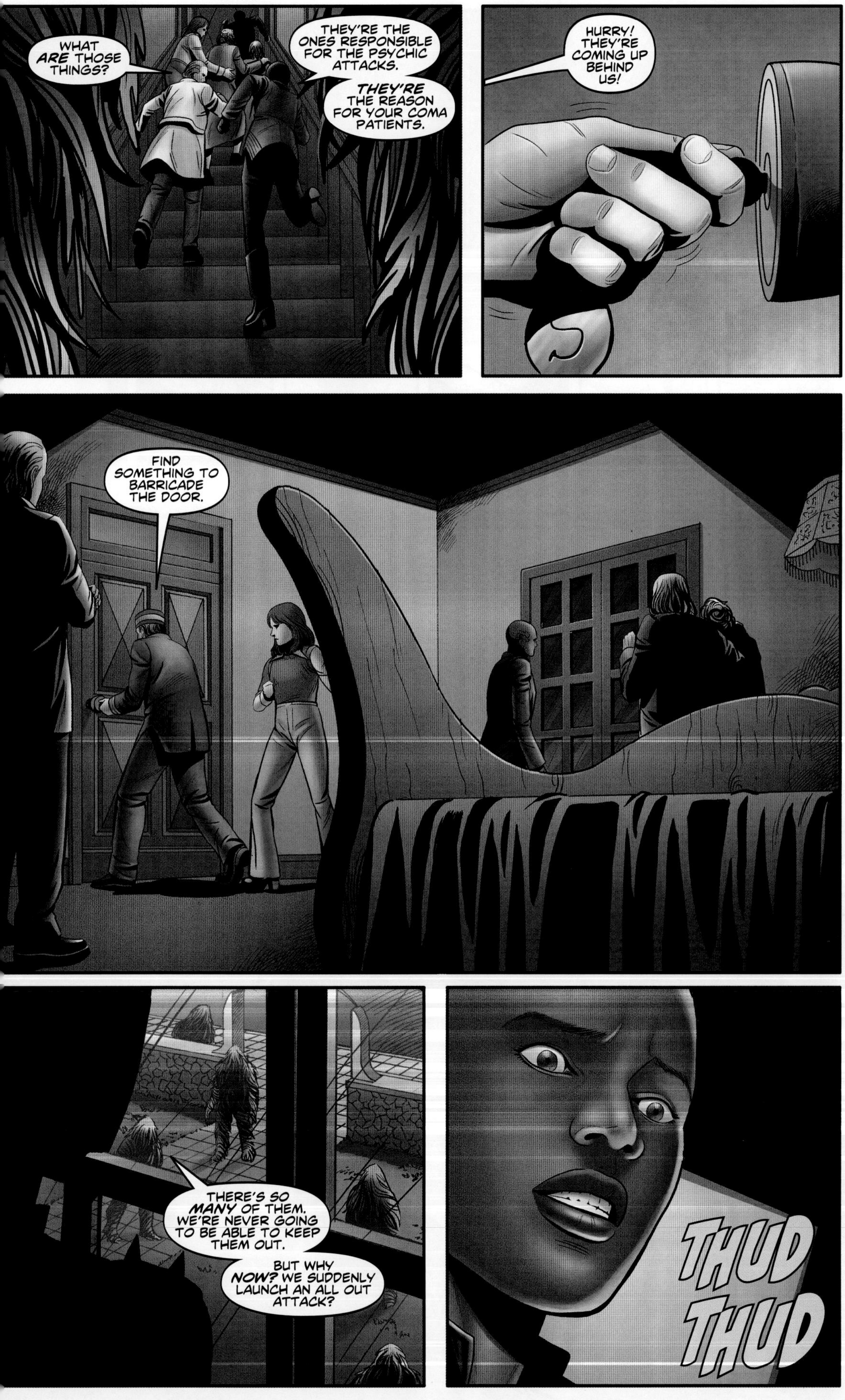
WHAT ARE THOSE THINGS?
THEY'RE THE ONES RESPONSIBLE FOR THE PSYCHIC ATTACKS.
THEY'RE THE REASON FOR YOUR COMA PATIENTS.
HURRY! THEY'RE COMING UP BEHIND US!
FIND SOMETHING TO BARRICADE THE DOOR.
THERE'S SO MANY OF THEM. WE'RE NEVER GOING TO BE ABLE TO KEEP THEM OUT.
BUT WHY NOW? WE SUDDENLY LAUNCH AN ALL OUT ATTACK?
THUD
THUD

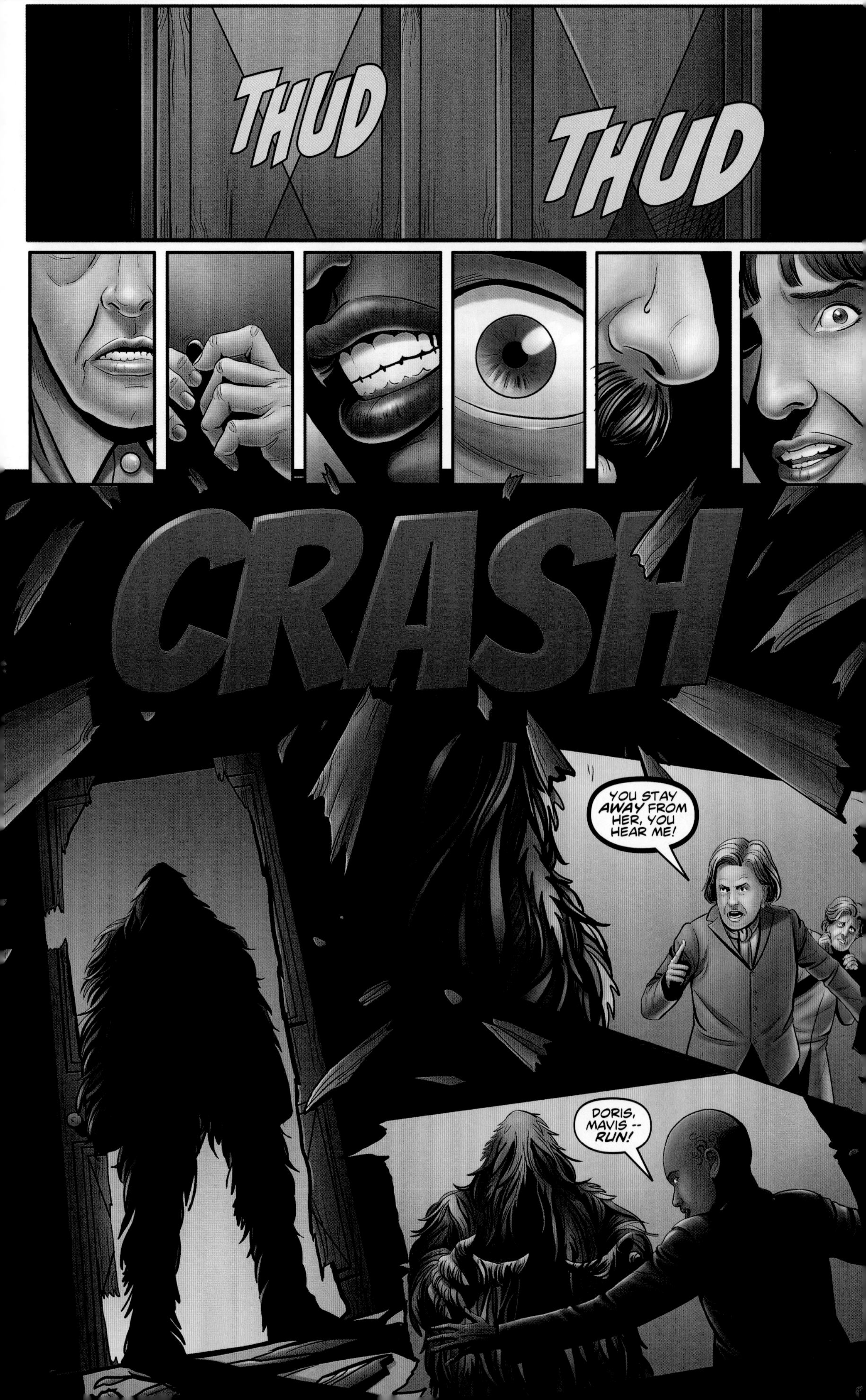
THUD
THUD
CRASH
YOU STAY AWAY FROM HER, YOU HEAR ME!
DORIS, MAVIS -- RUN!

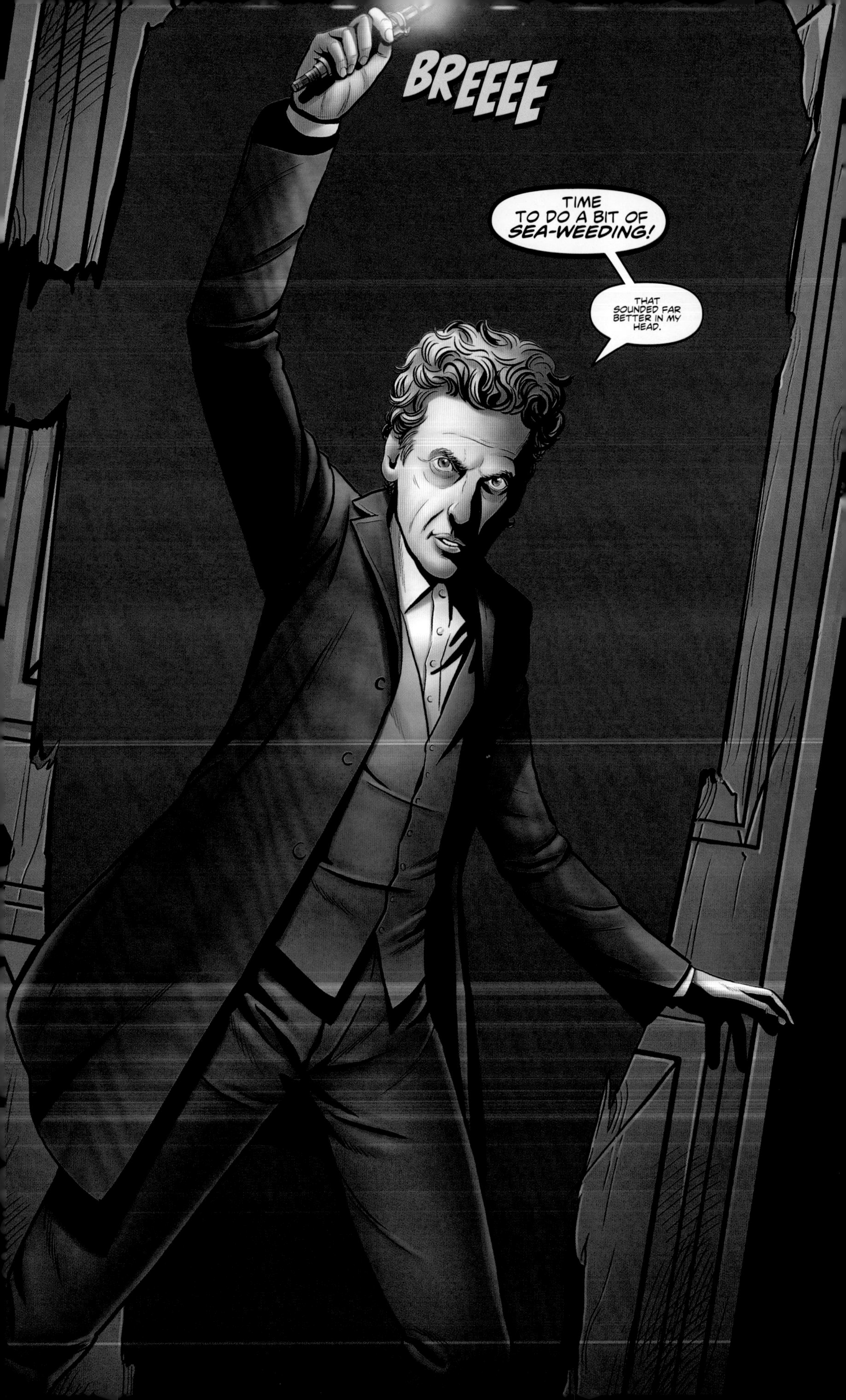
BREEEE
TIME TO DO A BIT OF SEA-WEEDING!
THAT SOUNDED FAR BETTER IN MY HEAD.

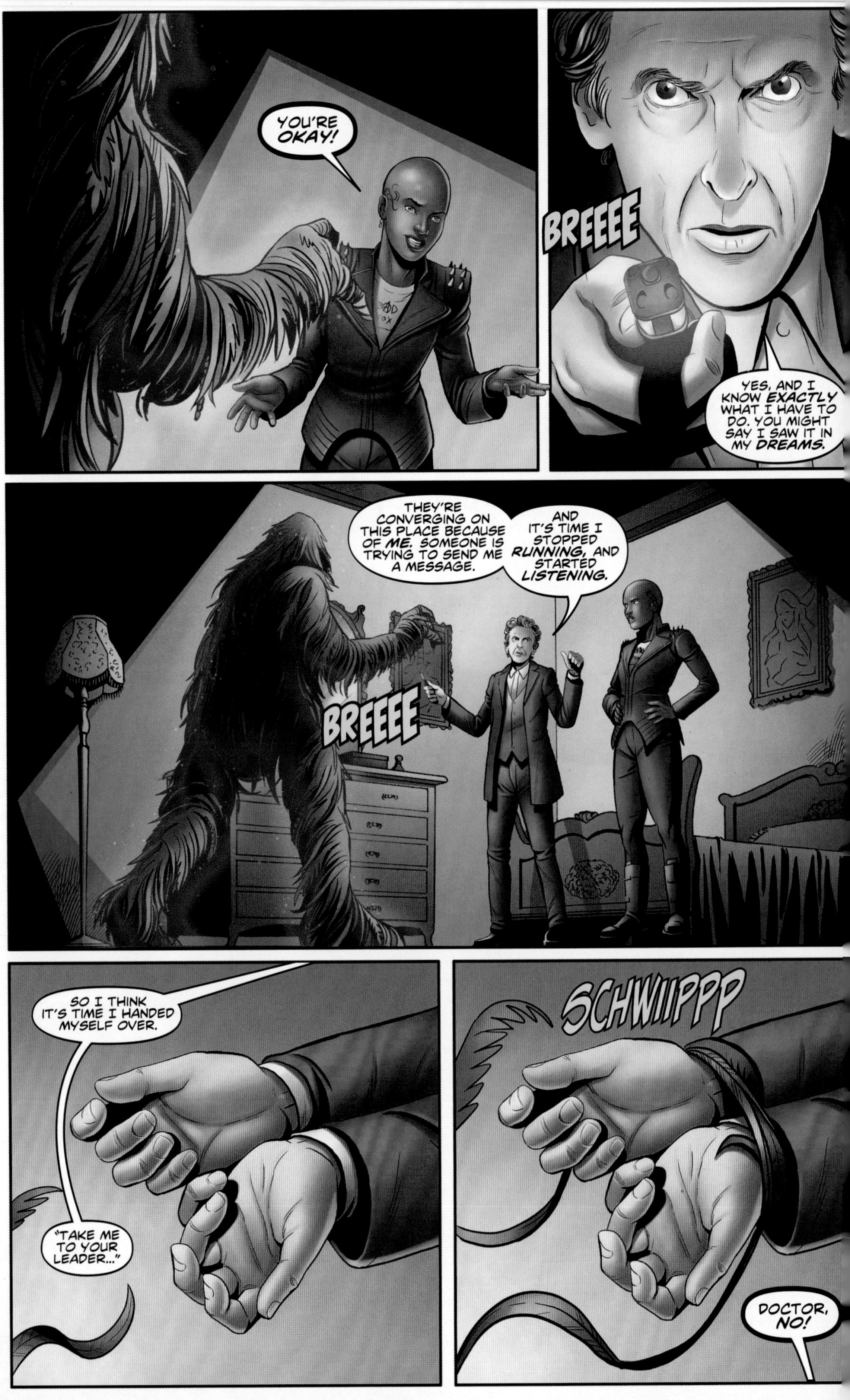
YOU'RE OKAY!
BREEEE
YES, AND I KNOW EXACTLY WHAT I HAVE TO DO. YOU MIGHT SAY I SAW IT IN MY DREAMS.
THEY'RE CONVERGING ON THIS PLACE BECAUSE OF ME. SOMEONE IS TRYING TO SEND ME A MESSAGE.
AND IT'S TIME I STOPPED RUNNING, AND STARTED LISTENING.
BREEEE
SO I THINK IT'S TIME I HANDED MYSELF OVER.
"TAKE ME TO YOUR LEADER..."
SCHWIIPPP
DOCTOR, NO!

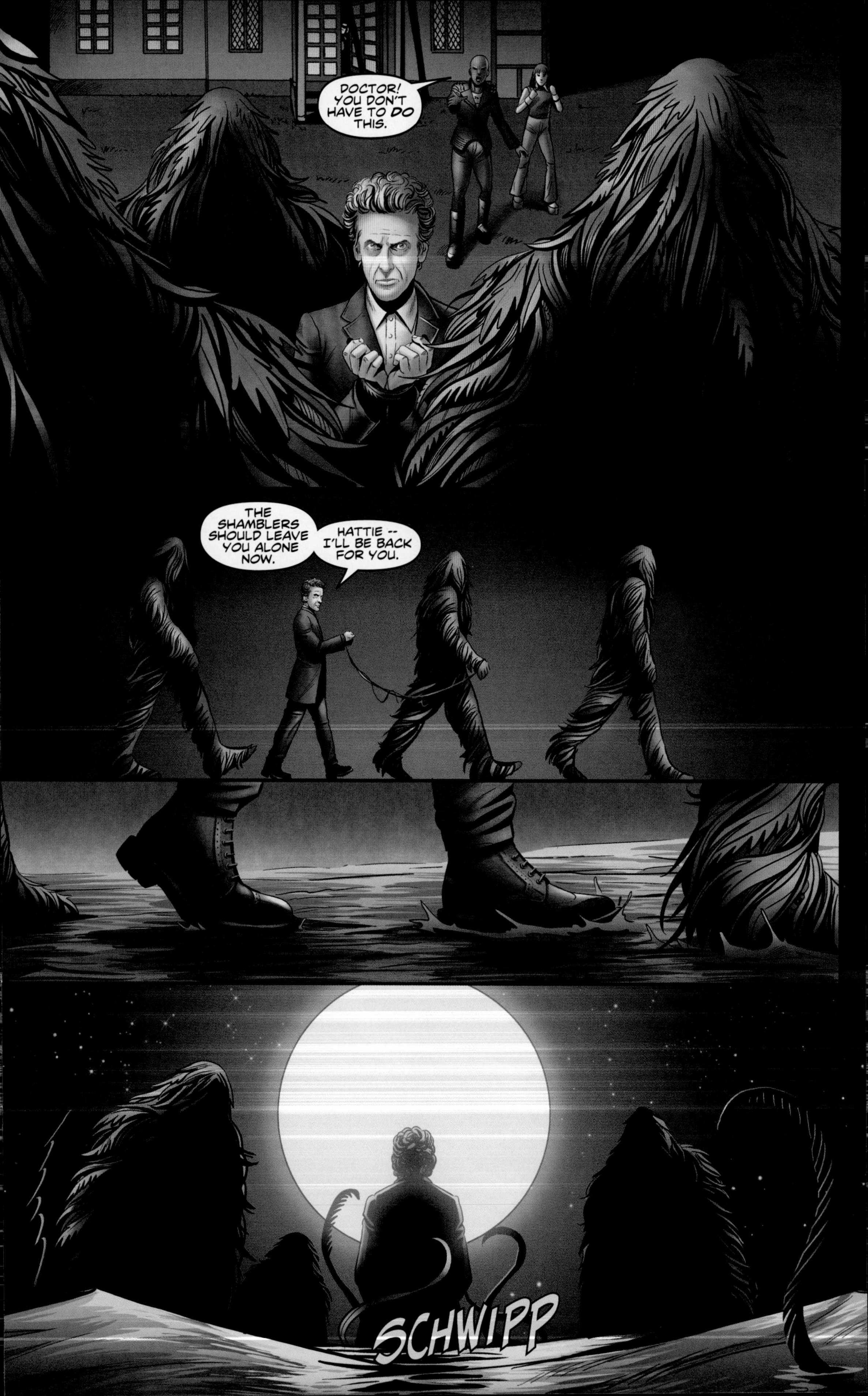
DOCTOR! YOU DON'T HAVE TO DO THIS.
THE SHAMBLERS SHOULD LEAVE YOU ALONE NOW.
HATTIE -- I'LL BE BACK FOR YOU.
SCHWIPP

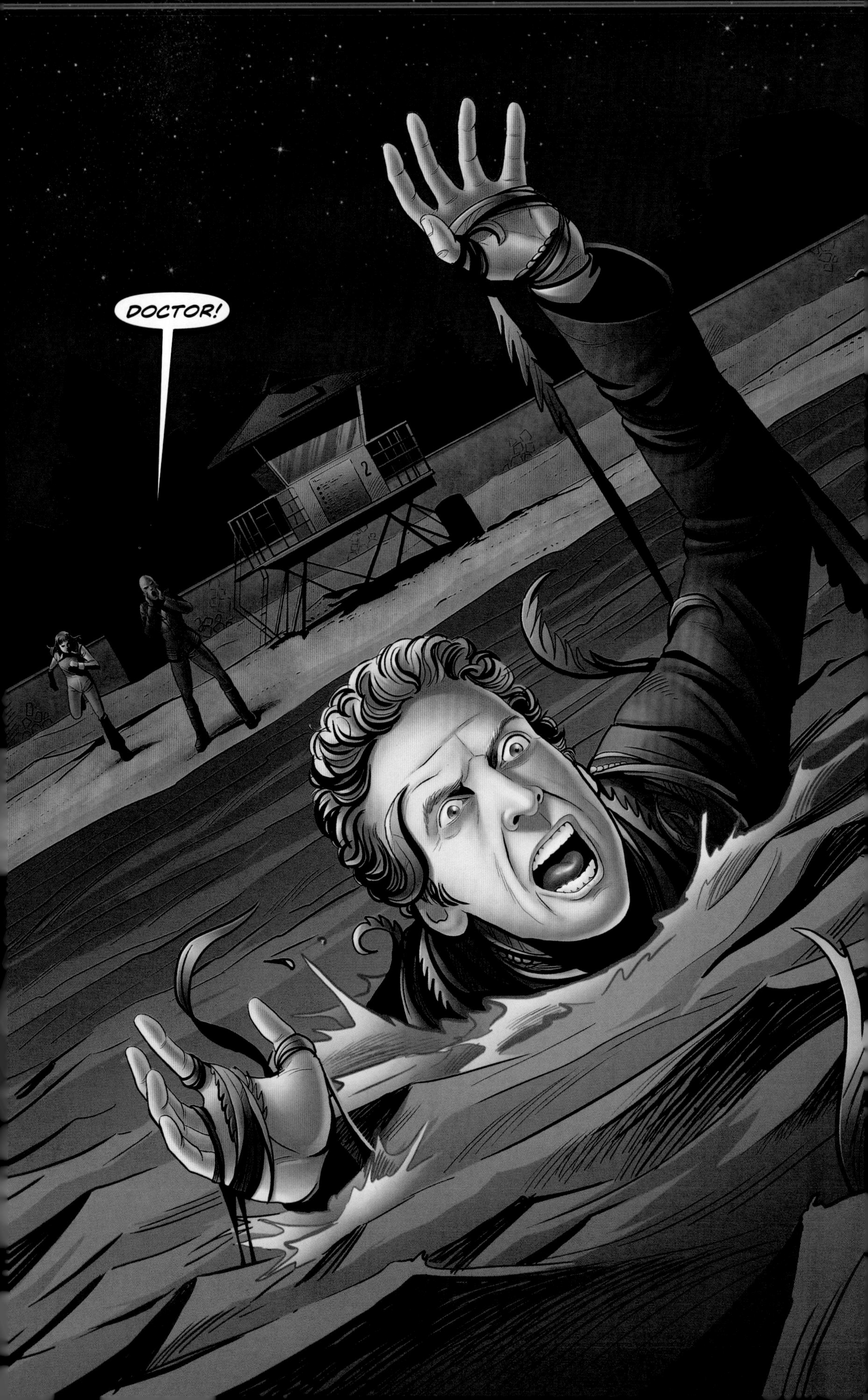
DOCTOR!

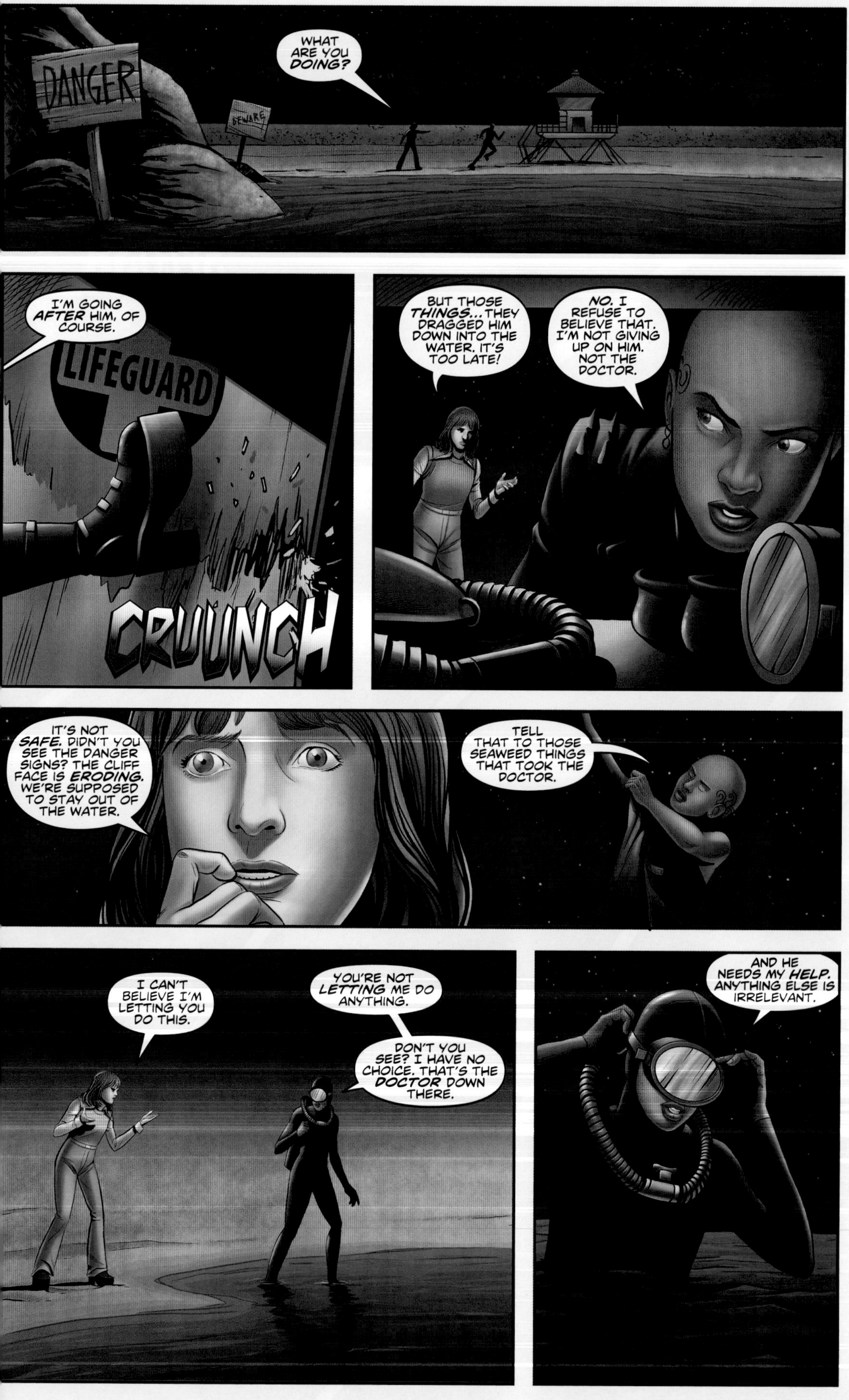
DANGER
BEWARE
WHAT ARE YOU *DOING?*
I'M GOING *AFTER* HIM, OF COURSE.
LIFEGUARD
CRUUNCH
BUT THOSE *THINGS...* THEY DRAGGED HIM DOWN INTO THE WATER. IT'S TOO LATE!
NO. I REFUSE TO BELIEVE THAT. I'M NOT GIVING UP ON HIM. NOT THE DOCTOR.
IT'S NOT *SAFE.* DIDN'T YOU SEE THE DANGER SIGNS? THE CLIFF FACE IS *ERODING.* WE'RE SUPPOSED TO STAY OUT OF THE WATER.
TELL THAT TO THOSE SEAWEED THINGS THAT TOOK THE DOCTOR.
I CAN'T BELIEVE I'M LETTING YOU DO THIS.
YOU'RE NOT *LETTING* ME DO ANYTHING.
DON'T YOU SEE? I HAVE NO CHOICE. THAT'S THE *DOCTOR* DOWN THERE.
AND HE NEEDS MY *HELP.* ANYTHING ELSE IS IRRELEVANT.

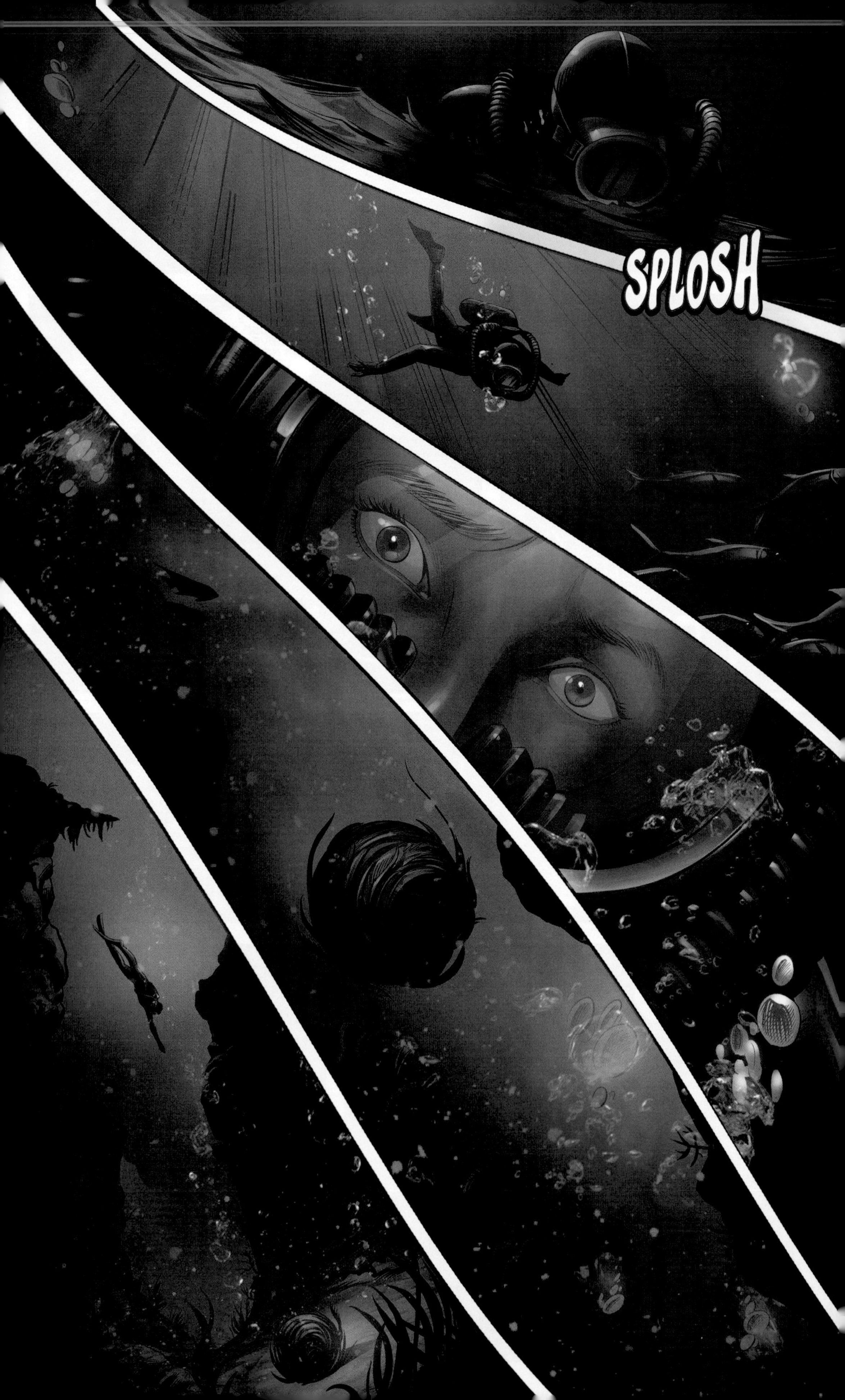
SPLOSH

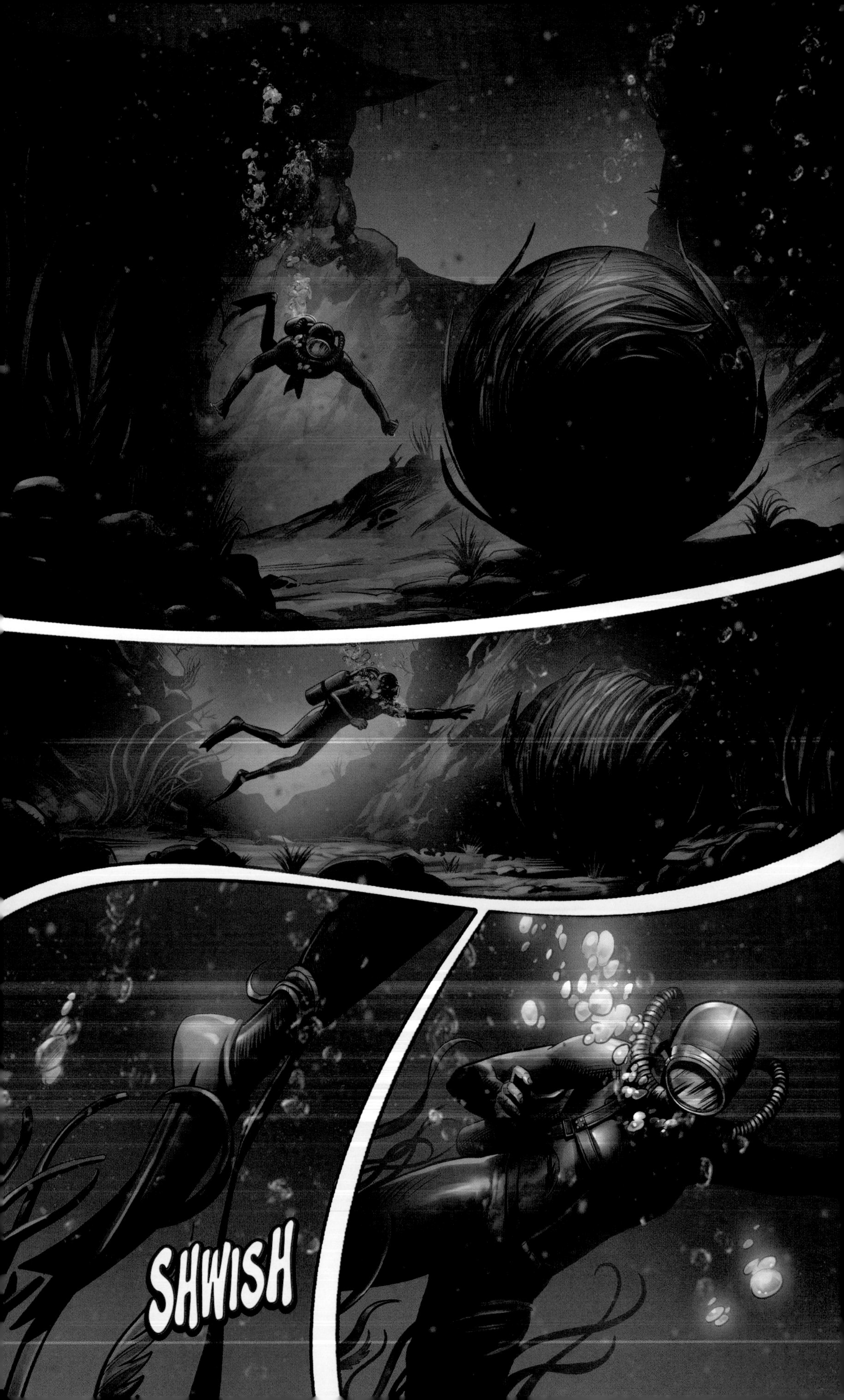
SHWISH

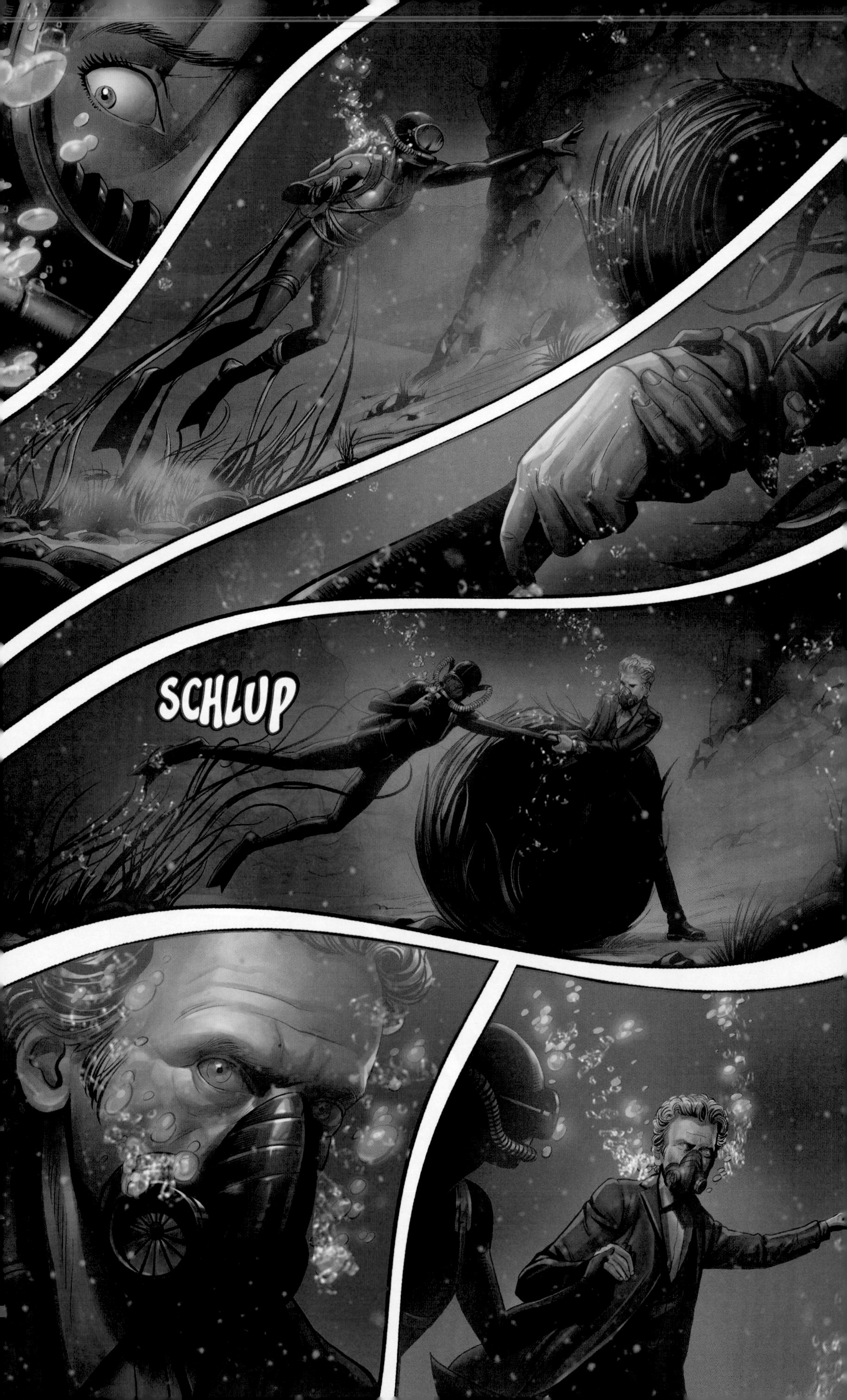
SCHLUP

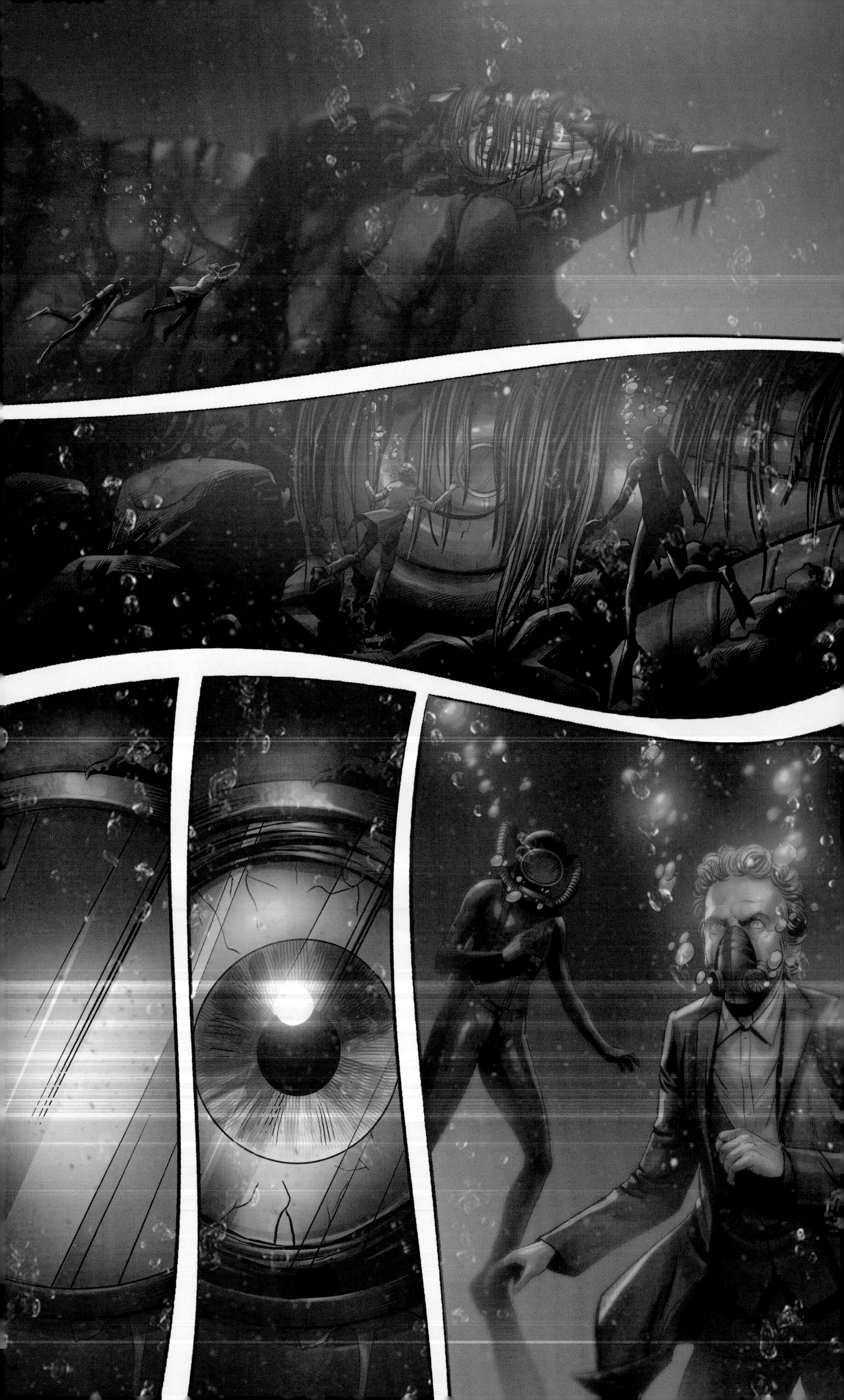

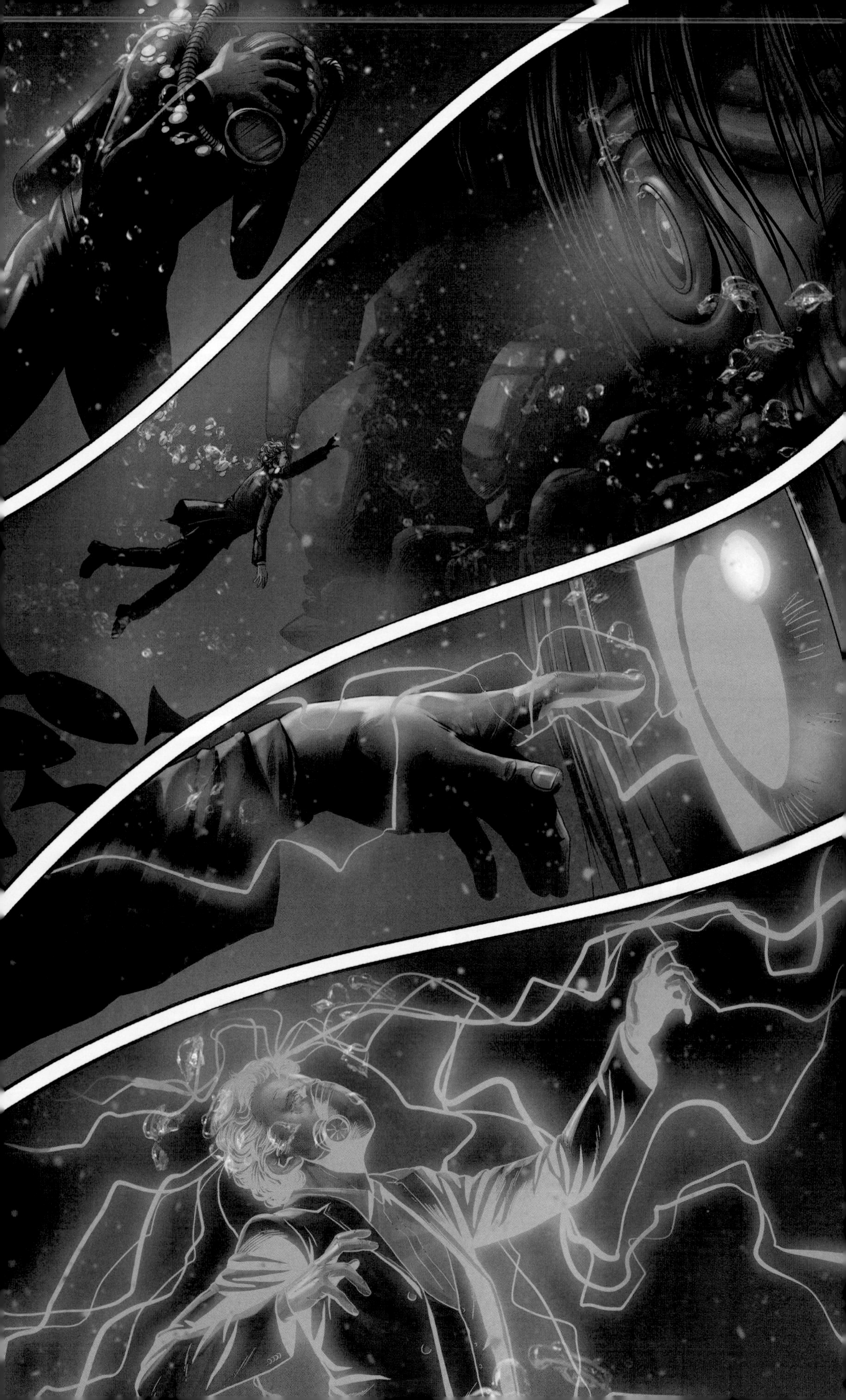

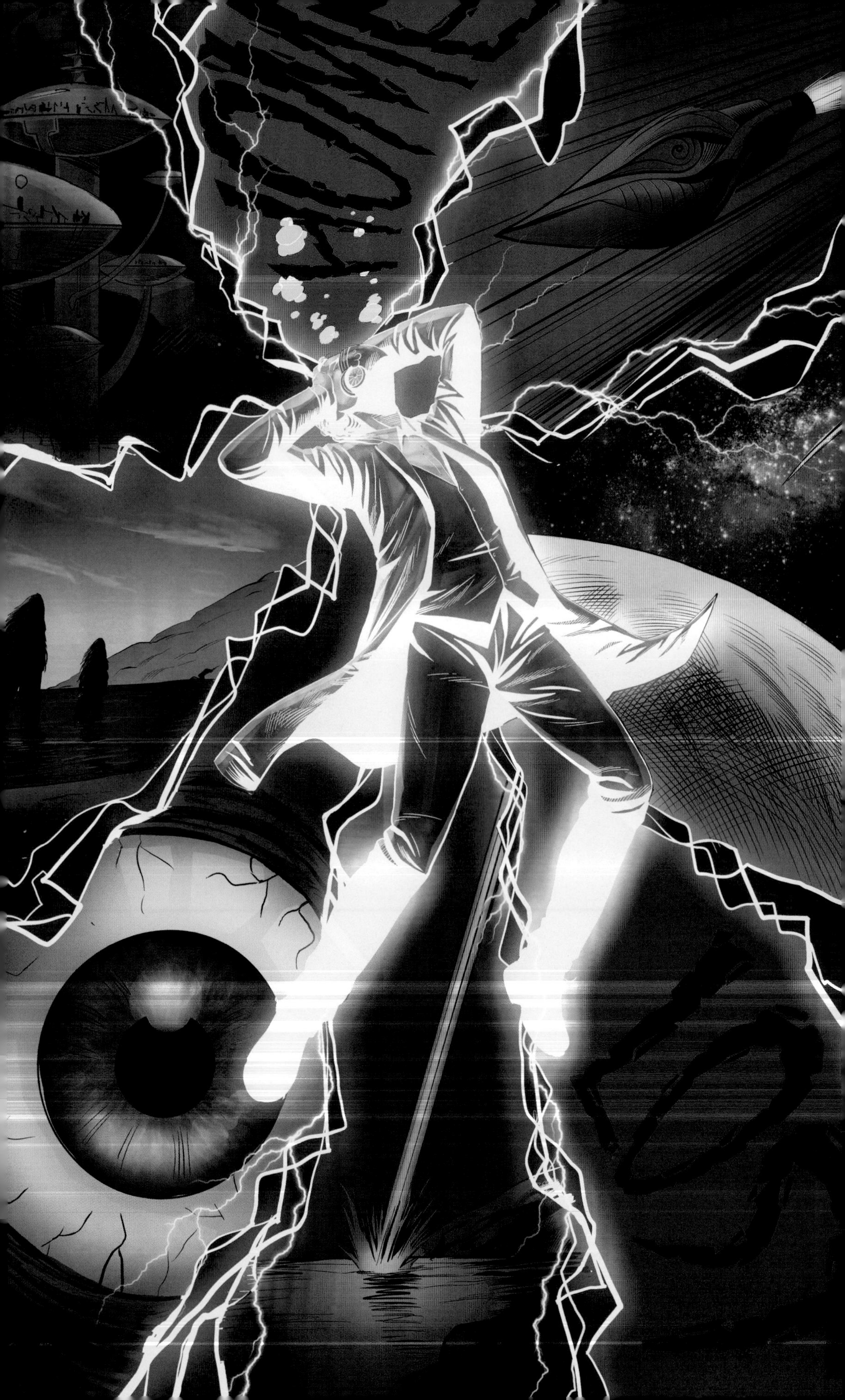

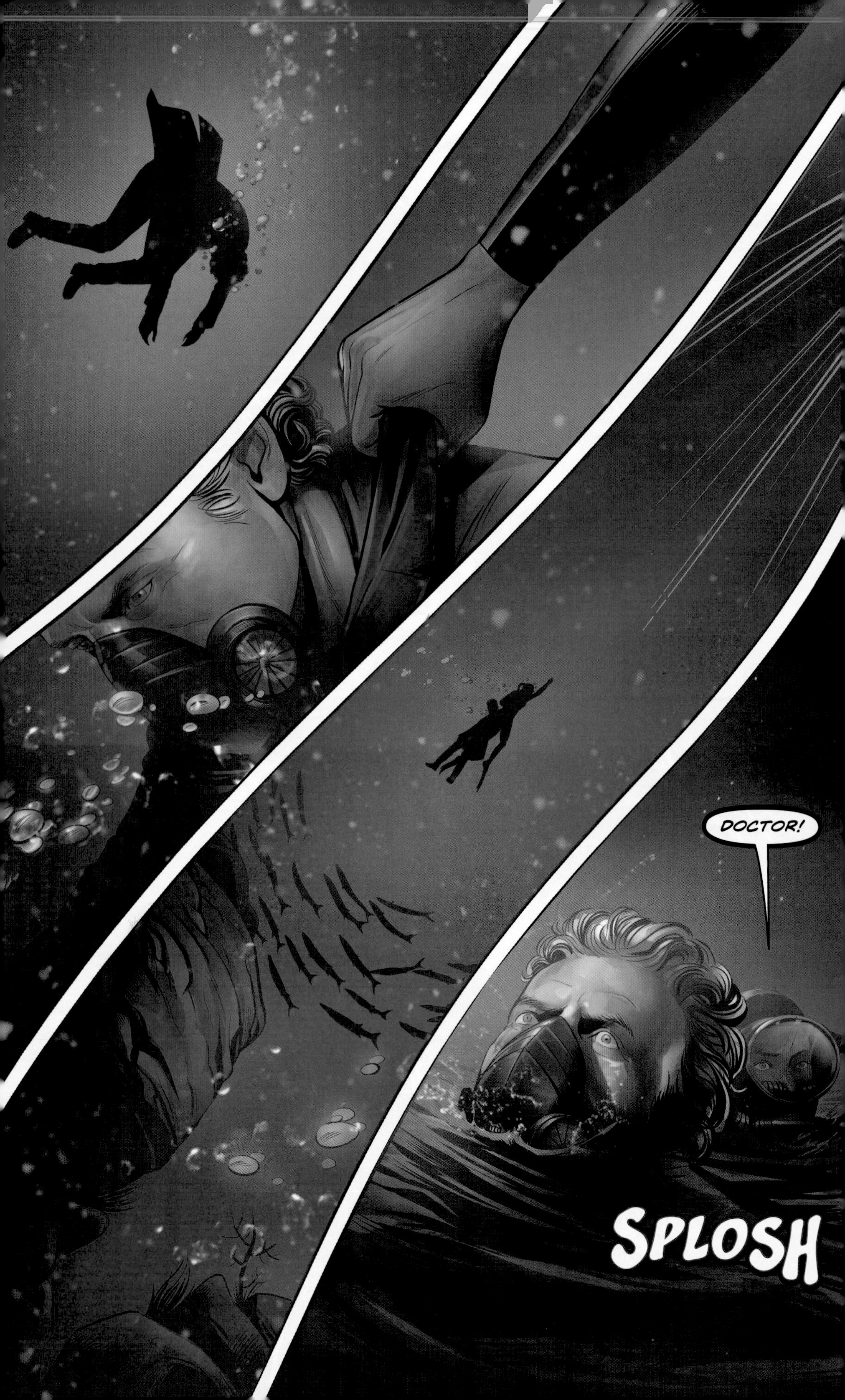
DOCTOR!
SPLOSH

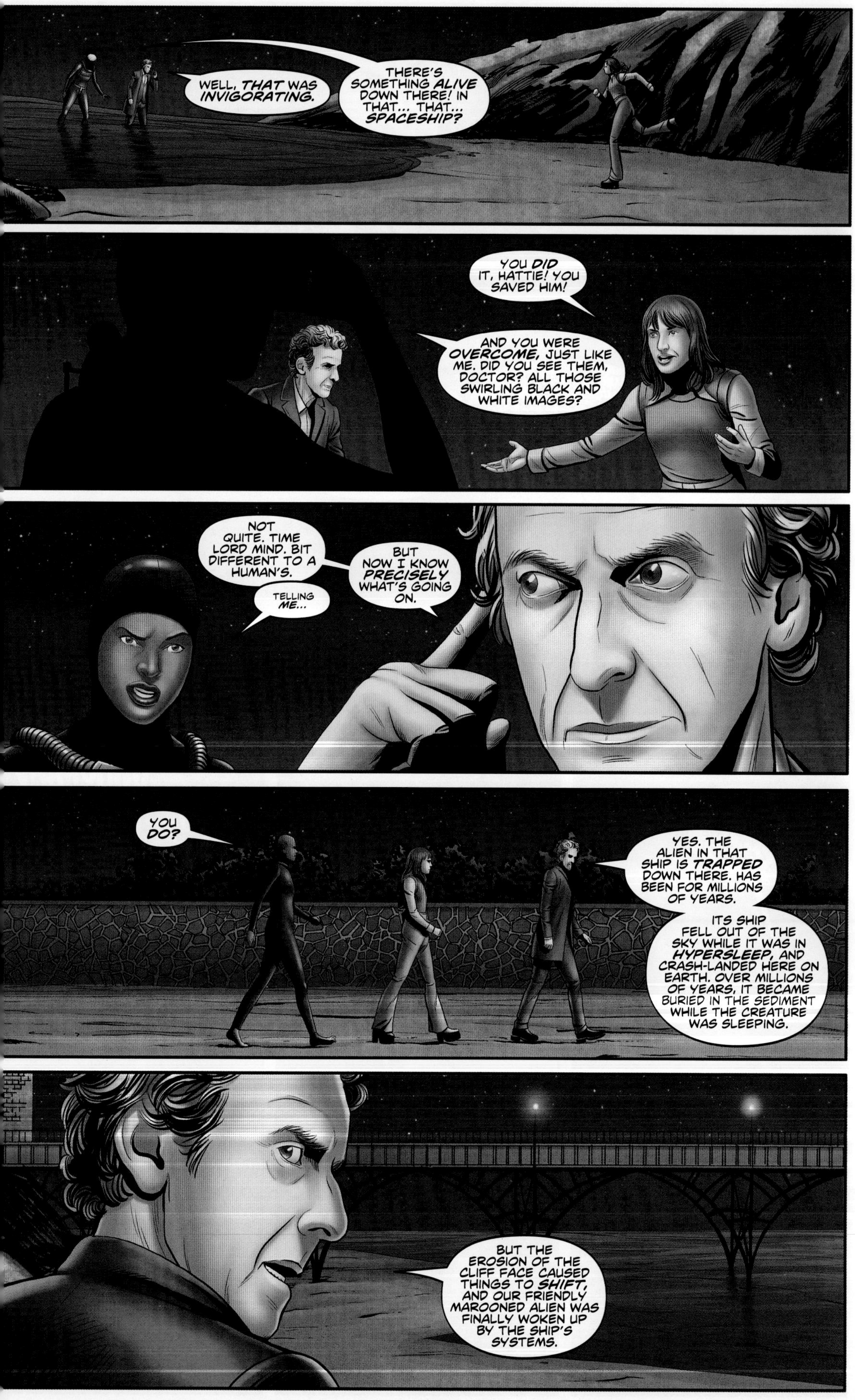
WELL, THAT WAS INVIGORATING.
THERE'S SOMETHING ALIVE DOWN THERE! IN THAT... THAT... SPACESHIP?
YOU DID IT, HATTIE! YOU SAVED HIM!
AND YOU WERE OVERCOME, JUST LIKE ME. DID YOU SEE THEM, DOCTOR? ALL THOSE SWIRLING BLACK AND WHITE IMAGES?
NOT QUITE. TIME LORD MIND. BIT DIFFERENT TO A HUMAN'S.
TELLING ME...
BUT NOW I KNOW PRECISELY WHAT'S GOING ON.
YOU DO?
YES. THE ALIEN IN THAT SHIP IS TRAPPED DOWN THERE. HAS BEEN FOR MILLIONS OF YEARS.
ITS SHIP FELL OUT OF THE SKY WHILE IT WAS IN HYPERSLEEP, AND CRASH-LANDED HERE ON EARTH. OVER MILLIONS OF YEARS, IT BECAME BURIED IN THE SEDIMENT WHILE THE CREATURE WAS SLEEPING.
BUT THE EROSION OF THE CLIFF FACE CAUSED THINGS TO SHIFT, AND OUR FRIENDLY MAROONED ALIEN WAS FINALLY WOKEN UP BY THE SHIP'S SYSTEMS.

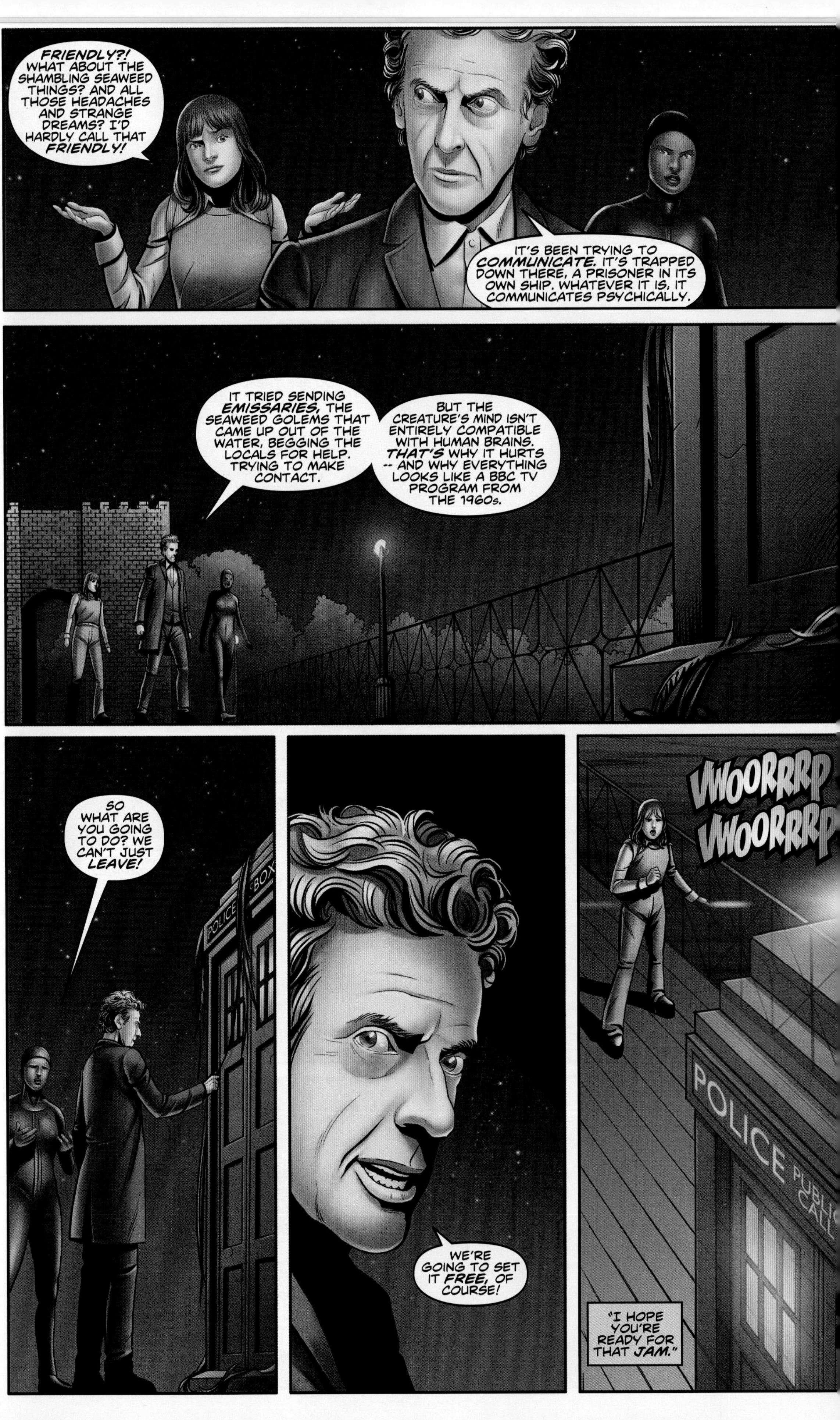
FRIENDLY?! WHAT ABOUT THE SHAMBLING SEAWEED THINGS? AND ALL THOSE HEADACHES AND STRANGE DREAMS? I'D HARDLY CALL THAT FRIENDLY!
IT'S BEEN TRYING TO COMMUNICATE. IT'S TRAPPED DOWN THERE, A PRISONER IN ITS OWN SHIP. WHATEVER IT IS, IT COMMUNICATES PSYCHICALLY.
IT TRIED SENDING EMISSARIES, THE SEAWEED GOLEMS THAT CAME UP OUT OF THE WATER, BEGGING THE LOCALS FOR HELP. TRYING TO MAKE CONTACT.
BUT THE CREATURE'S MIND ISN'T ENTIRELY COMPATIBLE WITH HUMAN BRAINS. THAT'S WHY IT HURTS -- AND WHY EVERYTHING LOOKS LIKE A BBC TV PROGRAM FROM THE 1960s.
SO WHAT ARE YOU GOING TO DO? WE CAN'T JUST LEAVE!
WE'RE GOING TO SET IT FREE, OF COURSE!
VWOORRRP VWOORRRP
"I HOPE YOU'RE READY FOR THAT JAM."

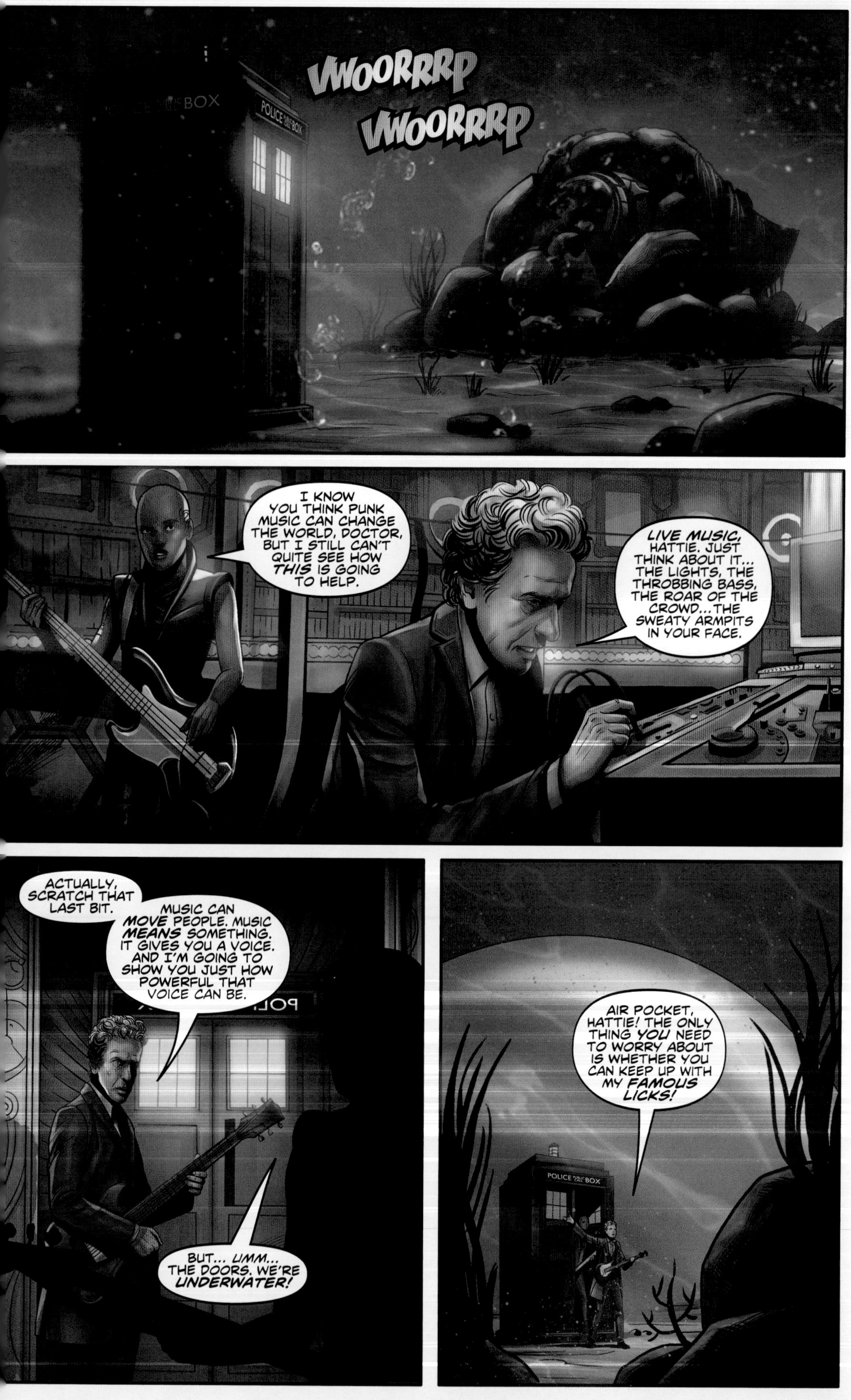
VWOORRRP
VWOORRRP
POLICE BOX
I KNOW YOU THINK PUNK MUSIC CAN CHANGE THE WORLD, DOCTOR, BUT I STILL CAN'T QUITE SEE HOW THIS IS GOING TO HELP.
LIVE MUSIC, HATTIE. JUST THINK ABOUT IT... THE LIGHTS, THE THROBBING BASS, THE ROAR OF THE CROWD... THE SWEATY ARMPITS IN YOUR FACE.
ACTUALLY, SCRATCH THAT LAST BIT.
MUSIC CAN MOVE PEOPLE. MUSIC MEANS SOMETHING. IT GIVES YOU A VOICE. AND I'M GOING TO SHOW YOU JUST HOW POWERFUL THAT VOICE CAN BE.
BUT... UMM... THE DOORS. WE'RE UNDERWATER!
AIR POCKET, HATTIE! THE ONLY THING YOU NEED TO WORRY ABOUT IS WHETHER YOU CAN KEEP UP WITH MY FAMOUS LICKS!
POLICE BOX

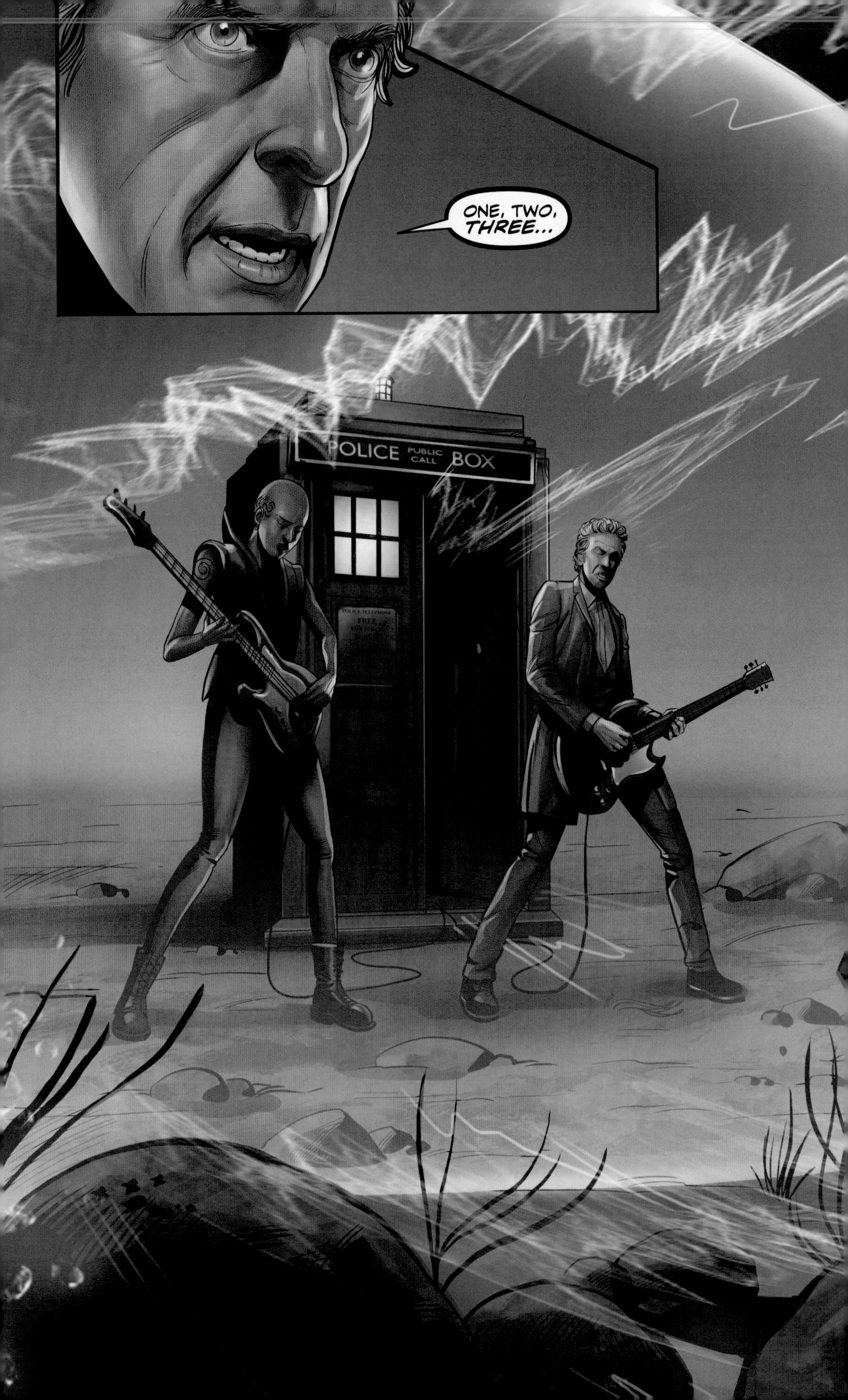
ONE, TWO, THREE...
POLICE PUBLIC CALL BOX

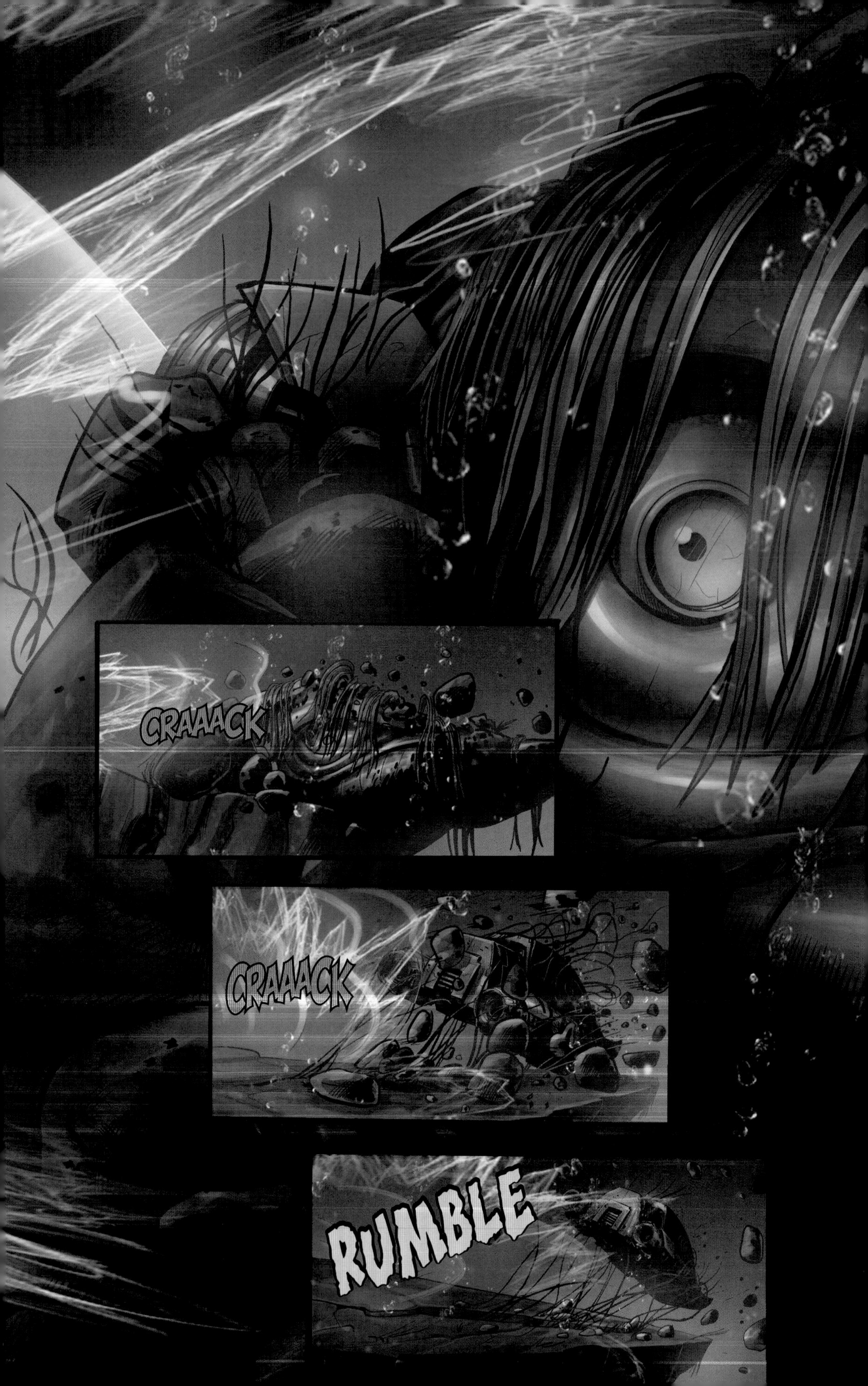
CRAAACK
CRAAACK
RUMBLE

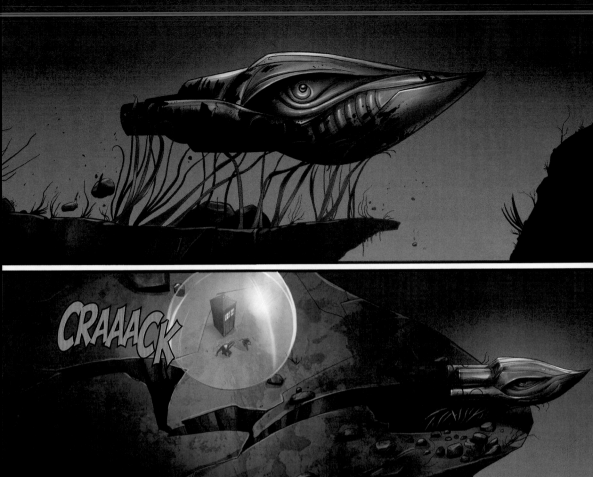

CRAAACK

DOCTOR? *THAT* DIDN'T SOUND PARTICULARLY ENCOURAGING.

I *DO* HOPE YOU'RE NOT TALKING ABOUT MY *SOLO.*

RUMBLE

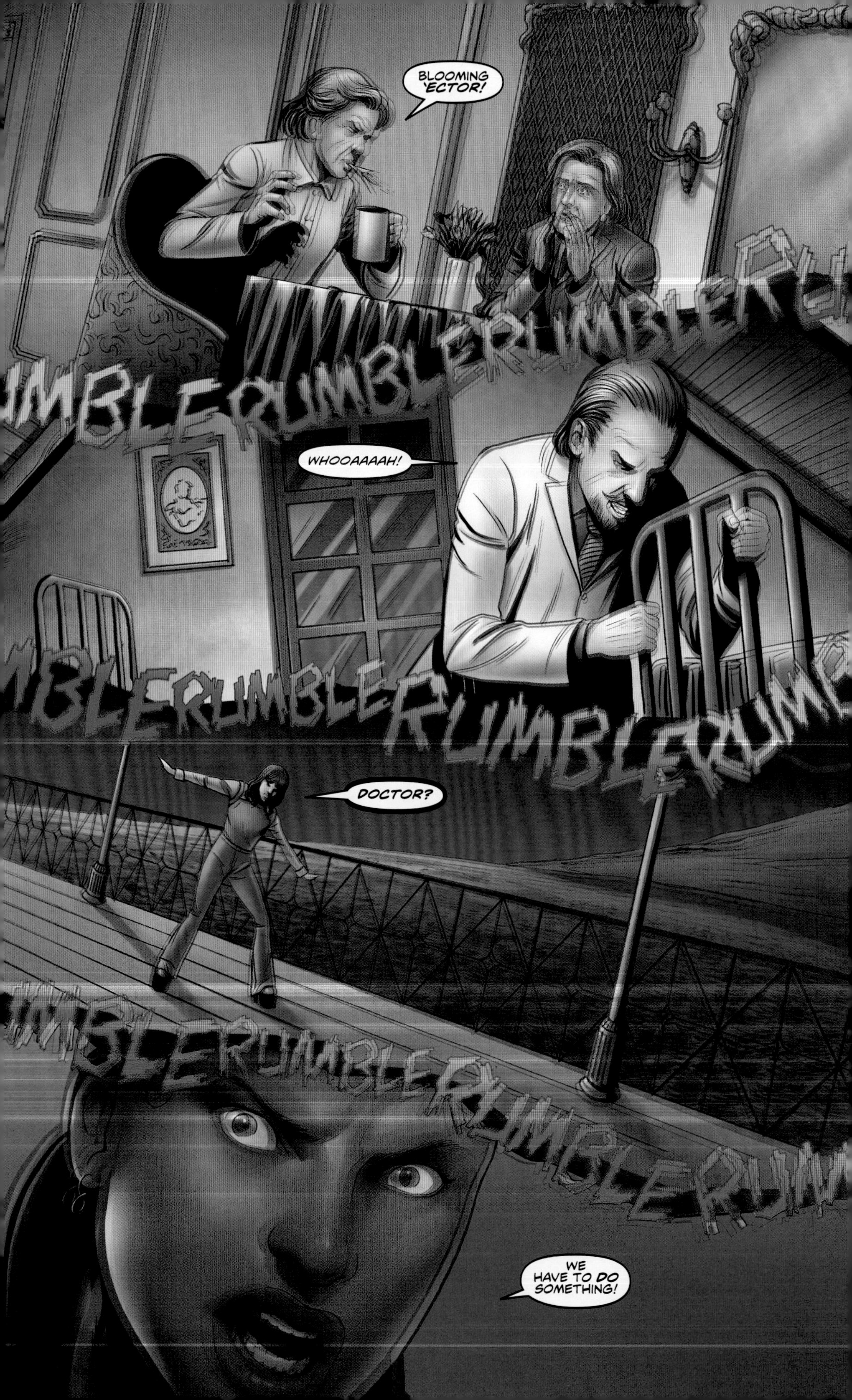
BLOOMING 'ECTOR!
UMBLERUMBLERUMBLERU
WHOOAAAAH!
MBLERUMBLERUMBLERUMB
DOCTOR?
UMBLERUMBLERUMBLERUMBLERUM
WE HAVE TO DO SOMETHING!

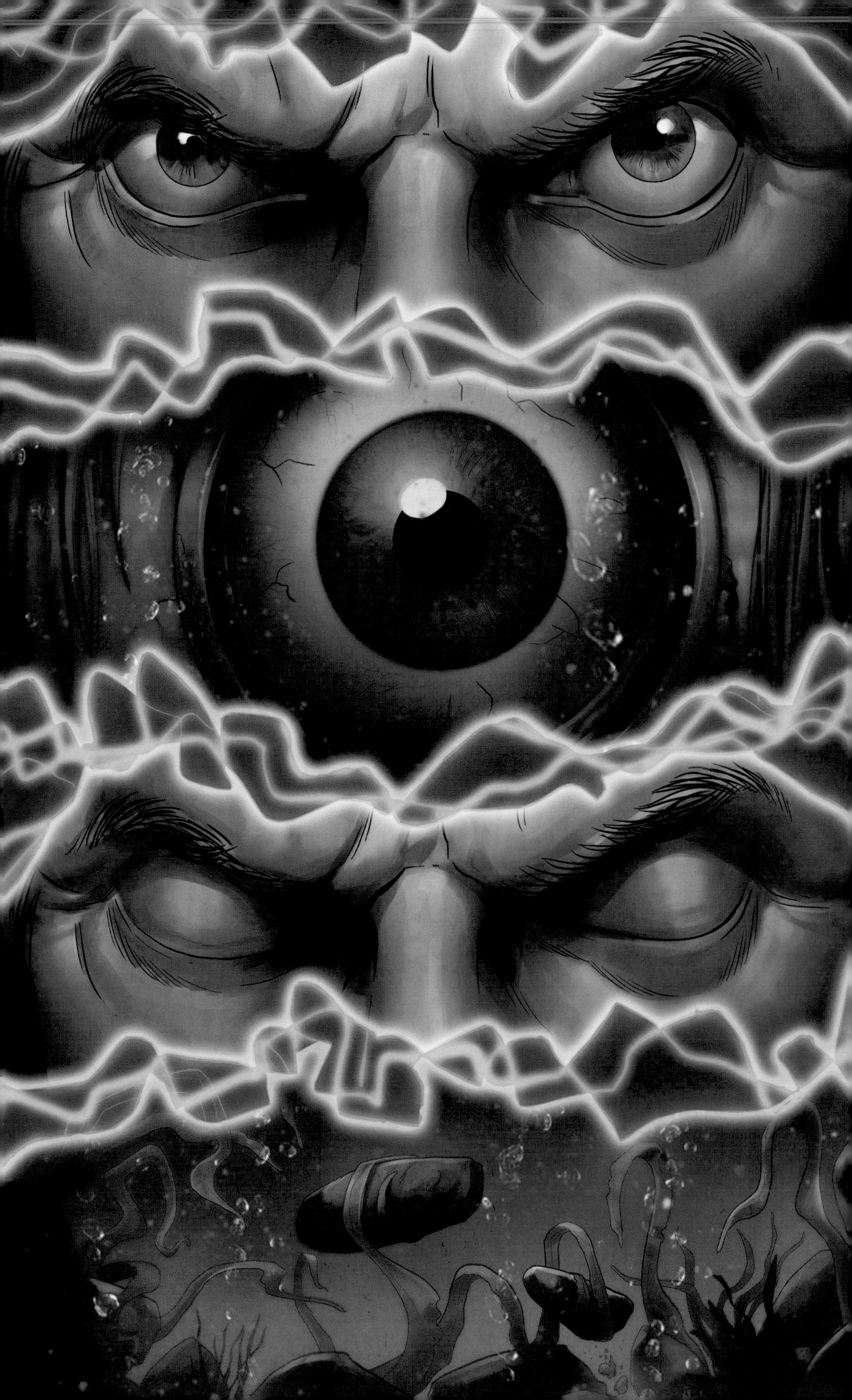

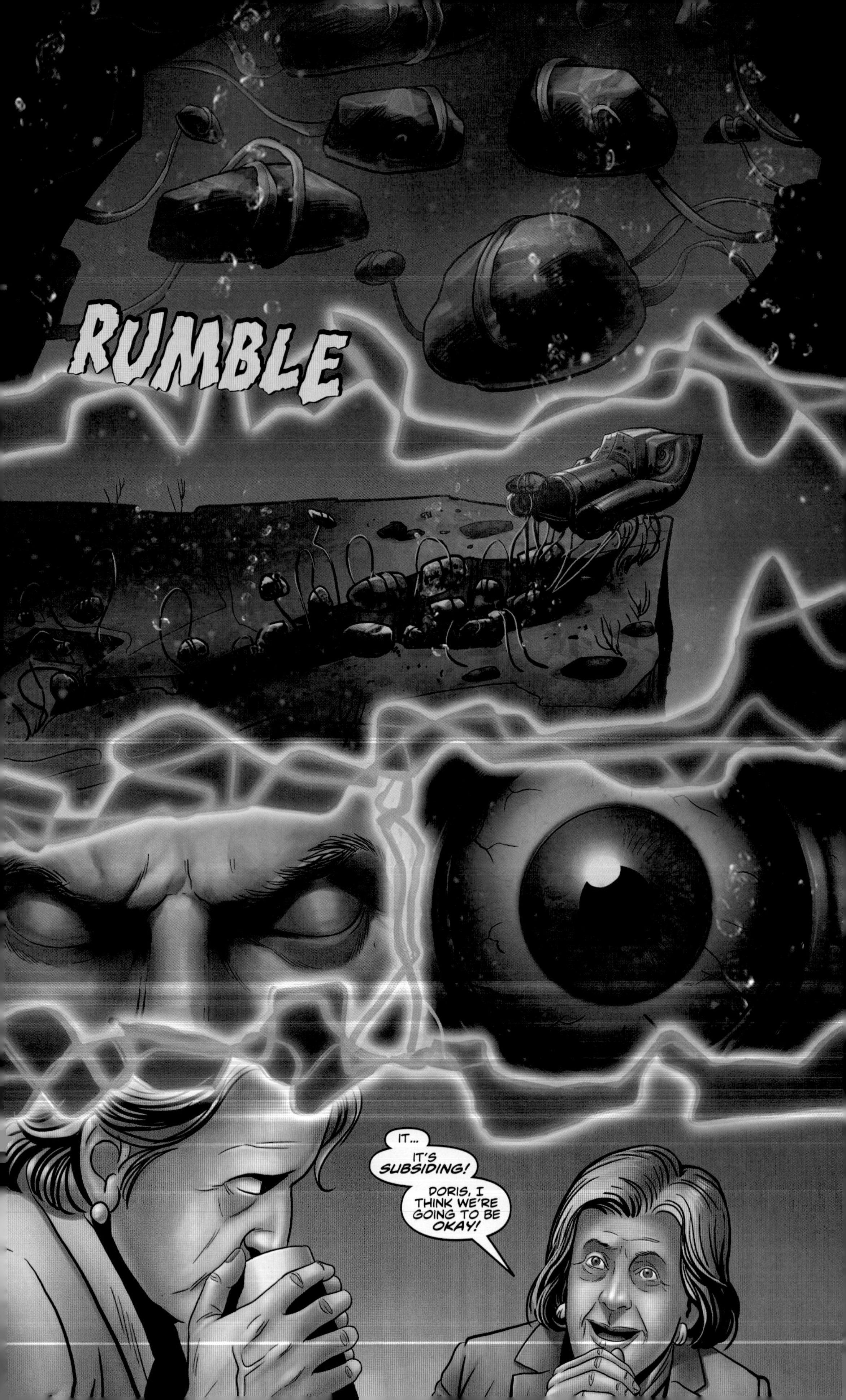
RUMBLE
IT...
IT'S SUBSIDING!
DORIS, I THINK WE'RE GOING TO BE OKAY!

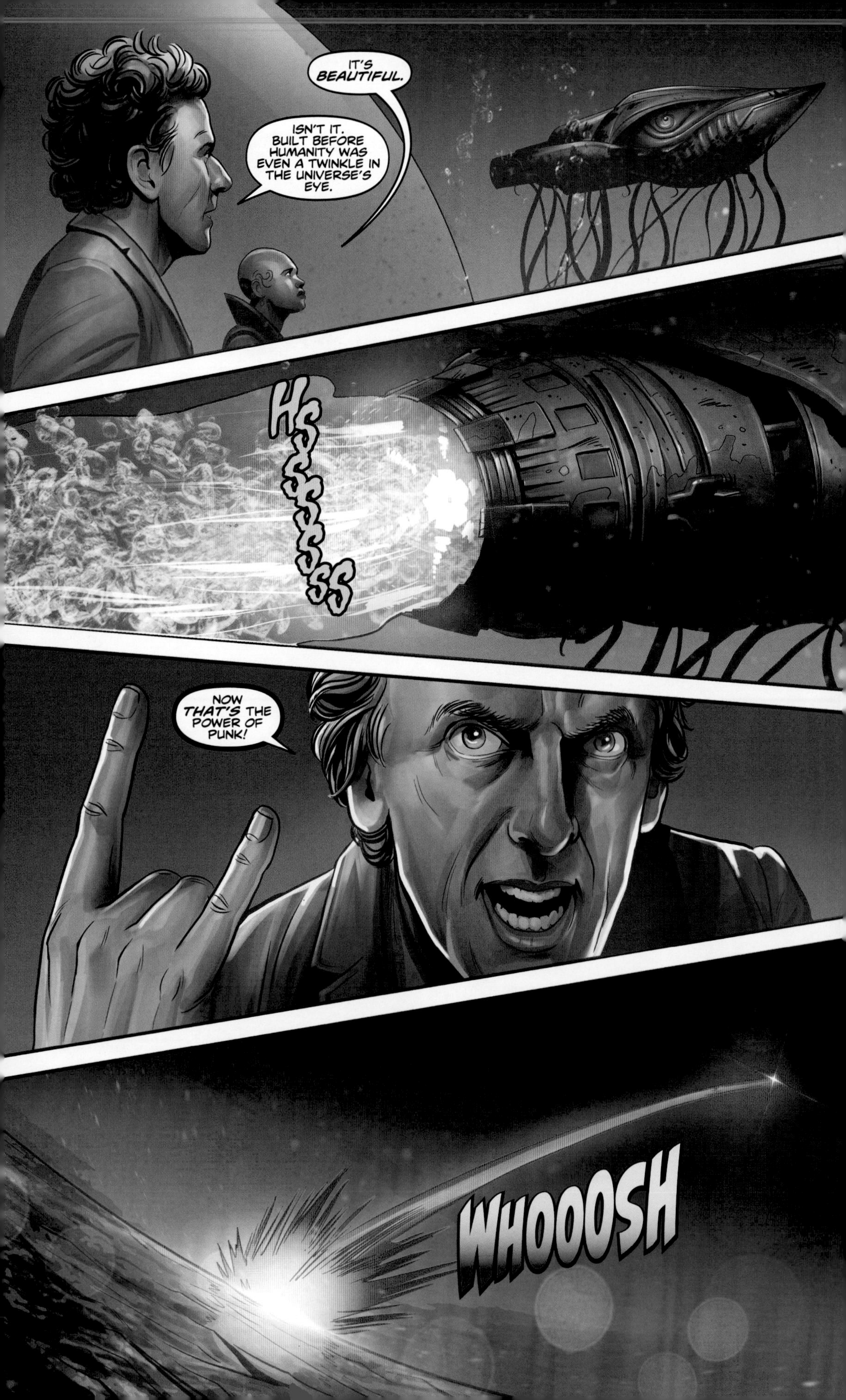

IT'S BEAUTIFUL.
ISN'T IT. BUILT BEFORE HUMANITY WAS EVEN A TWINKLE IN THE UNIVERSE'S EYE.
HSSSSSSS
NOW THAT'S THE POWER OF PUNK!
WHOOOSH

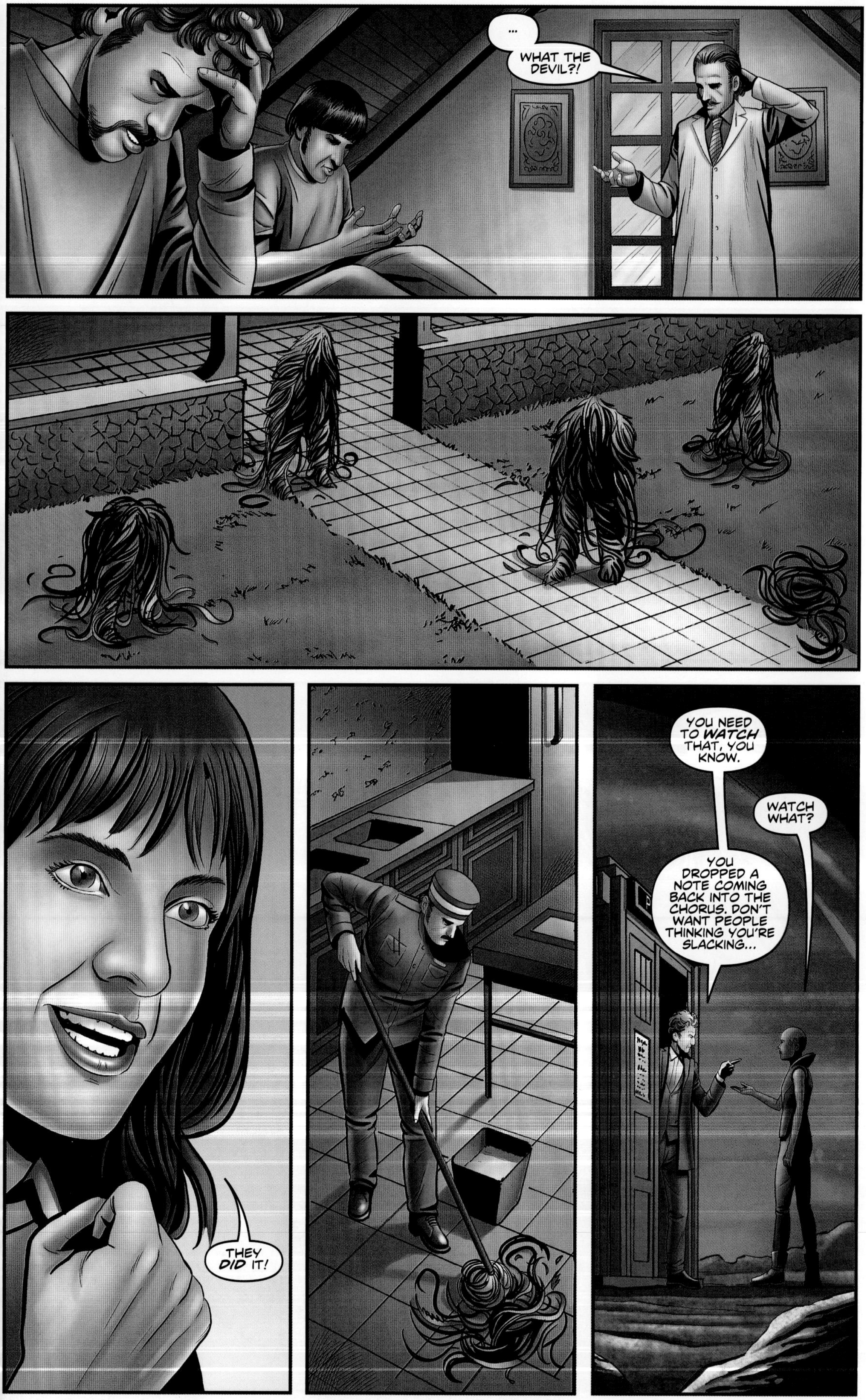
...
WHAT THE DEVIL?!
THEY DID IT!
YOU NEED TO WATCH THAT, YOU KNOW.
WATCH WHAT?
YOU DROPPED A NOTE COMING BACK INTO THE CHORUS. DON'T WANT PEOPLE THINKING YOU'RE SLACKING...

AND I HAVE HEARD THRUMMING THROUGH THE BOUGHS OF THE TREES AN ELECTRICAL HUMMING CALLING TO ME ♪

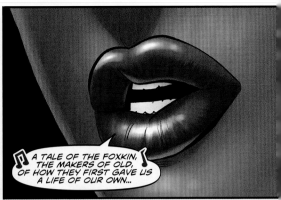

♪ A TALE OF THE FOXKIN, THE MAKERS OF OLD, OF HOW THEY FIRST GAVE US A LIFE OF OUR OWN... ♪

AHH... YOUR FIRST SOLO SINGLE.

HARDLY! IT'S JUST SOMETHING I'M MESSING ABOUT WITH.

TRUST ME. NUMBER ONE IN FIVE STAR SYSTEMS. NOT WHAT I CALL MESSING ABOUT.

WHAT?

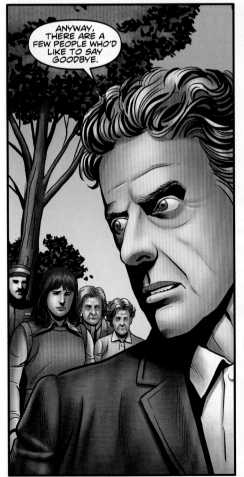

ANYWAY, THERE ARE A FEW PEOPLE WHO'D LIKE TO SAY GOODBYE.

YOU WERE SO BRAVE BACK THERE. I'M SORRY I DOUBTED YOU.

WE DID WHAT WE HAD TO DO. ALL OF US.

IT FEELS AS THOUGH A WEIGHT HAS BEEN LIFTED. THANK YOU, LOVIES.

WHAT NOW?

HOME, I THINK. DON'T YOU?

YEAH, I THINK IT'S TIME.

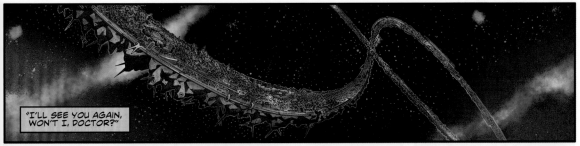

"I'LL SEE YOU AGAIN, WON'T I, DOCTOR?"

OH, I SHOULD THINK SO. YOU NEVER KNOW -- IF YOU'RE LUCKY, YOU MIGHT RUN INTO MY SPOON-PLAYING SELF AT SOME POINT. HE HAD *BRILLIANT* EYEBROWS, TOO.

WHAT ARE YOU--

OH, NEVER *MIND!* COME HERE!

OOMPH!

WELL, I CAN SEE *YOU'RE* FEELING BETTER.

YOU ALWAYS KNOW *JUST* WHAT TO DO, DON'T YOU?

TAKING ME SOMEWHERE TO MEET A CREATURE WITH NO VOICE, JUST TO SHOW ME HOW TO APPRECIATE THE PLATFORM I *DO* HAVE.

...

I REALLY DON'T KNOW *WHAT* YOU'RE TALKING ABOUT.

SEE YOU, DOCTOR. WHEN THE STARS ARE RIGHT.

CRACKING ALBUM, THAT ONE. I'LL BE BACK TO PICK UP A SIGNED COPY IN A COUPLE OF YEARS.

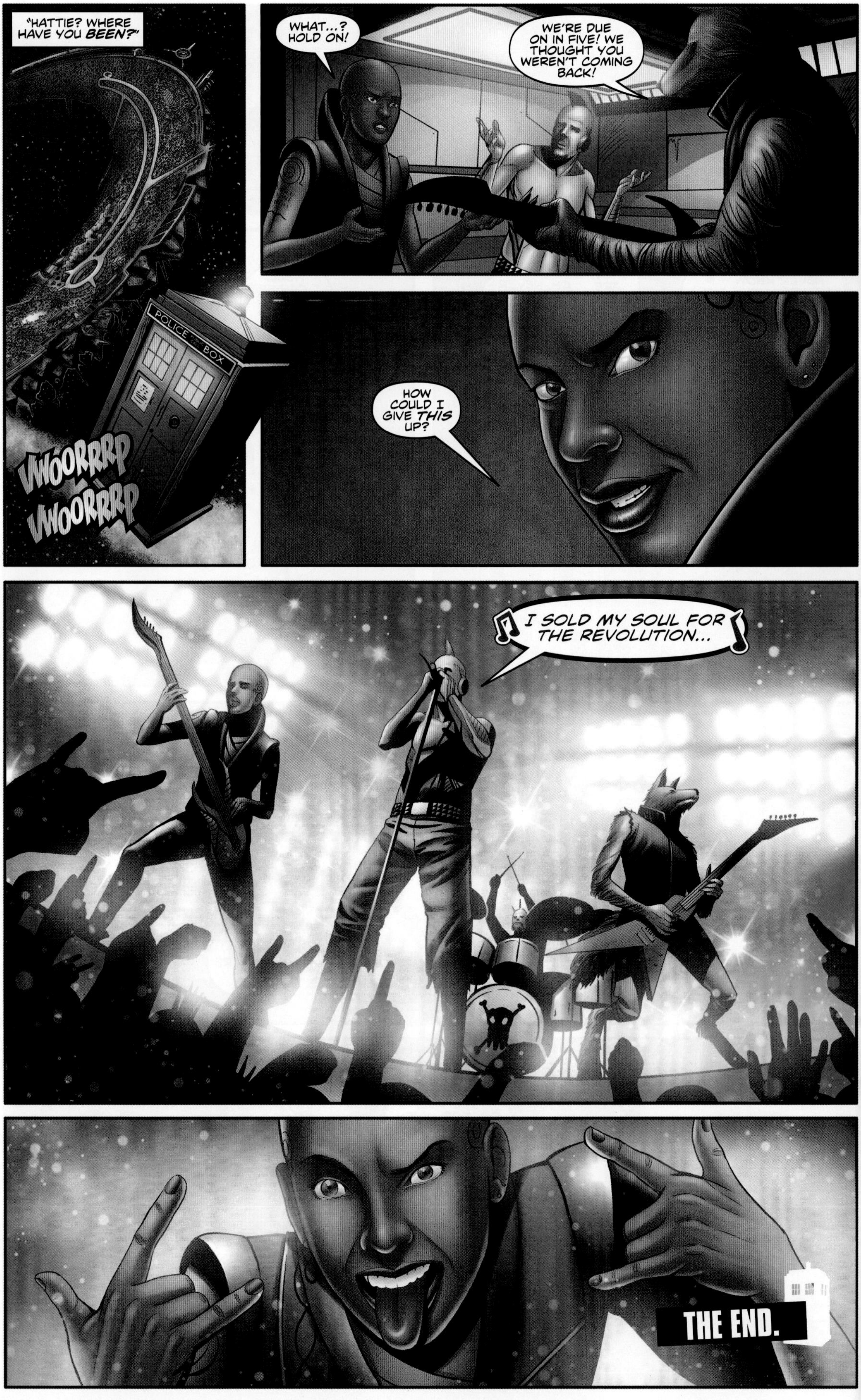
"HATTIE? WHERE HAVE YOU BEEN?"
POLICE BOX
VWOORRRP VWOORRRP
WHAT...? HOLD ON!
WE'RE DUE ON IN FIVE! WE THOUGHT YOU WEREN'T COMING BACK!
HOW COULD I GIVE THIS UP?
I SOLD MY SOUL FOR THE REVOLUTION...
THE END.

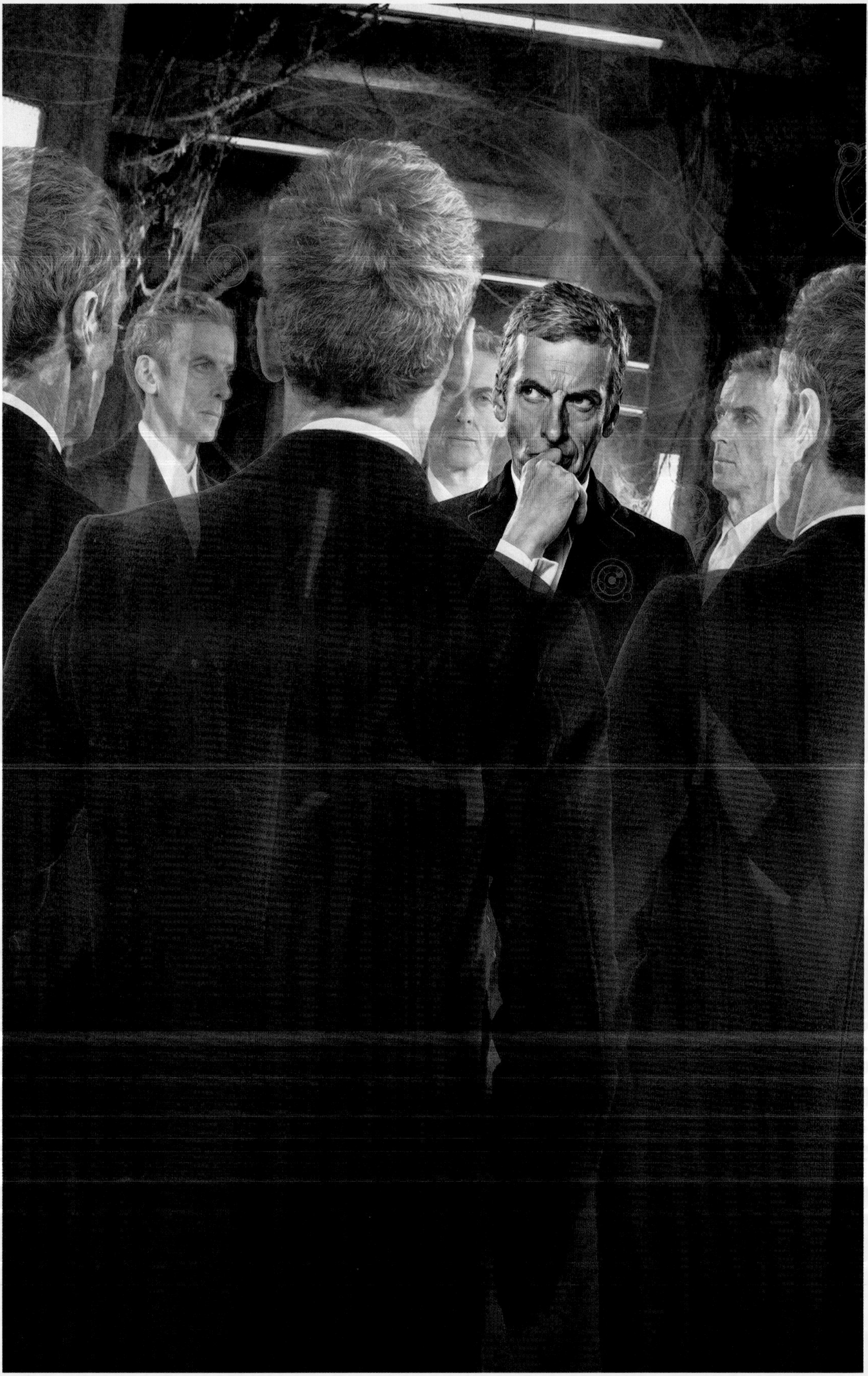

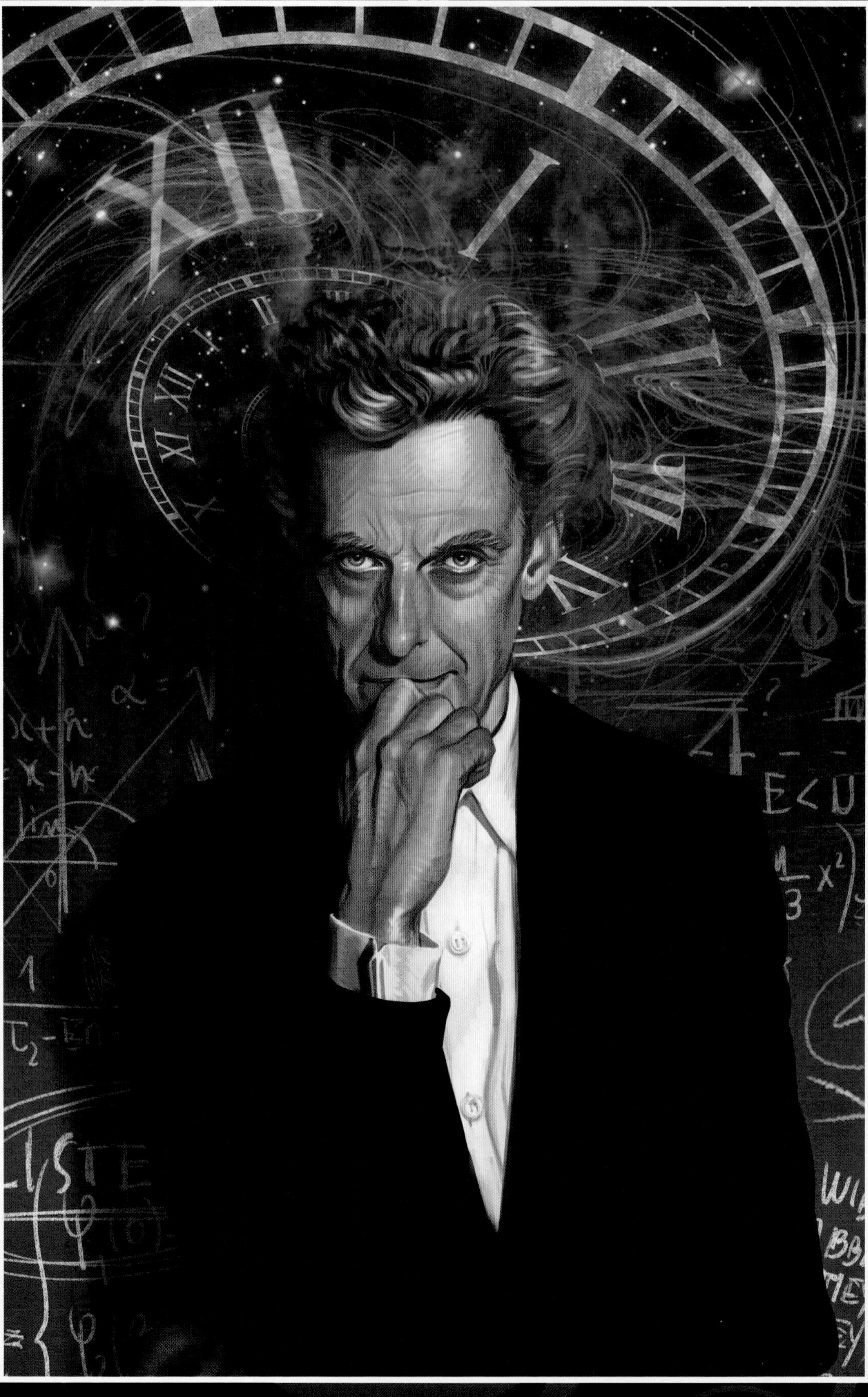

12D #3.2 Cover A: CLAUDIA IANNICIELLO

VWOORRRP

VWOORRRP

OH. WE'VE LANDED.

WHAT WAS ALL *THAT* ABOUT, EH?

NICE SIMPLE JAUNT BACK IN TIME AND YOU GET ALL MOODY LIKE WE'RE BREAKING THE FIFTH RULE OF THERMO--

POLICE PUBLIC BOX

THUD

AIIIIIIEEEEEE!!

LISTEN, JUST BECAUSE YOU'VE DROPPED ME SOMEWHERE *INTERESTING*, DON'T THINK THAT THIS GETS YOU--

POLICE PUBLIC BOX

--DYNAMICS.

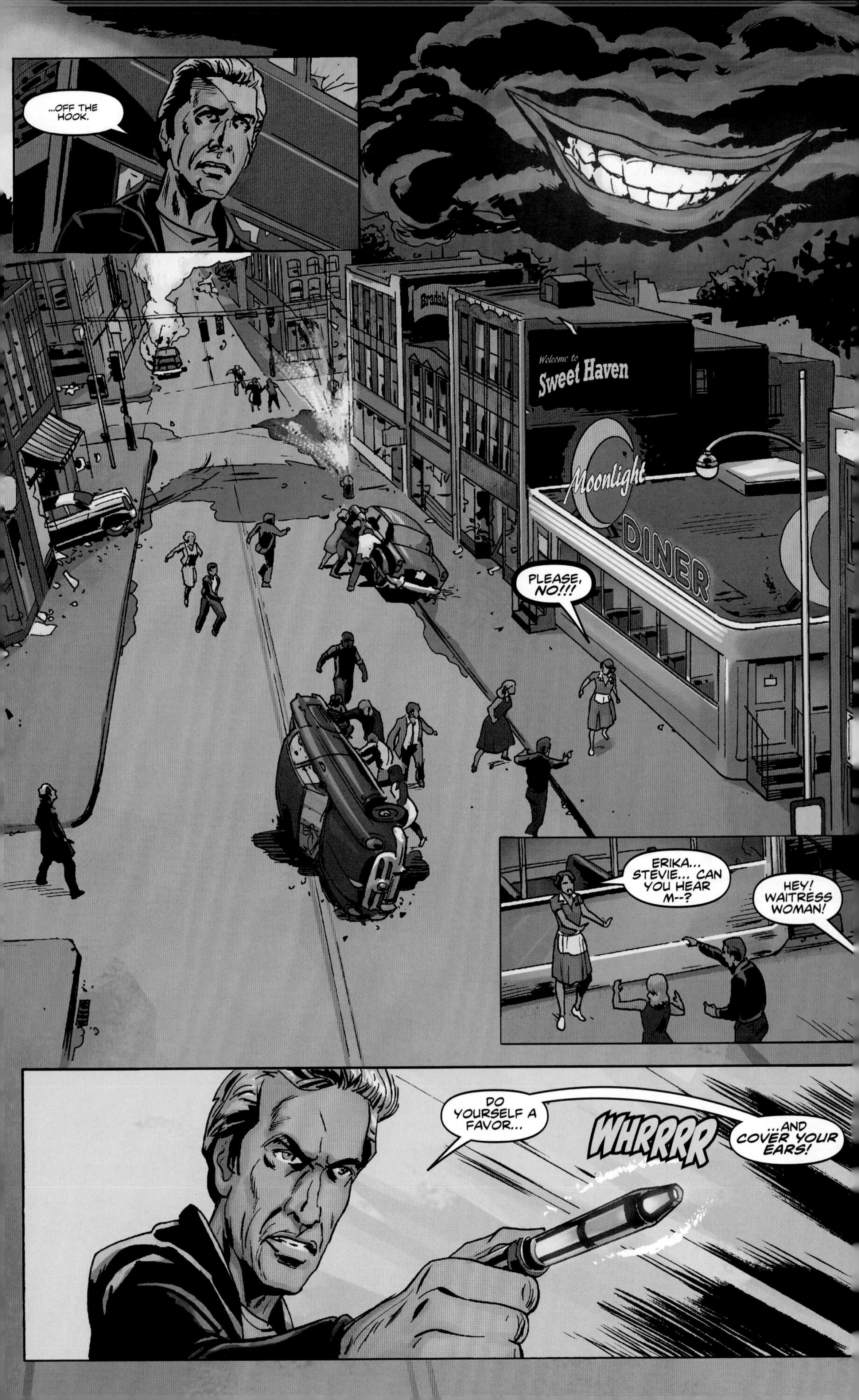
...OFF THE HOOK.
Welcome to
Sweet Haven
Moonlight
DINER
PLEASE, NO!!!
ERIKA... STEVIE... CAN YOU HEAR M--?
HEY! WAITRESS WOMAN!
DO YOURSELF A FAVOR...
WHRRRR
...AND COVER YOUR EARS!

SKRREEEEEEEEEE

ARRRGGGGGHHH!

SMASH

≥UNNNGH!≤

WH... WHAT DID YOU DO?

LOCALIZED SONIC BLAST.

I'M SORRY--?!

CALL IT A CLEVER THING.

WHERE ARE WE GOING?!

SOMEWHERE SAFE.

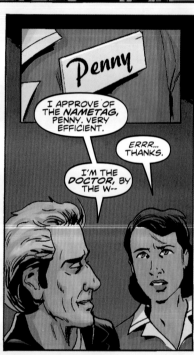

Penny

I APPROVE OF THE NAMETAG, PENNY. VERY EFFICIENT.

ERRR... THANKS.

I'M THE DOCTOR, BY THE W--

OH, THAT'S NOT GOOD.

NO COMMENT.

YOUR 'SAFE PLACE'. DOWN THAT ALLEY?

GREAT.

PENNY!!!!!

PENNY BARKER!!

HAPPEN TO KNOW ANYWHERE ELSE?

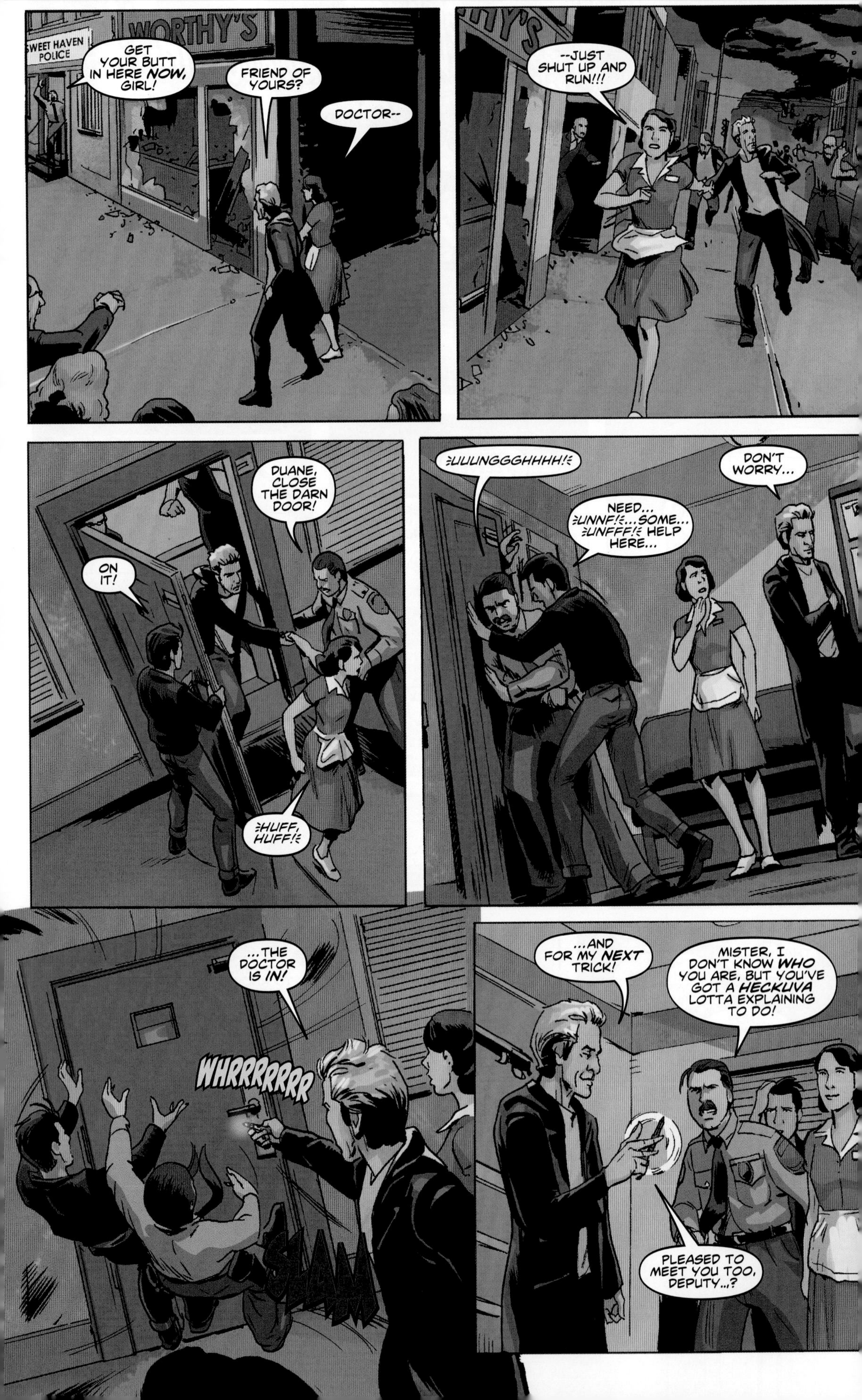
WORTHY'S
SWEET HAVEN POLICE
GET YOUR BUTT IN HERE NOW, GIRL!
FRIEND OF YOURS?
DOCTOR--
--JUST SHUT UP AND RUN!!!
DUANE, CLOSE THE DARN DOOR!
ON IT!
HUFF, HUFF!
UUUNGGGHHHH!
NEED... UNNF!...SOME... UNFFF! HELP HERE...
DON'T WORRY...
...THE DOCTOR IS IN!
WHRRRRRRR
SLAM
...AND FOR MY NEXT TRICK!
MISTER, I DON'T KNOW WHO YOU ARE, BUT YOU'VE GOT A HECKUVA LOTTA EXPLAINING TO DO!
PLEASED TO MEET YOU TOO, DEPUTY...?

DECKER. WHAT WERE YOU DOING OUTSIDE?

OH, Y'KNOW... LOCAL CUISINE RATED VERY HIGHLY. SEVEN STARS. VERY UNUSUAL. WANTED TO HAVE A TASTE.

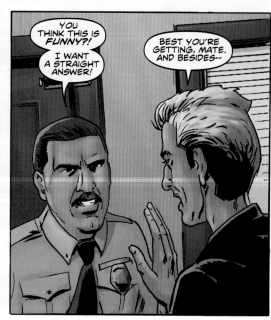

YOU THINK THIS IS *FUNNY*?! I WANT A STRAIGHT ANSWER!

BEST YOU'RE GETTING, MATE. AND BESIDES--

--I'VE GOT SOME QUESTIONS OF MY OWN.

LIKE, HOW COME THE LOCAL... *LOCALS* ARE NOW A GIBBERING HORDE?

AND WHY IS THERE A *GIANT TOOTHY GRIN* IN THE SKY?

BECAUSE FROM WHERE *I'M* SITTING, THAT LOOKS LIKE A SERIOUS FAILURE OF LOCAL LAW AND ORDER TO ME.

I OUGHTA WIPE THAT SMIRK CLEAN OFF YOUR--

IT STARTED A WEEK AGO.

JUST AN ORDINARY EVENING.

LIKE ANY *OTHER* EVENING IN SWEET HAVEN.

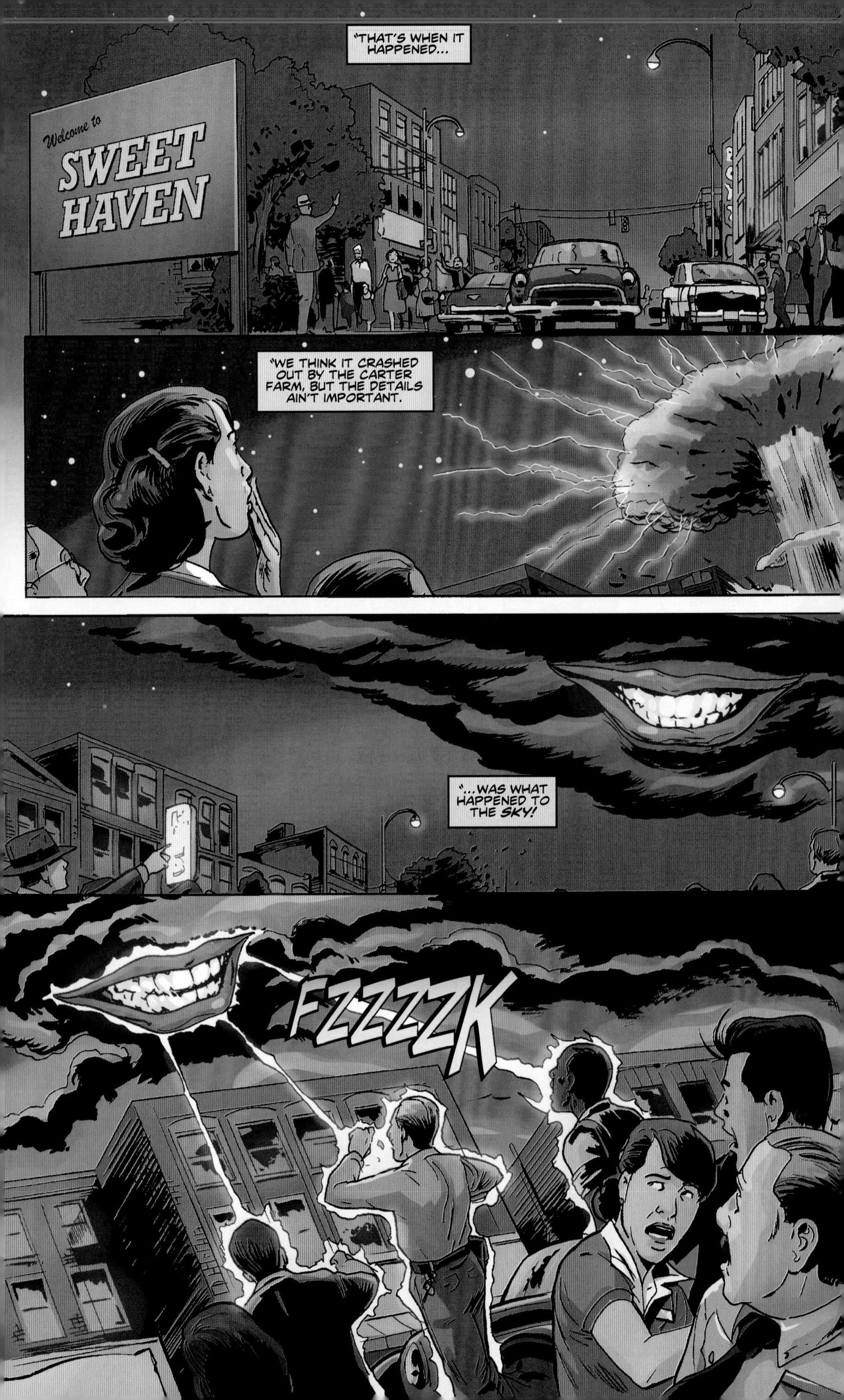

"THAT'S WHEN IT HAPPENED...
Welcome to
SWEET HAVEN
"WE THINK IT CRASHED OUT BY THE CARTER FARM, BUT THE DETAILS AIN'T IMPORTANT.
"...WAS WHAT HAPPENED TO THE SKY!
FZZZZK

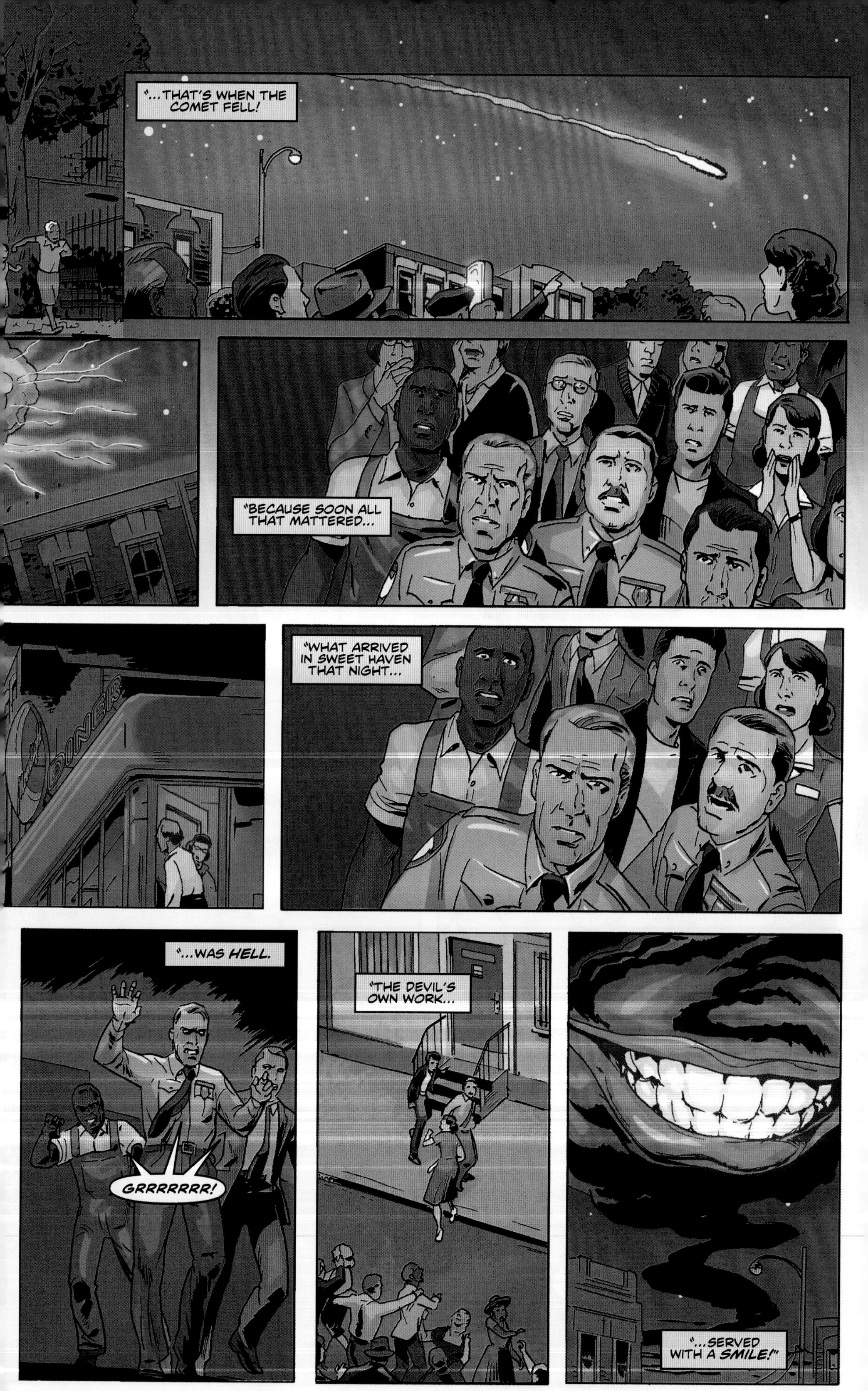
"...THAT'S WHEN THE COMET FELL!
"BECAUSE SOON ALL THAT MATTERED...
DINER
"WHAT ARRIVED IN SWEET HAVEN THAT NIGHT...
"...WAS HELL.
GRRRRRRR!
"THE DEVIL'S OWN WORK...
"...SERVED WITH A SMILE!"

SO, YOU'VE ALL BEEN HOLED UP IN HERE WHILE THE REST OF THE TOWN FELL TO THE SMILE?

WHAT ELSE WERE WE SUPPOSED TO DO?

YEAH, AND NO ONE OUT *THERE* SEEMS TO CARE WHAT'S GOING ON!

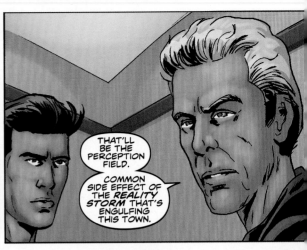

THAT'LL BE THE PERCEPTION FIELD.

COMMON SIDE EFFECT OF THE *REALITY STORM* THAT'S ENGULFING THIS TOWN.

WELL, THAT EXPLAINS EVERYTHING!

WHAT'S A REALITY STORM?

THE SOURCE OF ALL YOUR PROBLEMS.

WHICH I'M BETTING STARTED AT THE CRASH SITE OF YOUR COMET.

THE CARTER FARM.

THAT'S WHERE WE NEED TO GO.

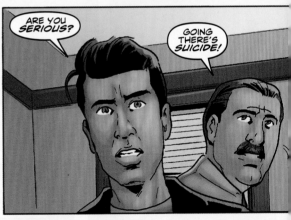

ARE YOU *SERIOUS?*

GOING THERE'S *SUICIDE!*

NO, STAYING *HERE* WOULD BE SUICIDE.

ESPECIALLY AS YOU'RE NEARLY OUT OF FOOD AND WATER.

HOW DID YOU--?

WHY ELSE WOULD PENNY BE OUTSIDE?

SHE'S NOT INSANE.

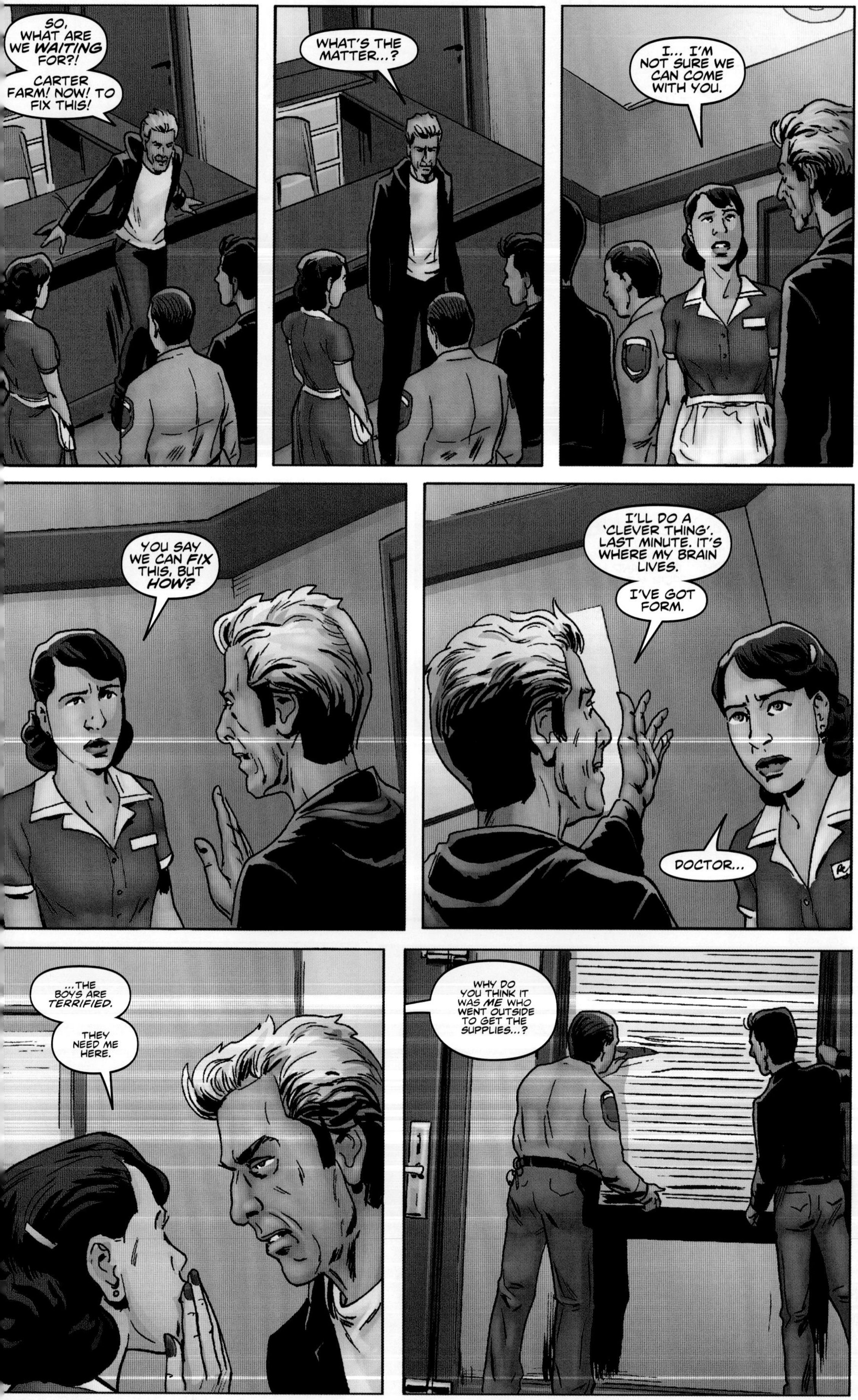
SO, WHAT ARE WE WAITING FOR?!
CARTER FARM! NOW! TO FIX THIS!
WHAT'S THE MATTER...?
I... I'M NOT SURE WE CAN COME WITH YOU.
YOU SAY WE CAN FIX THIS, BUT HOW?
I'LL DO A 'CLEVER THING'. LAST MINUTE. IT'S WHERE MY BRAIN LIVES.
I'VE GOT FORM.
DOCTOR...
...THE BOYS ARE TERRIFIED.
THEY NEED ME HERE.
WHY DO YOU THINK IT WAS ME WHO WENT OUTSIDE TO GET THE SUPPLIES...?

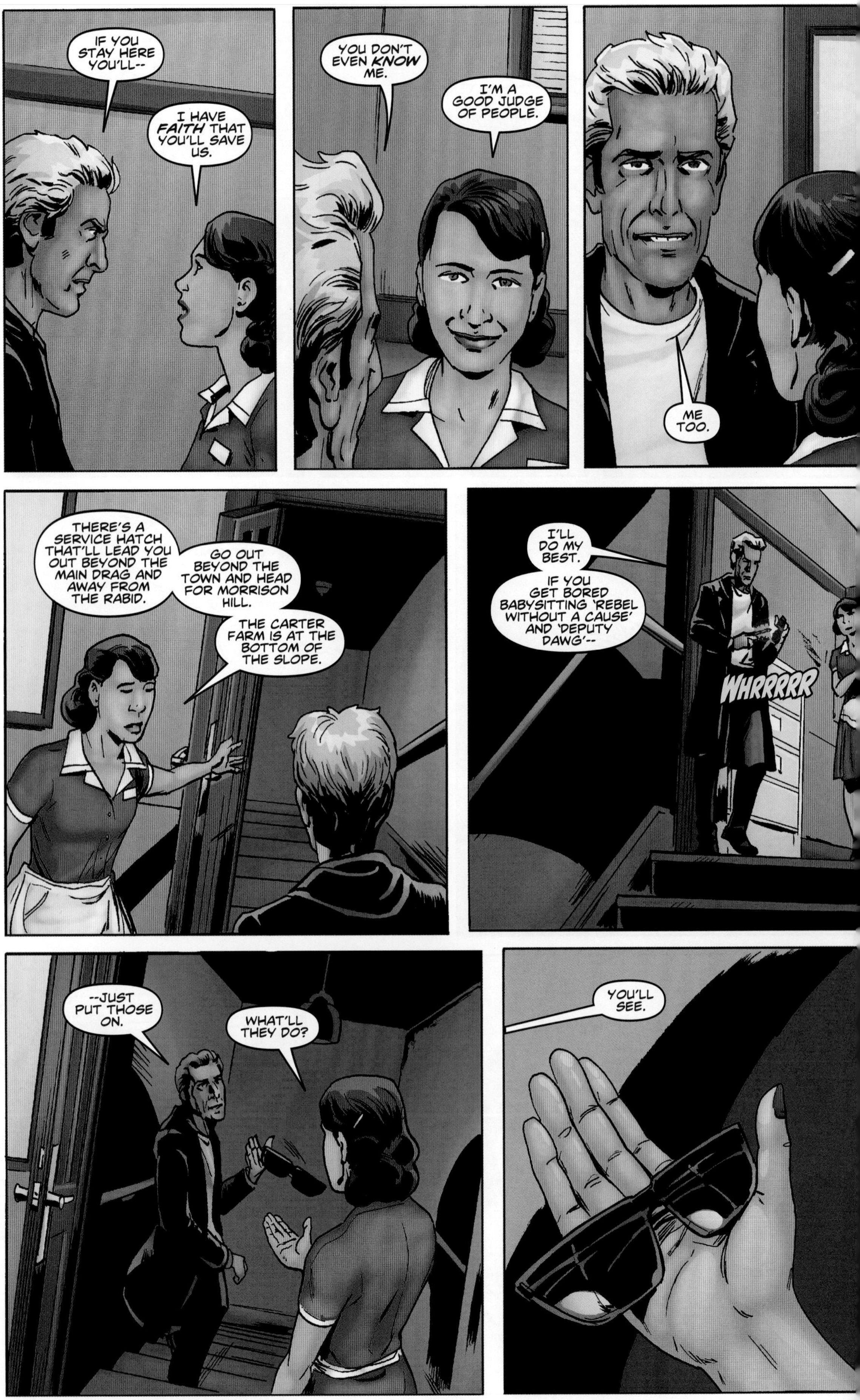
IF YOU STAY HERE YOU'LL--
I HAVE FAITH THAT YOU'LL SAVE US.
YOU DON'T EVEN KNOW ME.
I'M A GOOD JUDGE OF PEOPLE.
ME TOO.
THERE'S A SERVICE HATCH THAT'LL LEAD YOU OUT BEYOND THE MAIN DRAG AND AWAY FROM THE RABID.
GO OUT BEYOND THE TOWN AND HEAD FOR MORRISON HILL.
THE CARTER FARM IS AT THE BOTTOM OF THE SLOPE.
I'LL DO MY BEST.
IF YOU GET BORED BABYSITTING 'REBEL WITHOUT A CAUSE' AND 'DEPUTY DAWG'--
WHRRRRR
--JUST PUT THOSE ON.
WHAT'LL THEY DO?
YOU'LL SEE.

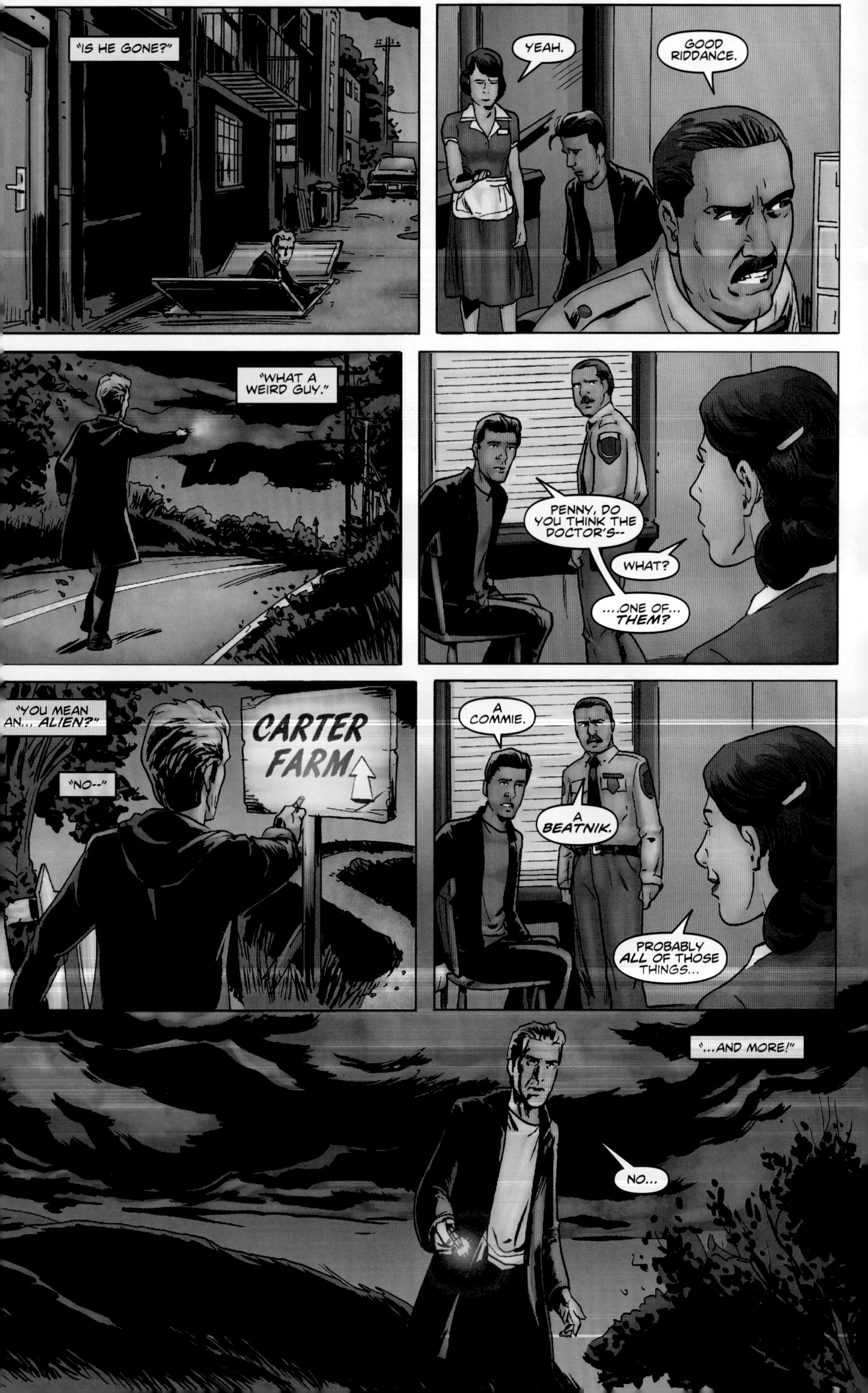
"IS HE GONE?"
YEAH.
GOOD RIDDANCE.
"WHAT A WEIRD GUY."
PENNY, DO YOU THINK THE DOCTOR'S--
WHAT?
....ONE OF... THEM?
"YOU MEAN AN... ALIEN?"
"NO--"
CARTER FARM
A COMMIE.
A BEATNIK.
PROBABLY ALL OF THOSE THINGS...
"...AND MORE!"
NO...

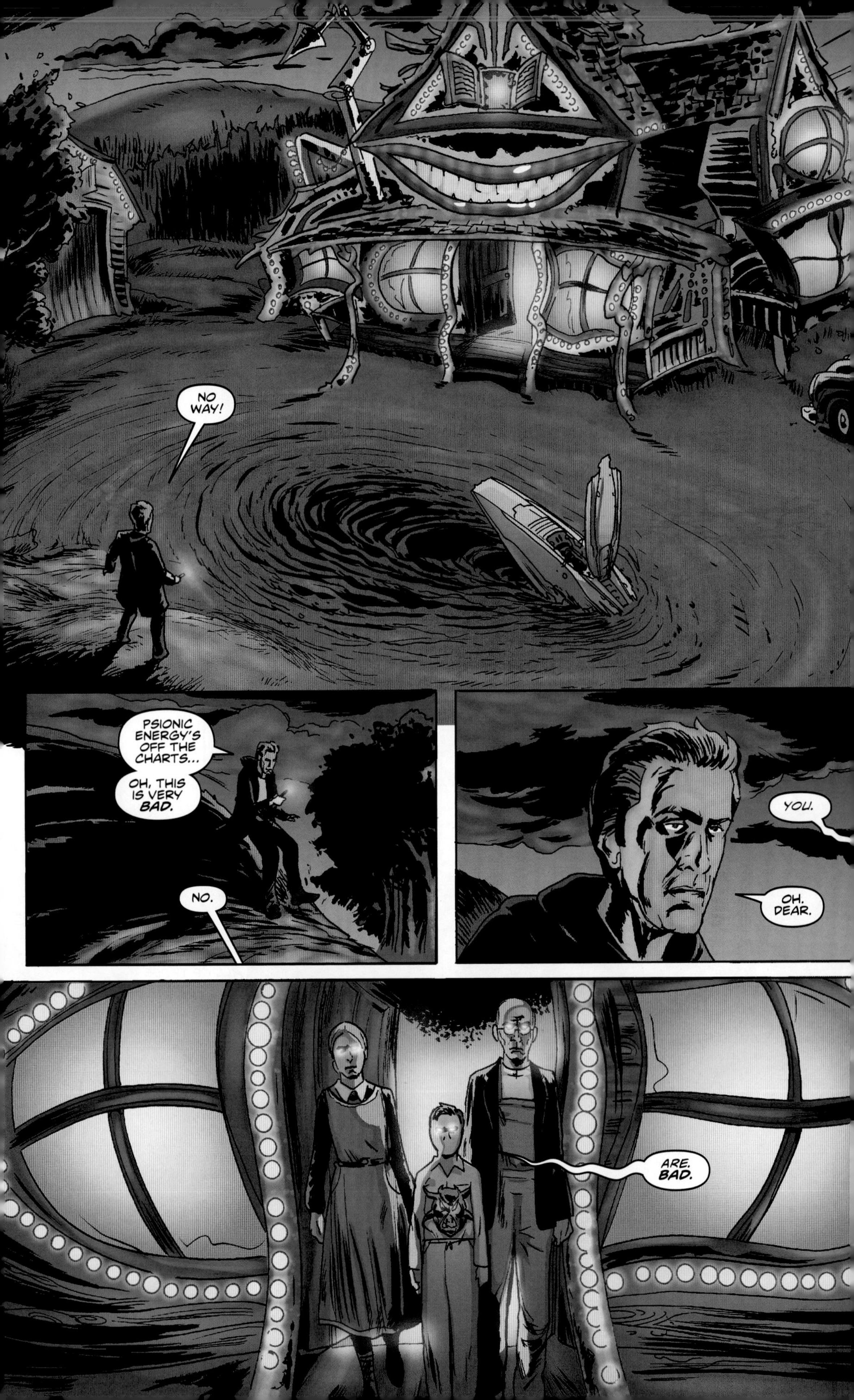
NO WAY!
PSIONIC ENERGY'S OFF THE CHARTS...
OH, THIS IS VERY BAD.
NO.
YOU.
OH. DEAR.
ARE. BAD.

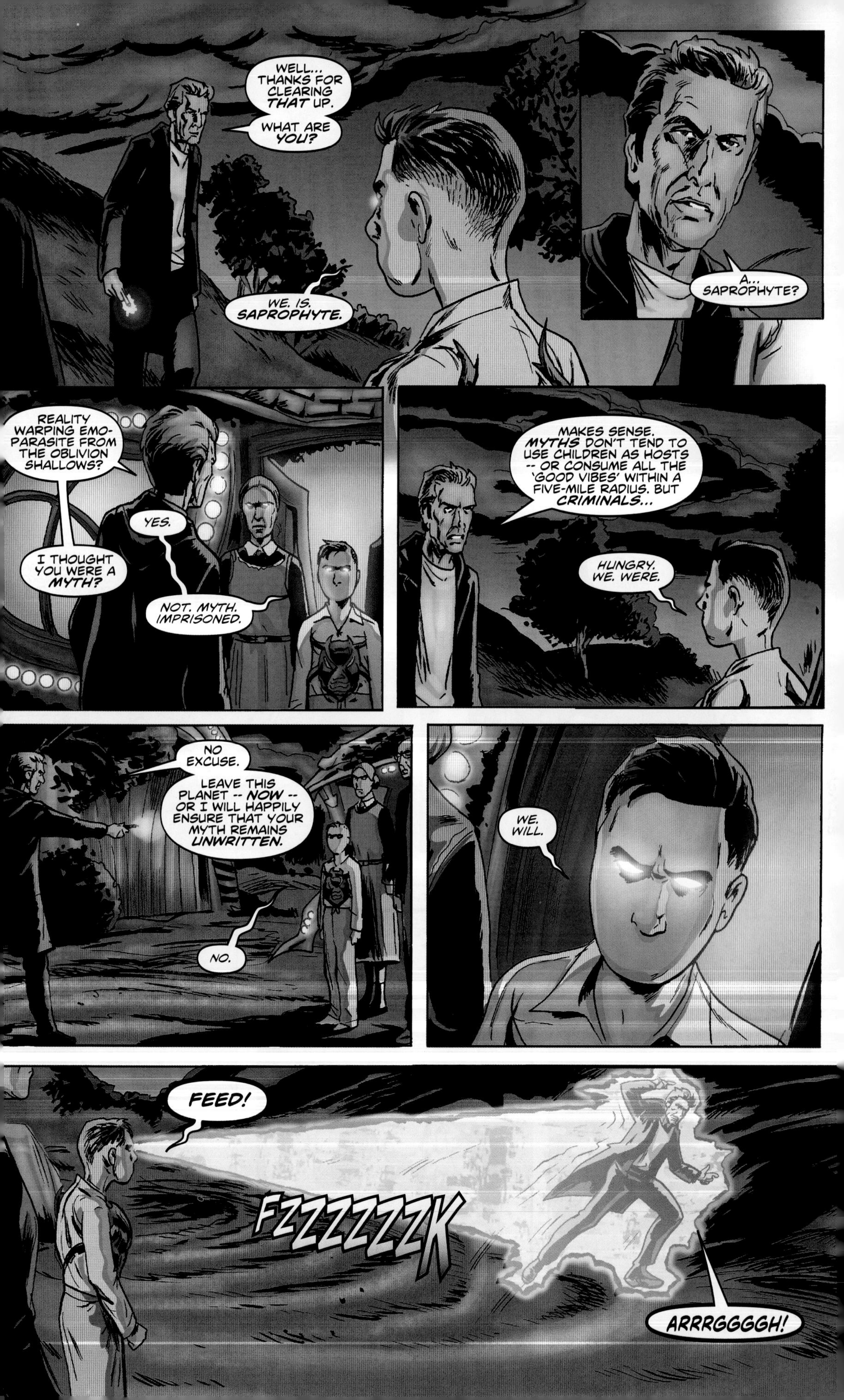
WELL... THANKS FOR CLEARING THAT UP.
WHAT ARE YOU?
WE. IS. SAPROPHYTE.
A... SAPROPHYTE?
REALITY WARPING EMO-PARASITE FROM THE OBLIVION SHALLOWS?
YES.
I THOUGHT YOU WERE A MYTH?
NOT. MYTH. IMPRISONED.
MAKES SENSE. MYTHS DON'T TEND TO USE CHILDREN AS HOSTS -- OR CONSUME ALL THE 'GOOD VIBES' WITHIN A FIVE-MILE RADIUS. BUT CRIMINALS...
HUNGRY. WE. WERE.
NO EXCUSE.
LEAVE THIS PLANET -- NOW -- OR I WILL HAPPILY ENSURE THAT YOUR MYTH REMAINS UNWRITTEN.
NO.
WE. WILL.
FEED!
FZZZZZZK
ARRRGGGGH!

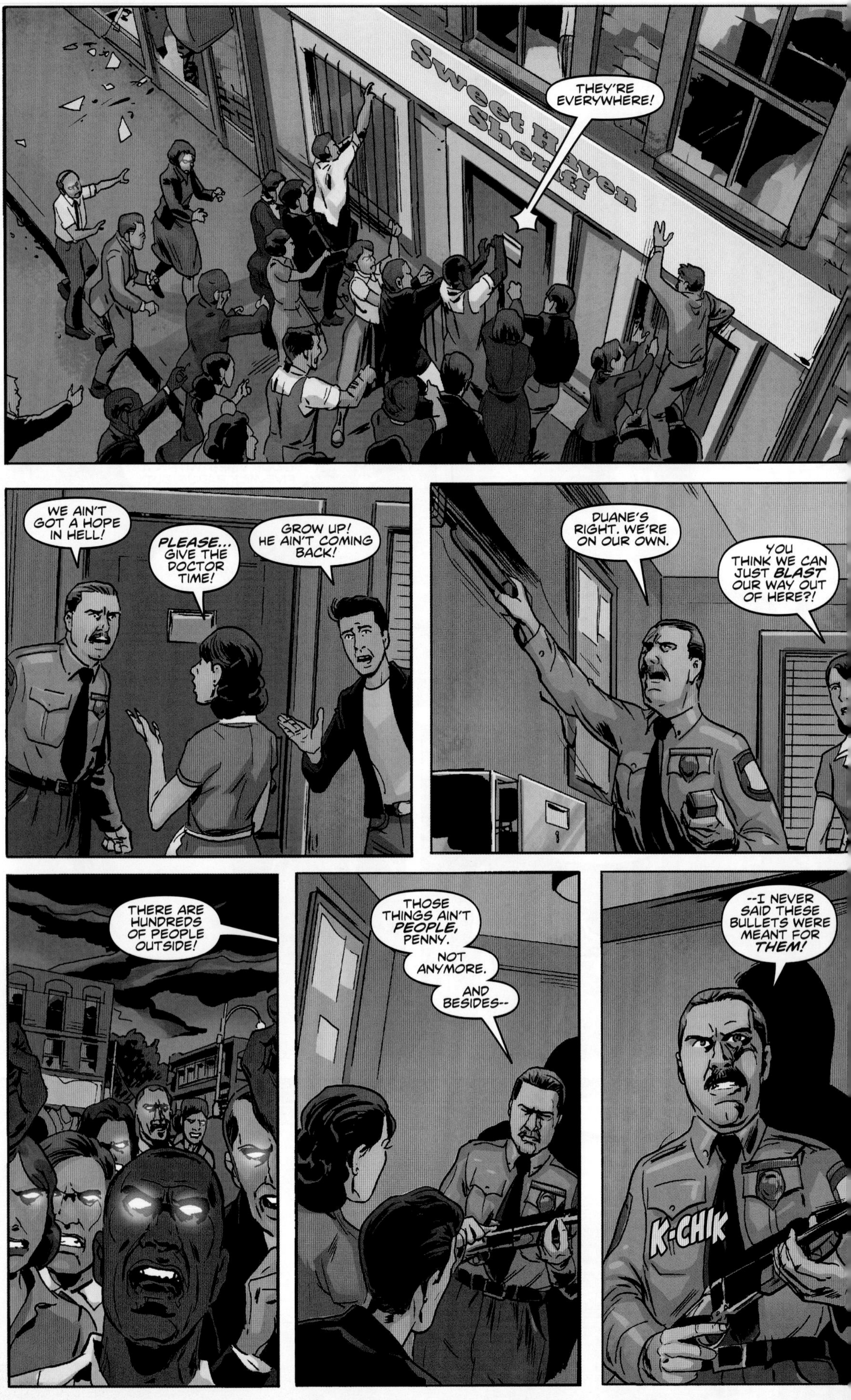
THEY'RE EVERYWHERE!
WE AIN'T GOT A HOPE IN HELL!
PLEASE... GIVE THE DOCTOR TIME!
GROW UP! HE AIN'T COMING BACK!
DUANE'S RIGHT. WE'RE ON OUR OWN.
YOU THINK WE CAN JUST BLAST OUR WAY OUT OF HERE?!
THERE ARE HUNDREDS OF PEOPLE OUTSIDE!
THOSE THINGS AIN'T PEOPLE, PENNY.
NOT ANYMORE.
AND BESIDES--
--I NEVER SAID THESE BULLETS WERE MEANT FOR THEM!
K-CHIK

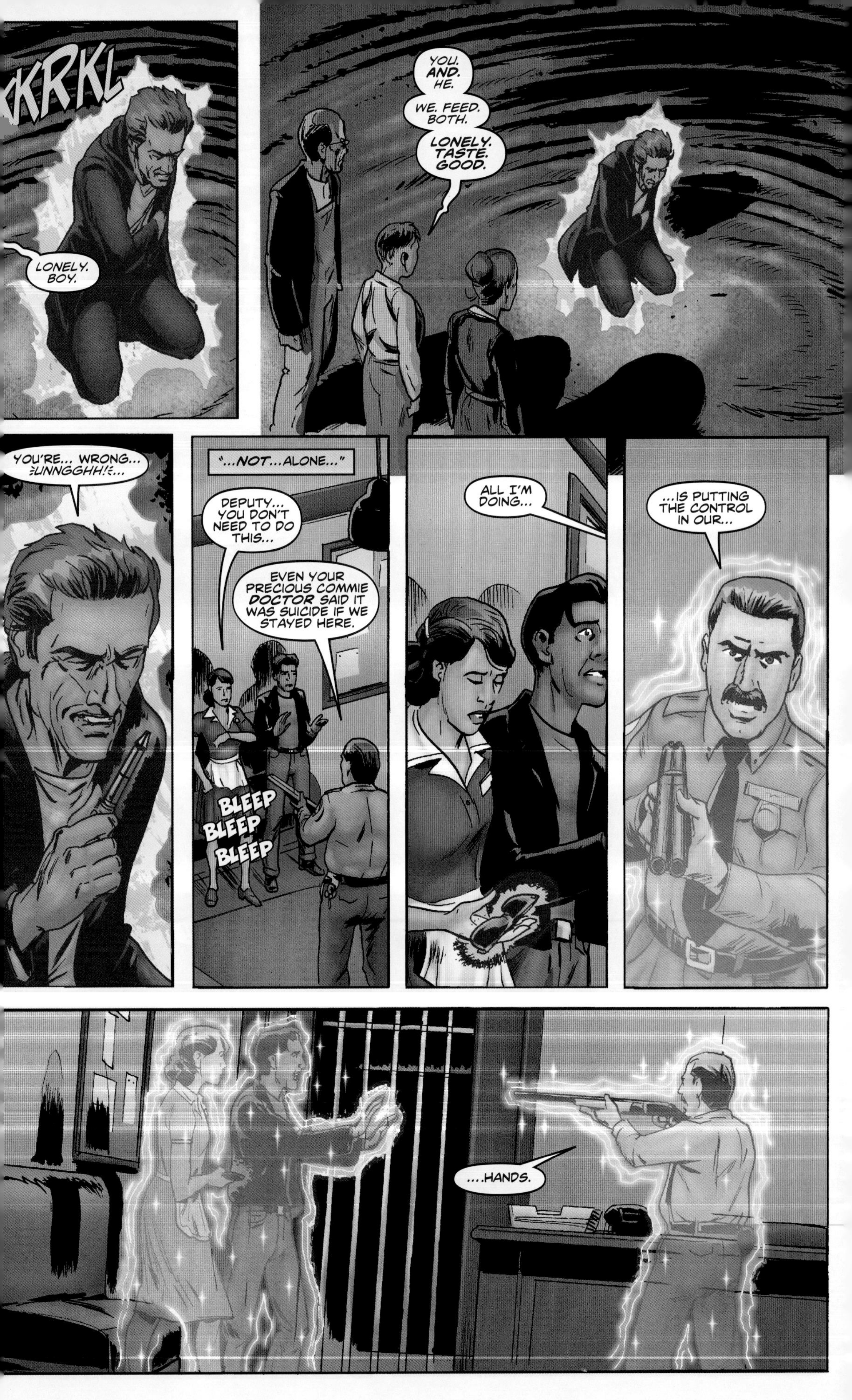
KRKL
LONELY. BOY.
YOU. AND. HE.
WE. FEED. BOTH.
LONELY. TASTE. GOOD.
YOU'RE... WRONG... UNNGGHH!...
"...NOT...ALONE..."
DEPUTY... YOU DON'T NEED TO DO THIS...
EVEN YOUR PRECIOUS COMMIE DOCTOR SAID IT WAS SUICIDE IF WE STAYED HERE.
BLEEP BLEEP BLEEP
ALL I'M DOING...
...IS PUTTING THE CONTROL IN OUR...
....HANDS.

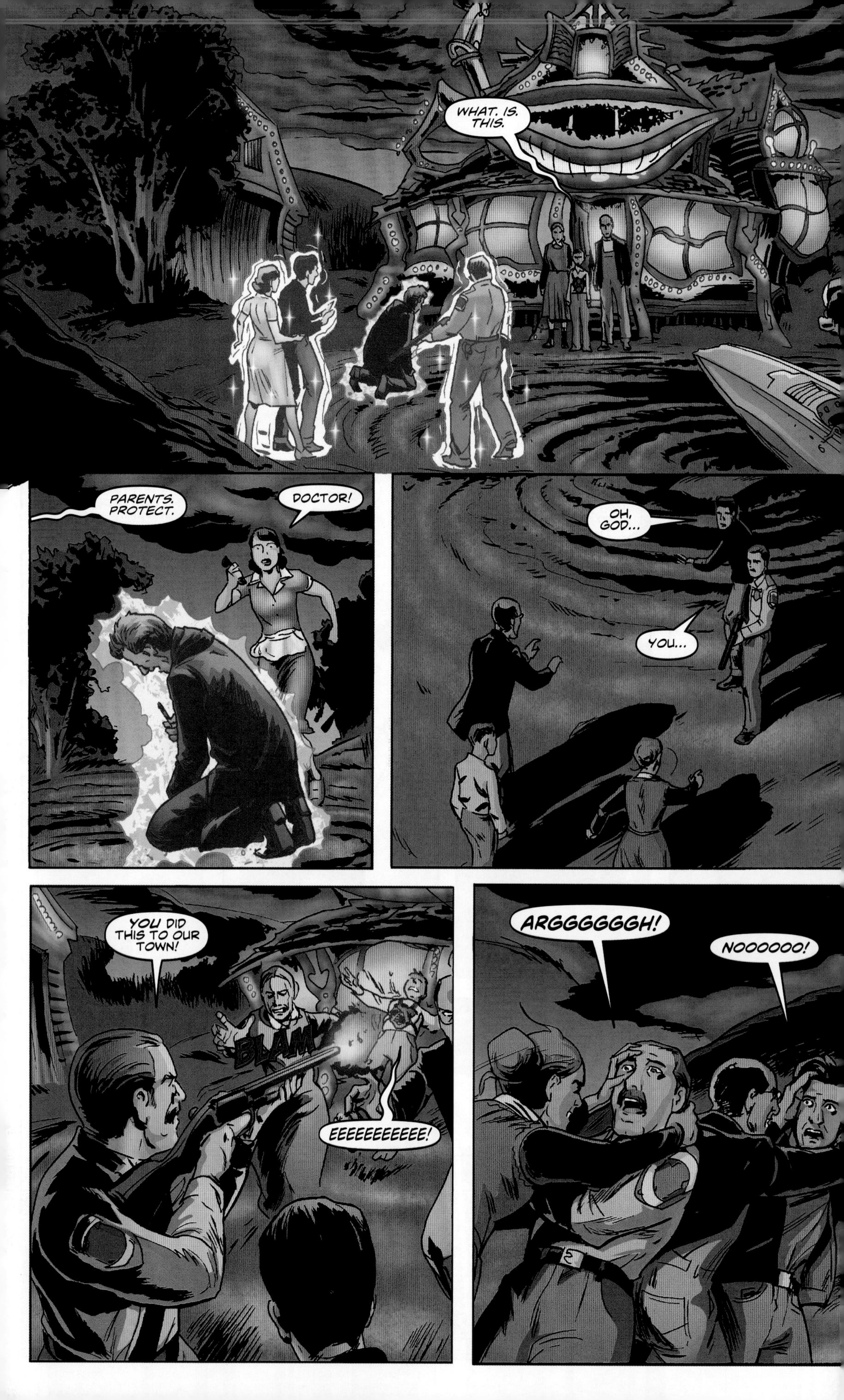
WHAT. IS. THIS.
PARENTS. PROTECT.
DOCTOR!
OH, GOD...
YOU...
YOU DID THIS TO OUR TOWN!
BLAM
EEEEEEEEEEE!
ARGGGGGGH!
NOOOOOO!

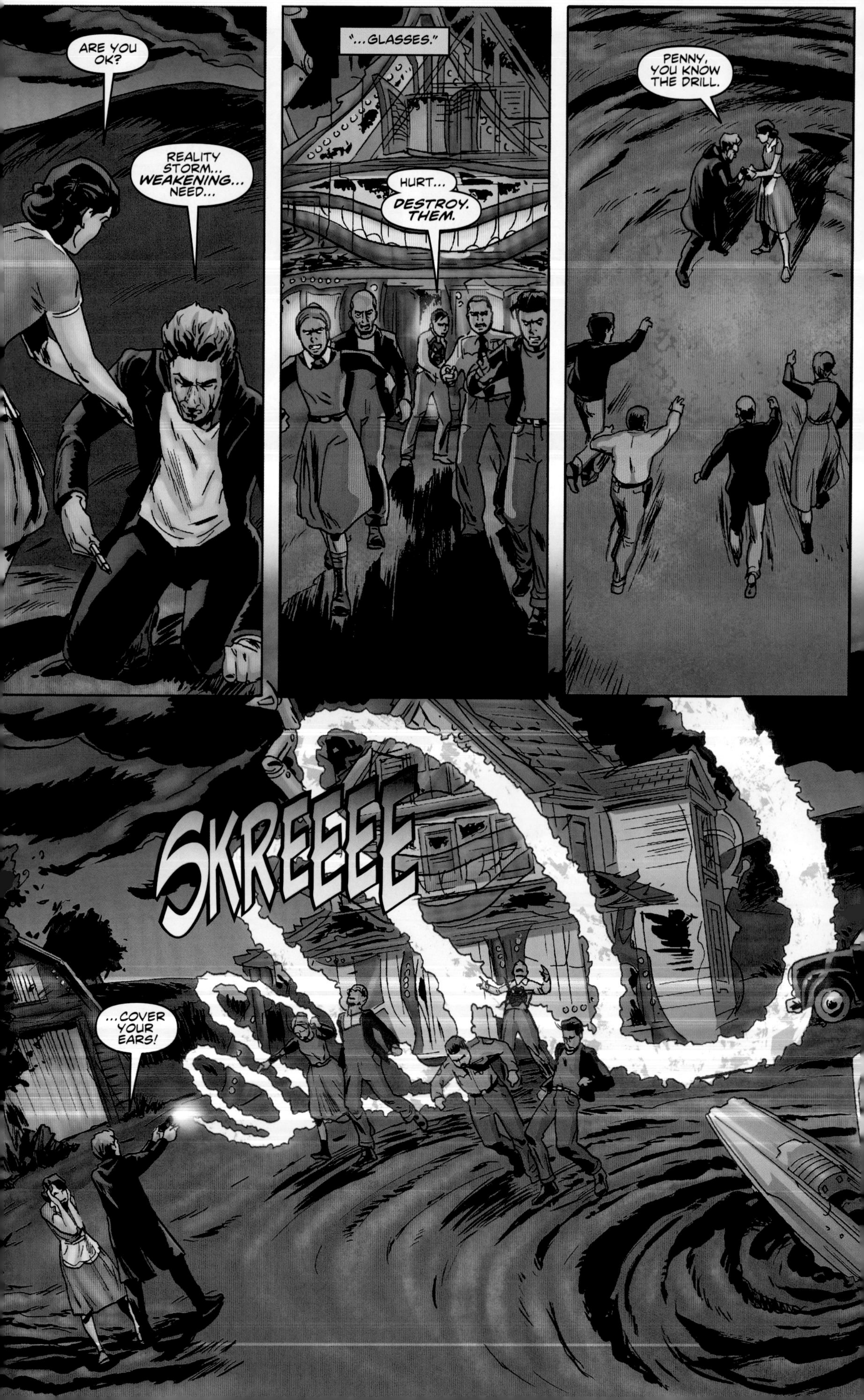
ARE YOU OK?
REALITY STORM... WEAKENING... NEED...
"...GLASSES."
HURT... DESTROY. THEM.
PENNY, YOU KNOW THE DRILL.
SKREEEE
...COVER YOUR EARS!

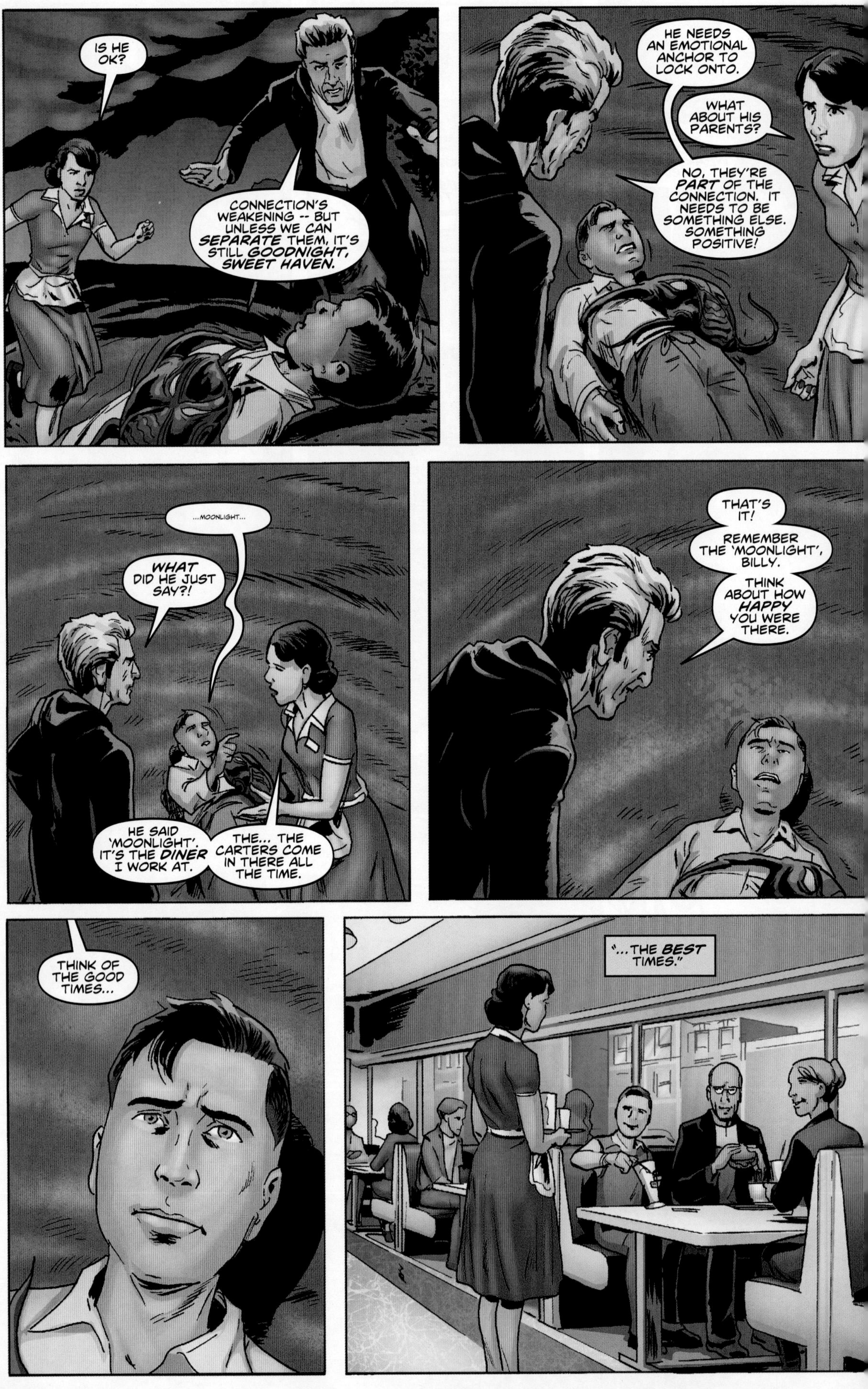
IS HE OK?
CONNECTION'S WEAKENING -- BUT UNLESS WE CAN SEPARATE THEM, IT'S STILL GOODNIGHT, SWEET HAVEN.
HE NEEDS AN EMOTIONAL ANCHOR TO LOCK ONTO.
WHAT ABOUT HIS PARENTS?
NO, THEY'RE PART OF THE CONNECTION. IT NEEDS TO BE SOMETHING ELSE. SOMETHING POSITIVE!
...MOONLIGHT...
WHAT DID HE JUST SAY?!
HE SAID 'MOONLIGHT'. IT'S THE DINER I WORK AT.
THE... THE CARTERS COME IN THERE ALL THE TIME.
THAT'S IT!
REMEMBER THE 'MOONLIGHT', BILLY.
THINK ABOUT HOW HAPPY YOU WERE THERE.
THINK OF THE GOOD TIMES...
"...THE BEST TIMES."

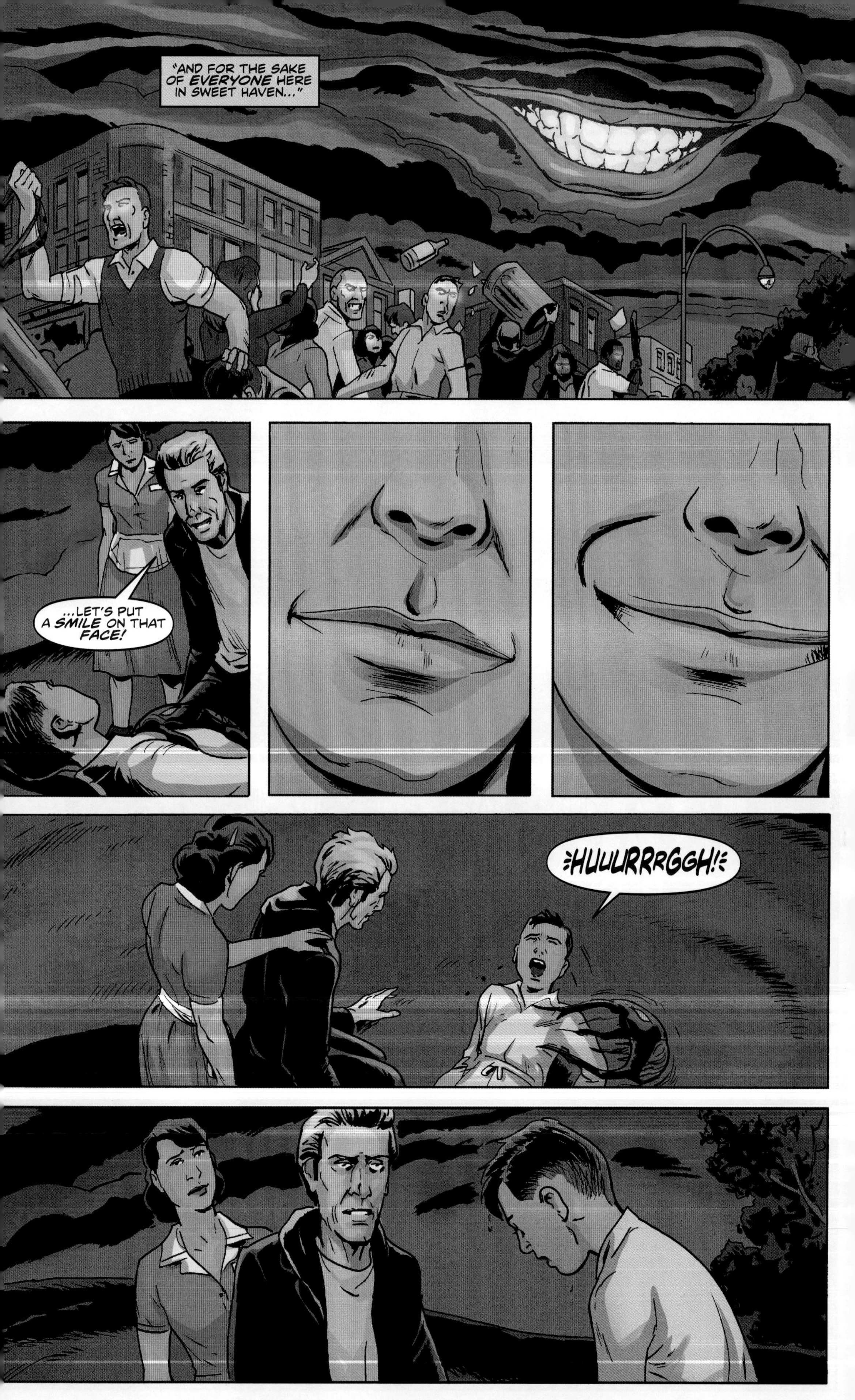
"AND FOR THE SAKE OF EVERYONE HERE IN SWEET HAVEN..."
...LET'S PUT A SMILE ON THAT FACE!
HUUURRRGGH!

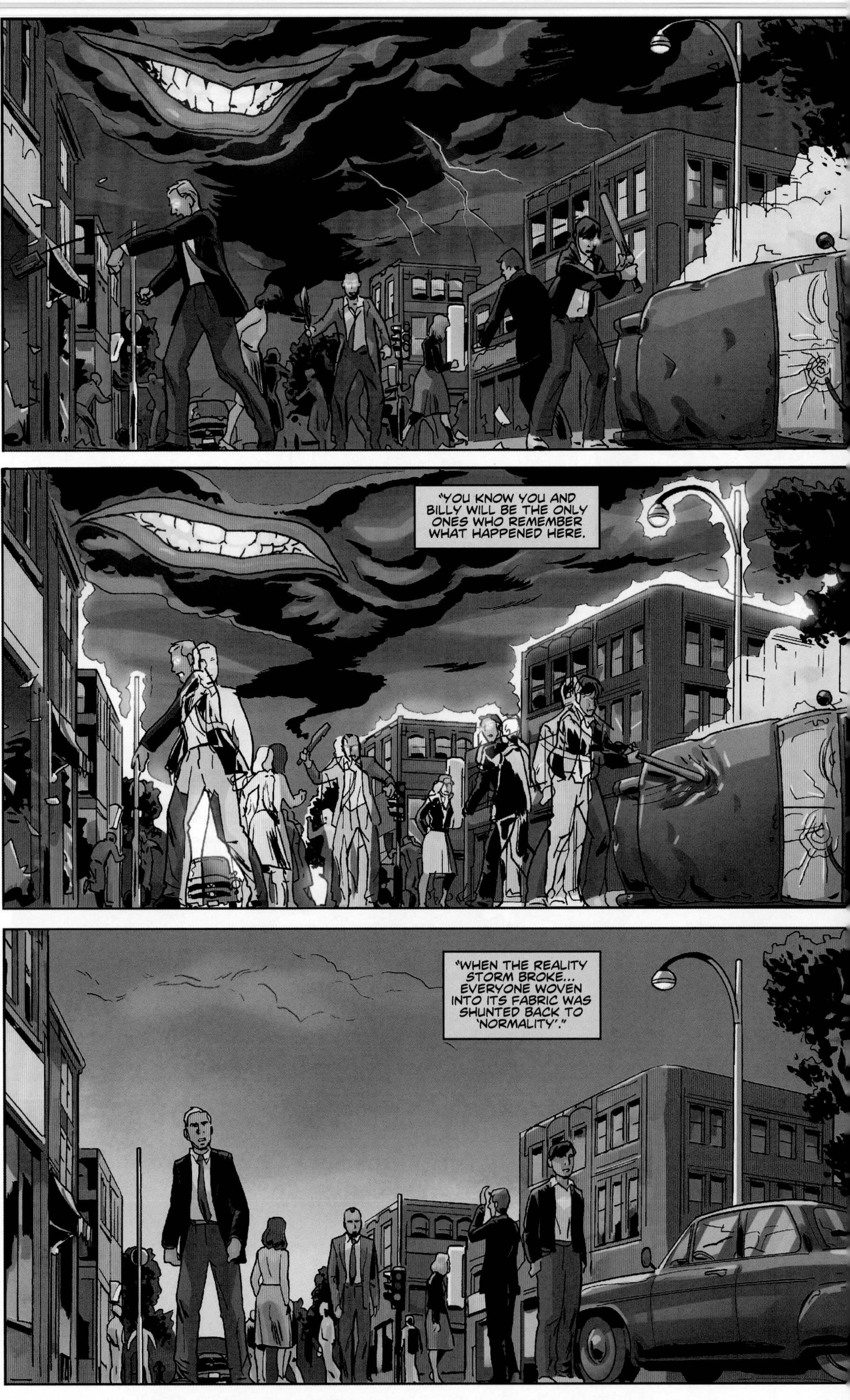
"YOU KNOW YOU AND BILLY WILL BE THE ONLY ONES WHO REMEMBER WHAT HAPPENED HERE.
"WHEN THE REALITY STORM BROKE... EVERYONE WOVEN INTO ITS FABRIC WAS SHUNTED BACK TO 'NORMALITY'."

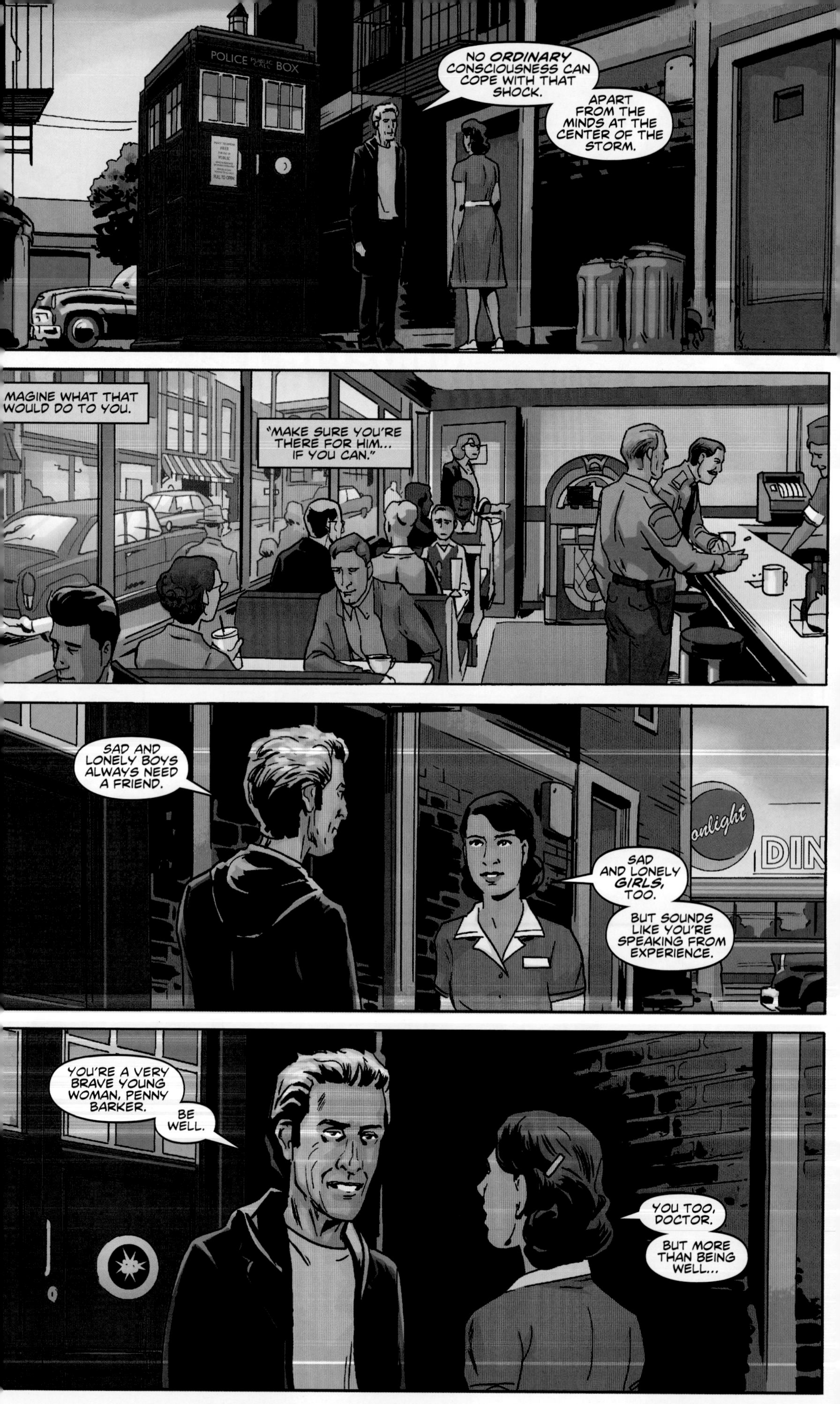
POLICE PUBLIC CALL BOX
NO ORDINARY CONSCIOUSNESS CAN COPE WITH THAT SHOCK.
APART FROM THE MINDS AT THE CENTER OF THE STORM.
MAGINE WHAT THAT WOULD DO TO YOU.
"MAKE SURE YOU'RE THERE FOR HIM... IF YOU CAN."
SAD AND LONELY BOYS ALWAYS NEED A FRIEND.
SAD AND LONELY GIRLS, TOO.
BUT SOUNDS LIKE YOU'RE SPEAKING FROM EXPERIENCE.
onlight
DIN
YOU'RE A VERY BRAVE YOUNG WOMAN, PENNY BARKER.
BE WELL.
YOU TOO, DOCTOR.
BUT MORE THAN BEING WELL...

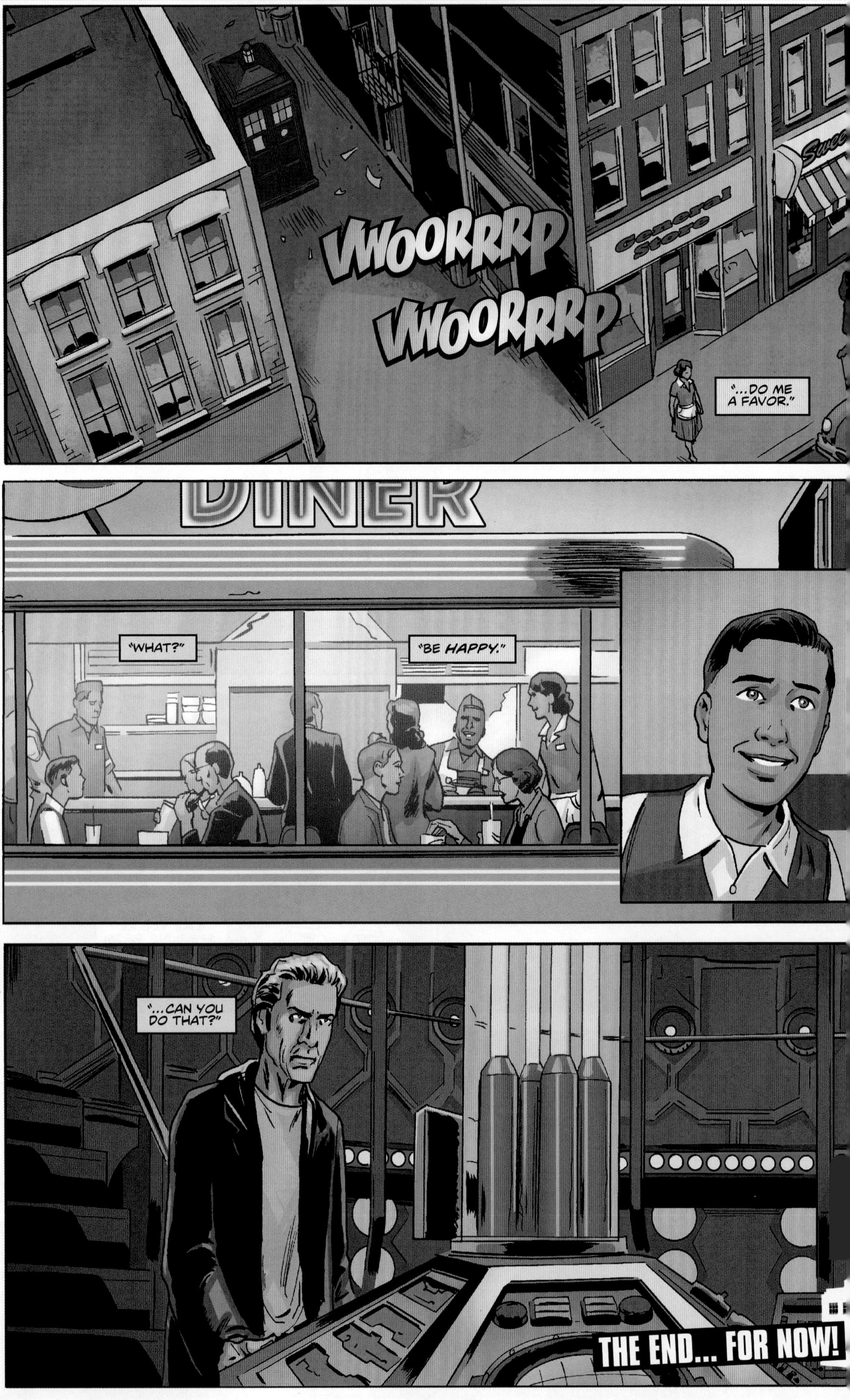
VWOORRRP
VWOORRRP
General Store
"...DO ME A FAVOR."
DINER
"WHAT?"
"BE HAPPY."
"...CAN YOU DO THAT?"
THE END... FOR NOW!

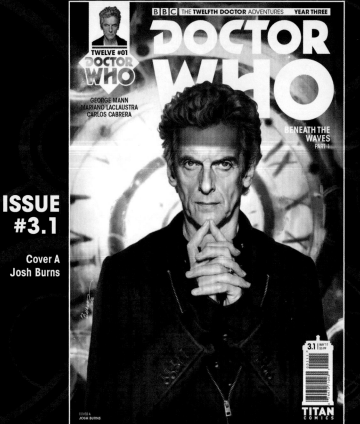

COVER GALLERY

DOCTOR WHO
THE TWELFTH DOCTOR

ISSUE #3.1

BBC THE TWELFTH DOCTOR ADVENTURES YEAR THREE
DOCTOR WHO
TWELVE #01
DOCTOR WHO
GEORGE MANN
MARIANO LACLAUSTRA
CARLOS CABRERA
BENEATH THE WAVES
PART 1
3.1 MAY '17 $3.99
TITAN COMICS
COVER A
JOSH BURNS

Cover A
Josh Burns

BBC THE TWELFTH DOCTOR ADVENTURES YEAR THREE
DOCTOR WHO
TWELVE #01
DOCTOR WHO
GEORGE MANN
MARIANO LACLAUSTRA
CARLOS CABRERA
BENEATH THE WAVES
PART 1
3.1 MAY '17 $3.99
PUBLIC BOX
RACHAEL SMITH

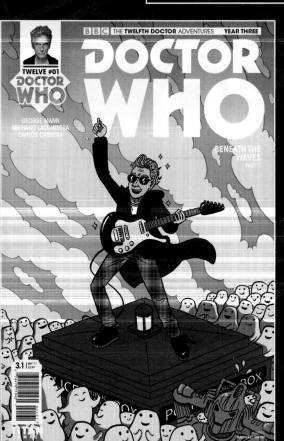

Cover C
Rachael Smith

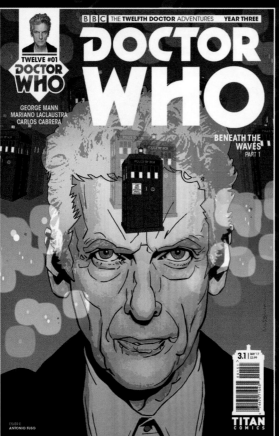

COVER GALLERY

DOCTOR WHO
THE TWELFTH DOCTOR

Cover D
Mariano Laclaustra

Cover E
Antonio Fuso

COVER GALLERY

BBC THE TWELFTH DOCTOR ADVENTURES YEAR THREE
DOCTOR WHO
TWELVE #01
DOCTOR WHO
GEORGE MANN
MARIANO LACLAUSTRA
CARLOS CABRERA
BENEATH THE WAVES
PART 1
POLICE BOX
3.1 MAY '17 $3.99
TITAN COMICS
COVER F
PASQUALE QUALANO

Cover F
Pasquale Qualano

ISSUE #3.2

Cover B
Will Brooks

BBC THE TWELFTH DOCTOR ADVENTURES YEAR THREE
DOCTOR WHO
TWELVE #02
DOCTOR WHO
JAMES PEATY
WARREN PLEECE
HI-FI
3.2 2017 $3.99
TITAN COMICS
COVER B
WILL BROOKS

COVER GALLERY

BBC THE TWELFTH DOCTOR ADVENTURES YEAR THREE
TWELVE #02
DOCTOR WHO
DOCTOR WHO
JAMES PEATY
WARREN PLEECE
HI-FI
THE BOY WITH THE DISPLACED SMILE
POLICE BOX
POLICE BOX
3.2 2017 $3.99
TITAN COMICS
COVER C
RYAN HALL

Cover C
Ryan Hall

BBC THE TWELFTH DOCTOR ADVENTURES YEAR THREE
TWELVE #02
DOCTOR WHO
DOCTOR WHO
JAMES PEATY
WARREN PLEECE
HI-FI
3.2 2017 $3.99
TITAN COMICS
PASQUALE QUALANO & AMOONA SAOHIN

Cover D
Pasquale Qualano &
Amoona Saohin

DOCTOR WHO
THE TWELFTH DOCTOR

COVER GALLERY

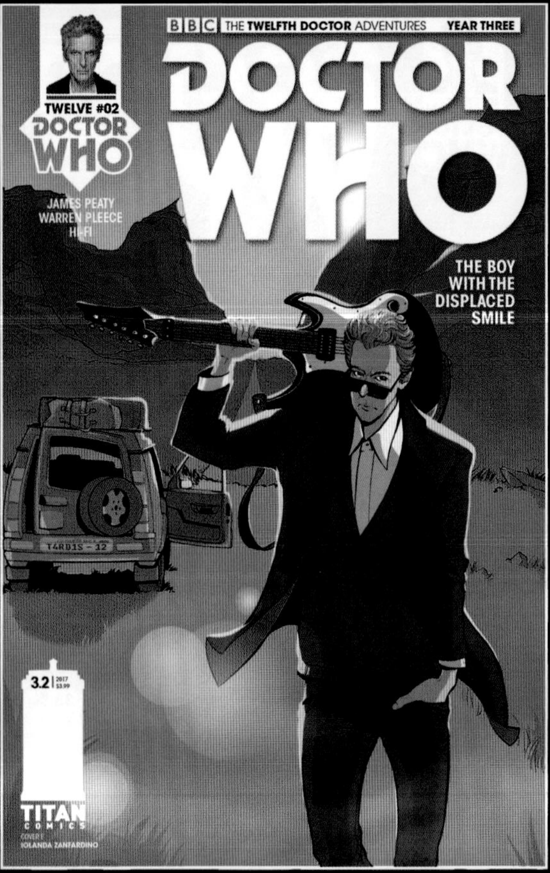
BBC THE TWELFTH DOCTOR ADVENTURES YEAR THREE
DOCTOR WHO
TWELVE #02
DOCTOR WHO
JAMES PEATY
WARREN PLEECE
HI-FI
THE BOY WITH THE DISPLACED SMILE
T4RD1S - 12
3.2 2017 $3.99
TITAN COMICS
COVER E
IOLANDA ZANFARDINO

Cover E
Iolanda Zanfardino

ISSUE #3.3

Cover A
Wellington Diaz &
Rod Fernandes

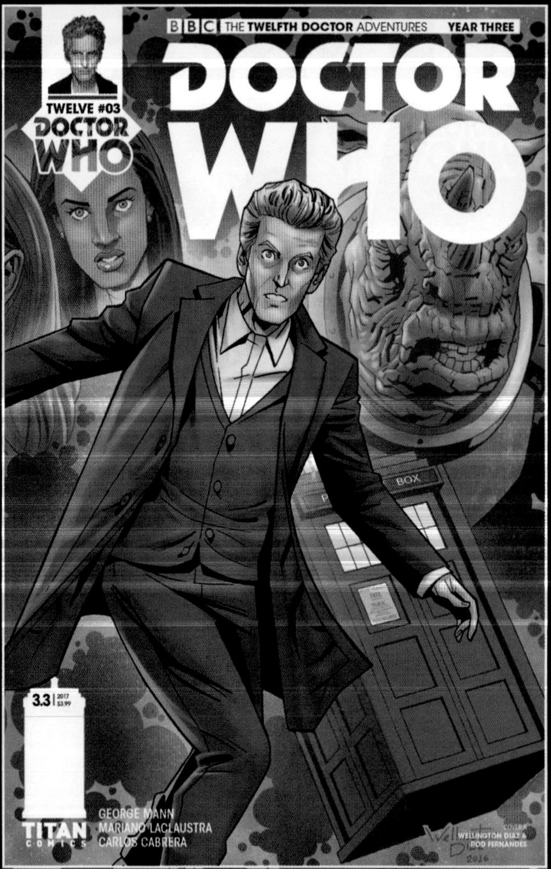
BBC THE TWELFTH DOCTOR ADVENTURES YEAR THREE
DOCTOR WHO
TWELVE #03
DOCTOR WHO
BOX
3.3 2017 $3.99
TITAN COMICS
GEORGE MANN
MARIANO LACLAUSTRA
CARLOS CABRERA
COVER A
WELLINGTON DIAZ &
ROD FERNANDES

BBC DOCTOR WHO THE TWELFTH DOCTOR

COVER GALLERY

BBC THE TWELFTH DOCTOR ADVENTURES YEAR THREE
DOCTOR WHO
TWELVE #03
DOCTOR WHO
GEORGE MANN
MARIANO LACLAUSTRA
CARLOS CABRERA
3.3 2017 $3.99
COVER B
WILL BROOKS
TITAN COMICS

Cover B
Will Brooks

BBC THE TWELFTH DOCTOR ADVENTURES YEAR THREE
DOCTOR WHO
TWELVE #03
DOCTOR WHO
GEORGE MANN
MARIANO LACLAUSTRA
CARLOS CABRERA
BENEATH THE WAVES
PART 2
3.3 2017 $3.99
SIMON 2015
COVER C
SIMON MYERS
TITAN COMICS

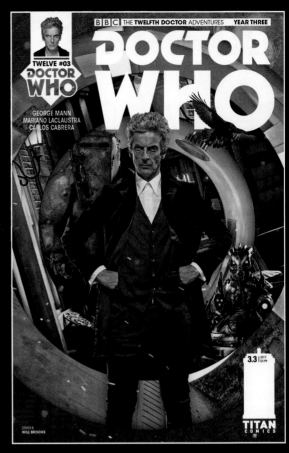

Cover C
Simon Myers

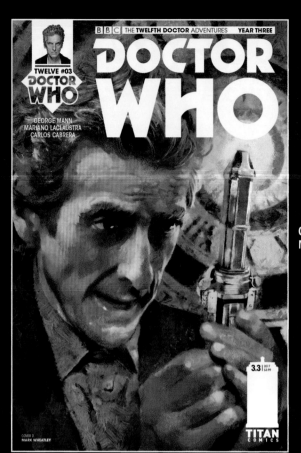

Cover D
Mark Wheatley

ISSUE
#3.4

Cover A
Simon Myers

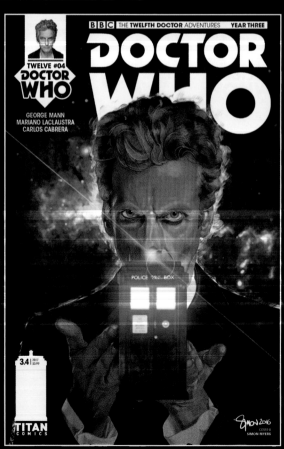

COVER GALLERY

Cover B
Will Brooks

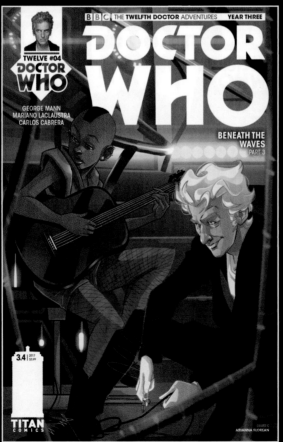

Cover C
Arianna Florean

COVER GALLERY

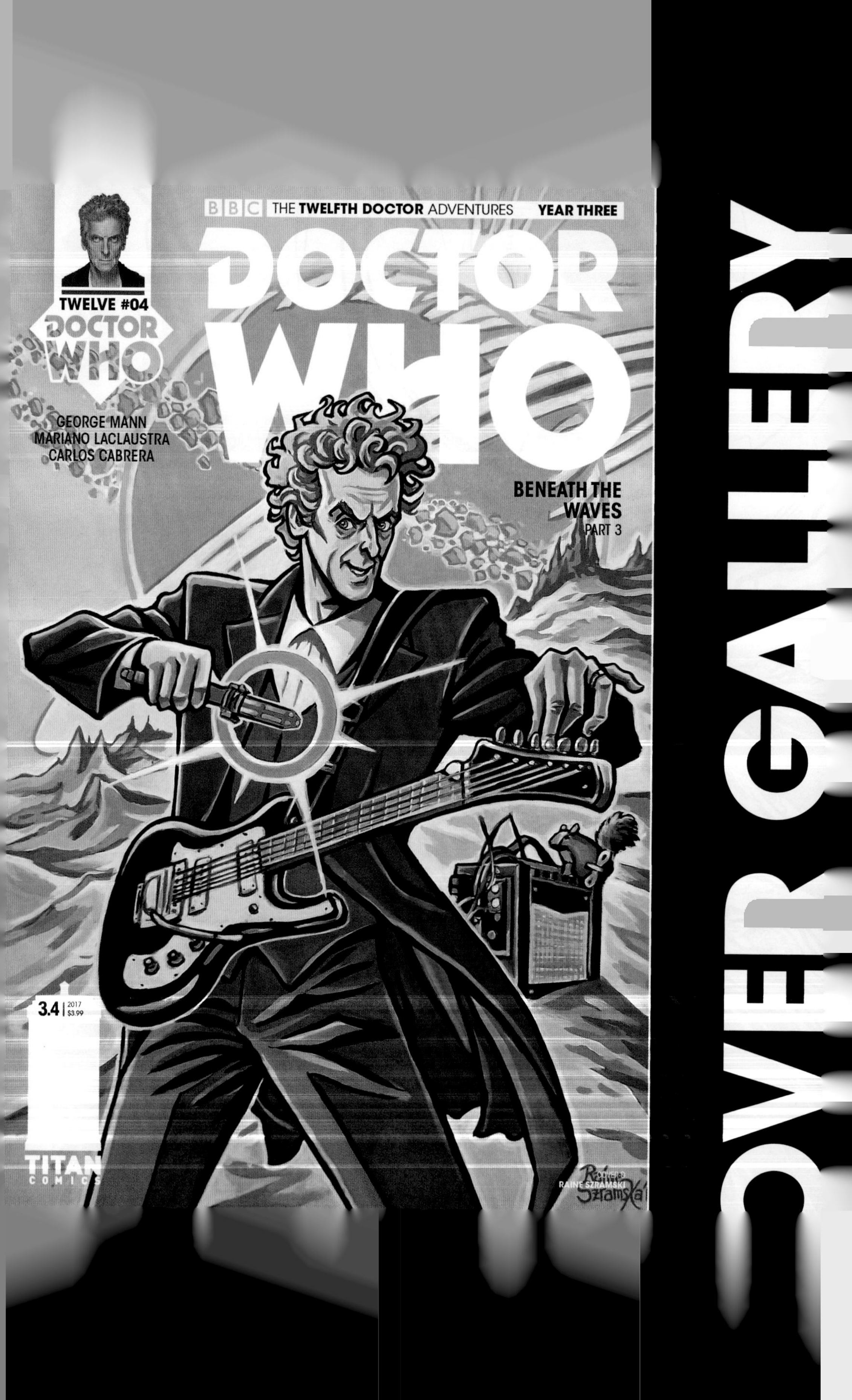

BBC
THE TWELFTH DOCTOR ADVENTURES
YEAR THREE
DOCTOR WHO
TWELVE #04
DOCTOR WHO
GEORGE MANN
MARIANO LACLAUSTRA
CARLOS CABRERA
BENEATH THE WAVES
PART 3
3.4
2017
$3.99
TITAN
COMICS
COVER B
RAINE SZRAMSKI

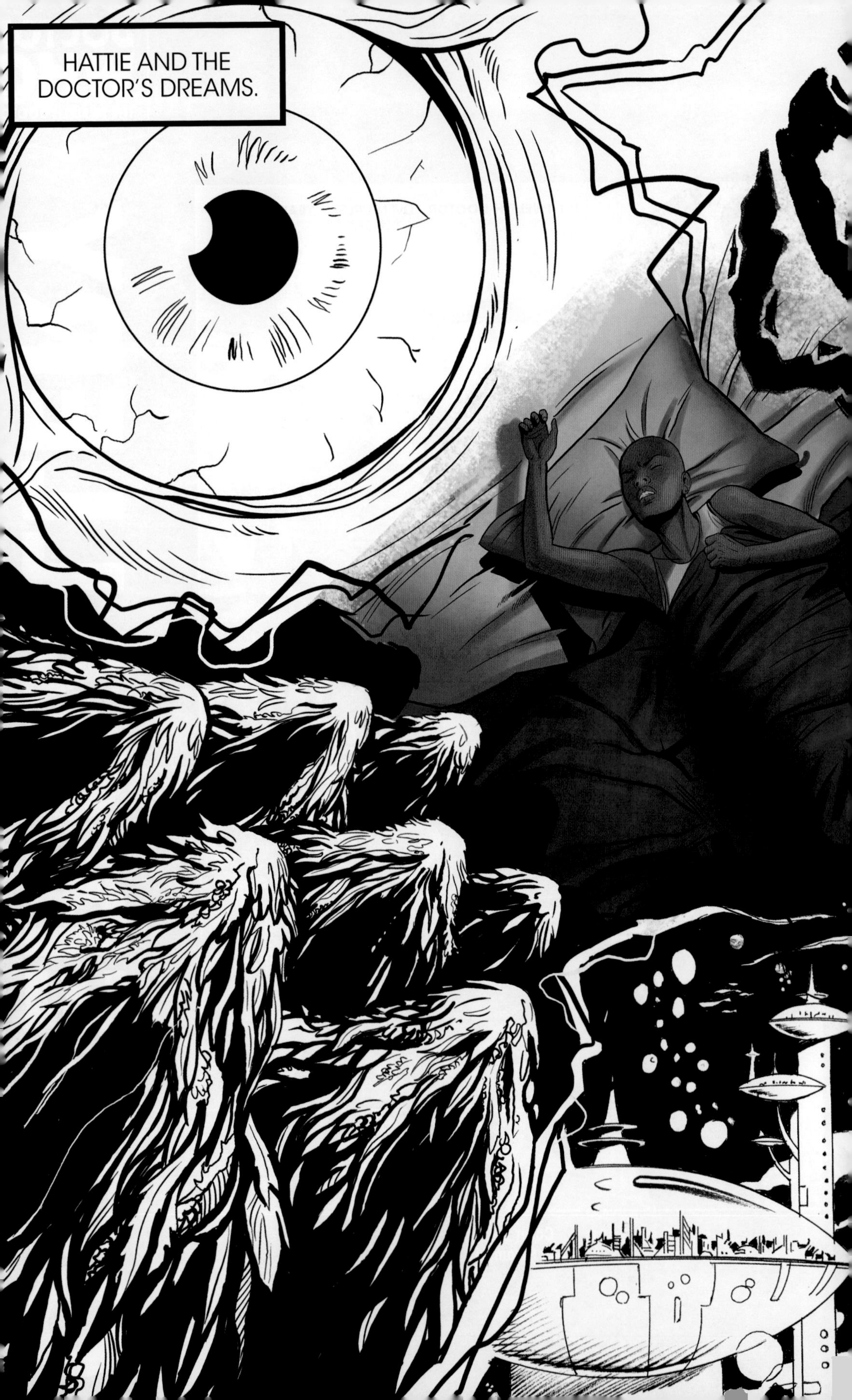
HATTIE AND THE DOCTOR'S DREAMS.

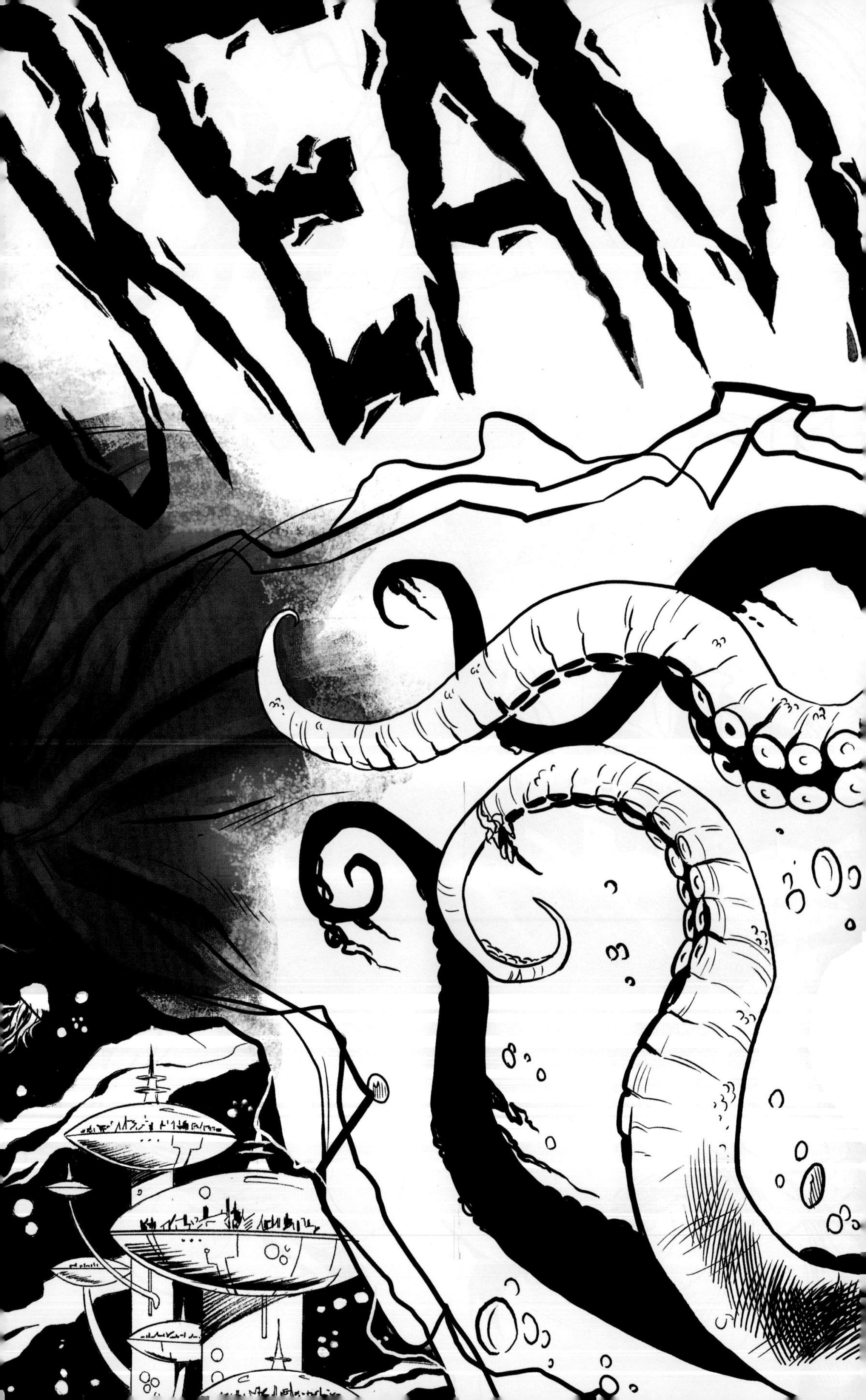

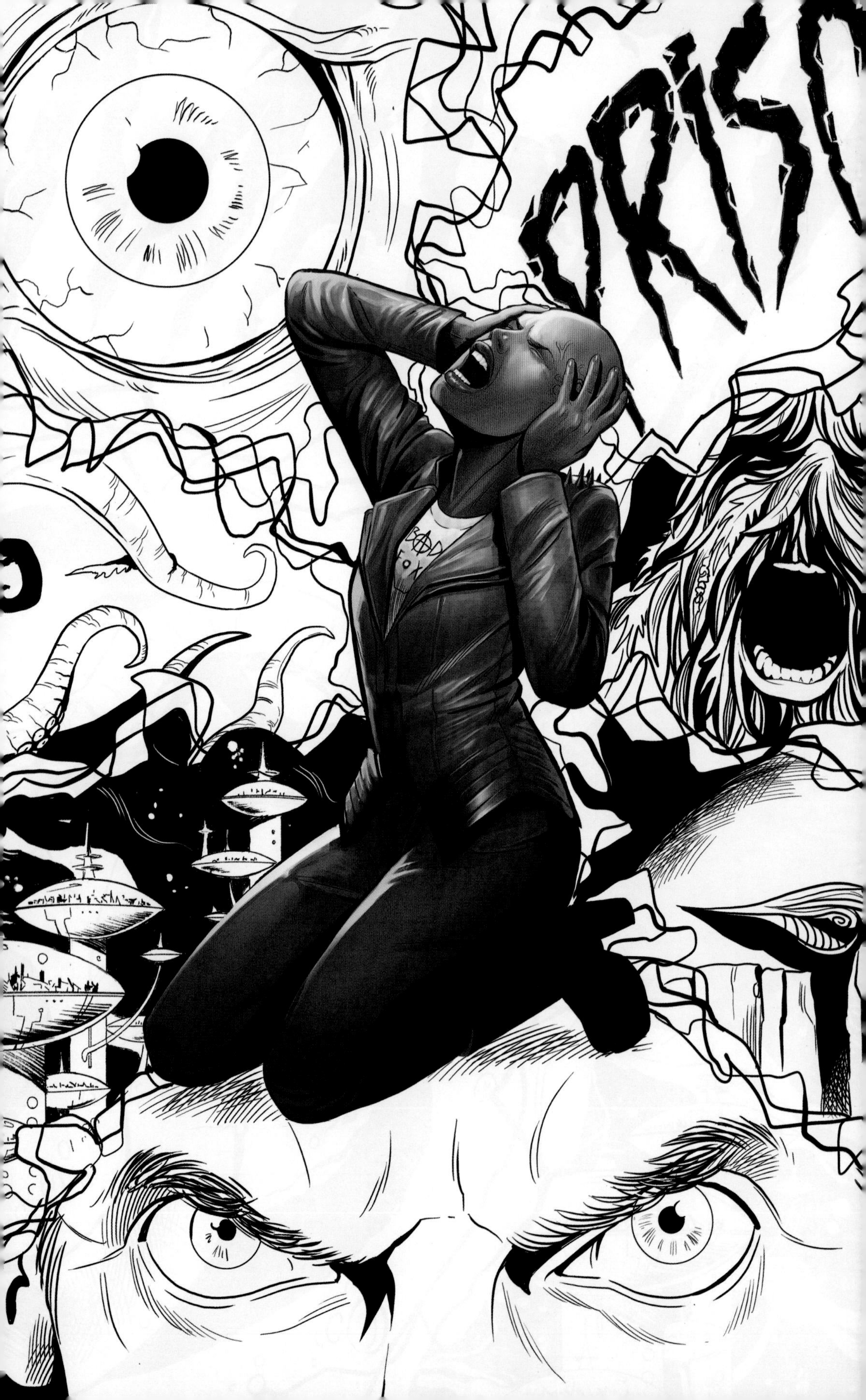
CRIS
BAD
FOX

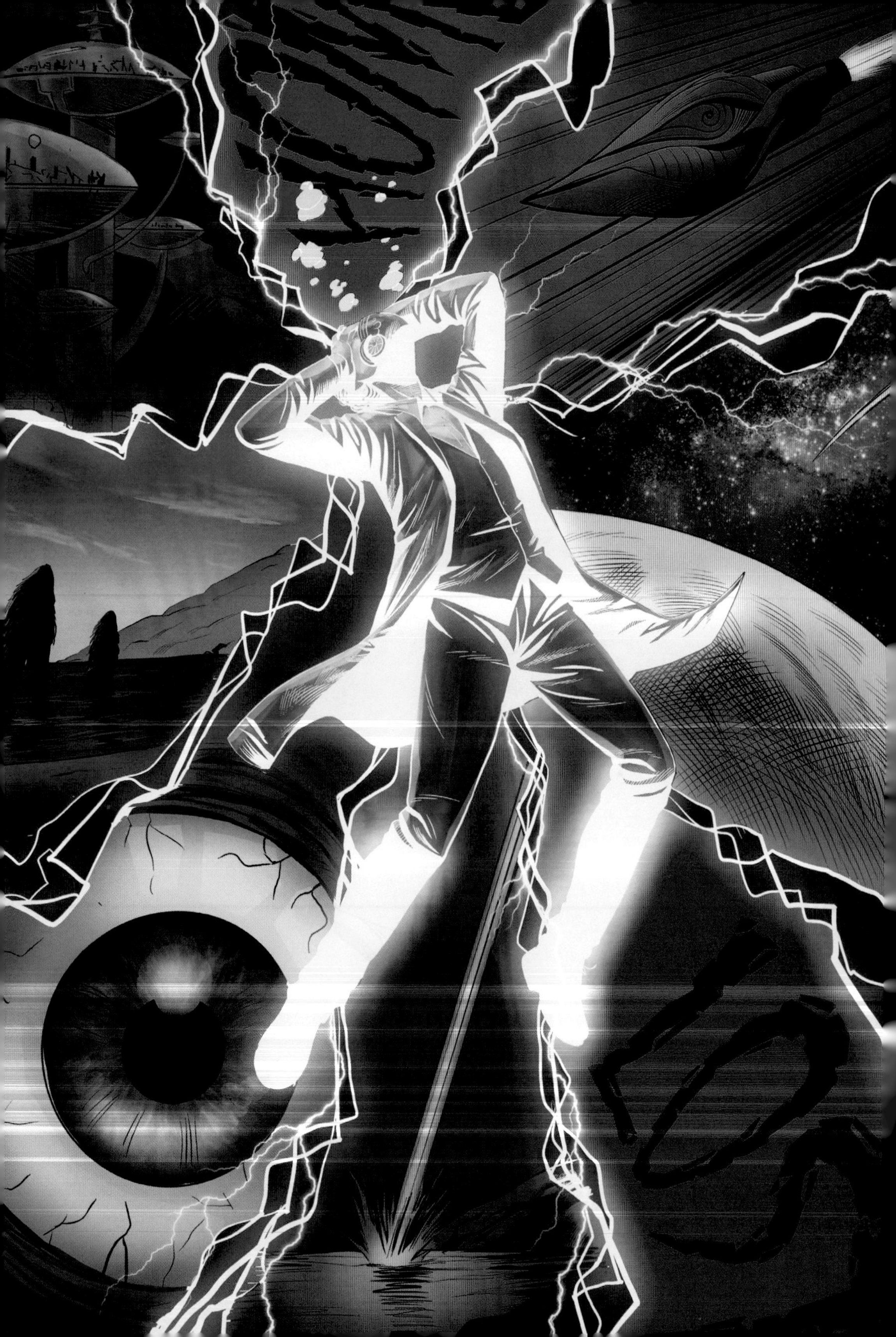

MARIANO LACLAUSTRA'S UNDERWATER SCENES ARE BROUGHT TO VIVID LIFE BY THE BEAUTIFUL COLORS OF **CARLOS CABRERA**.

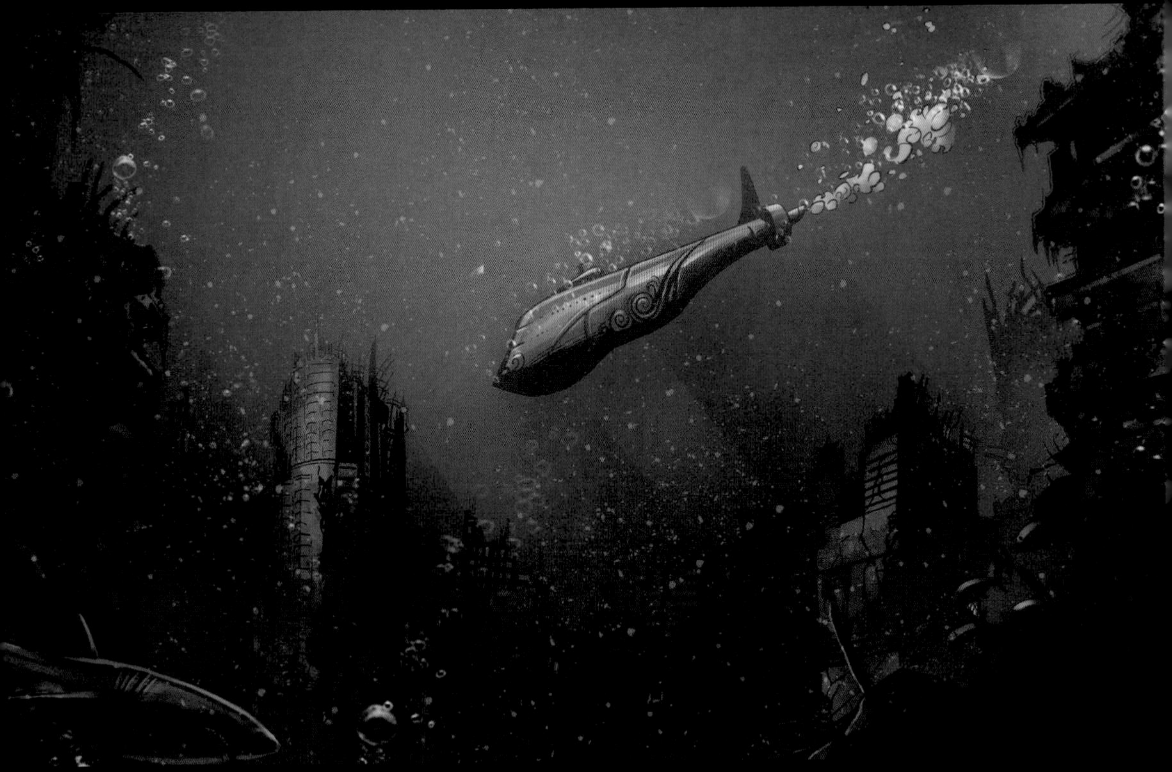

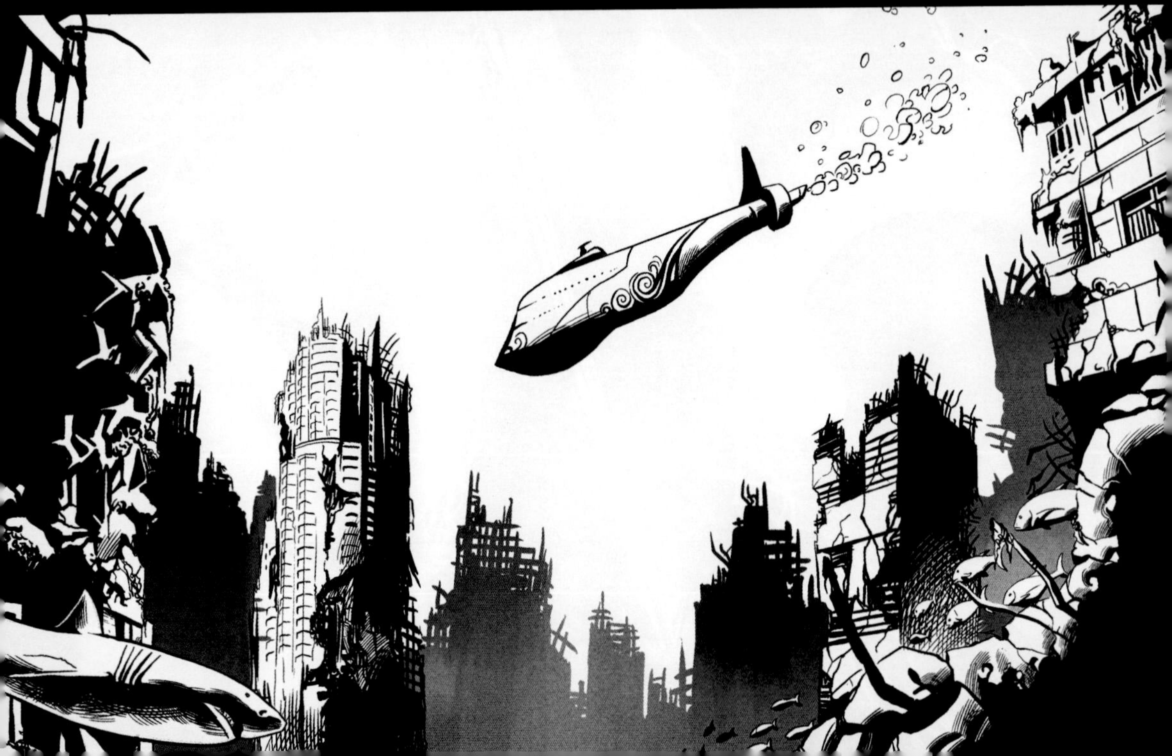

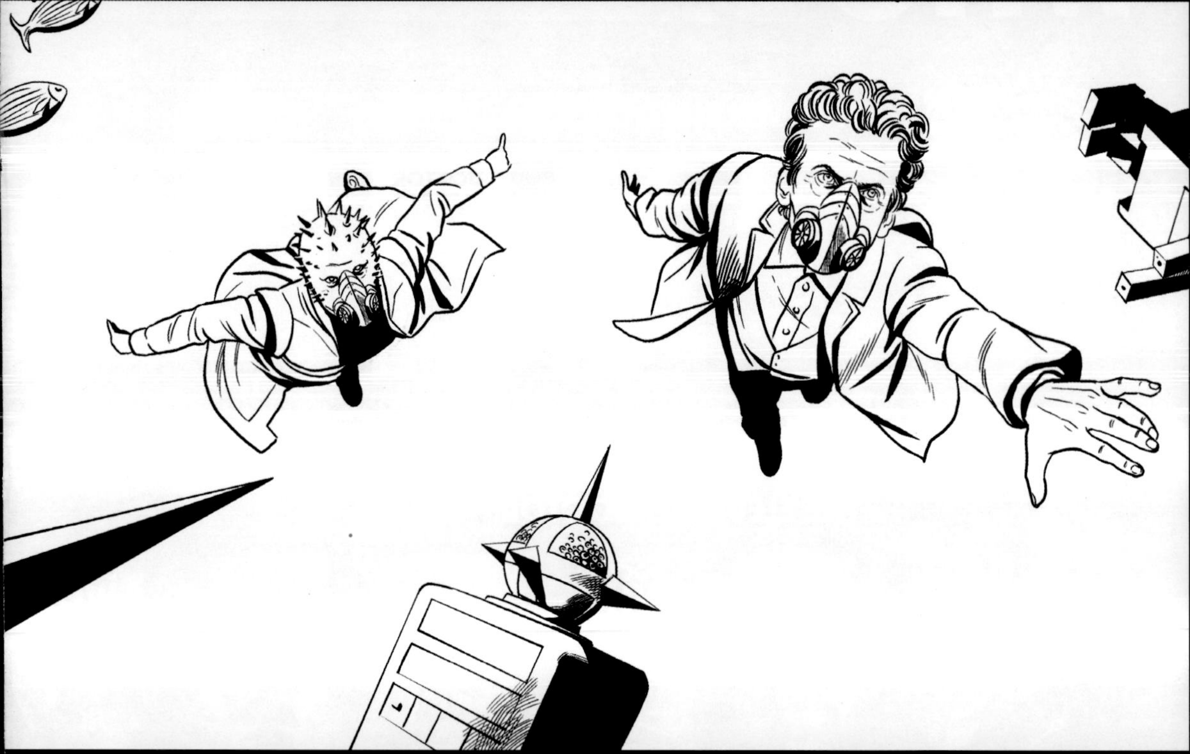

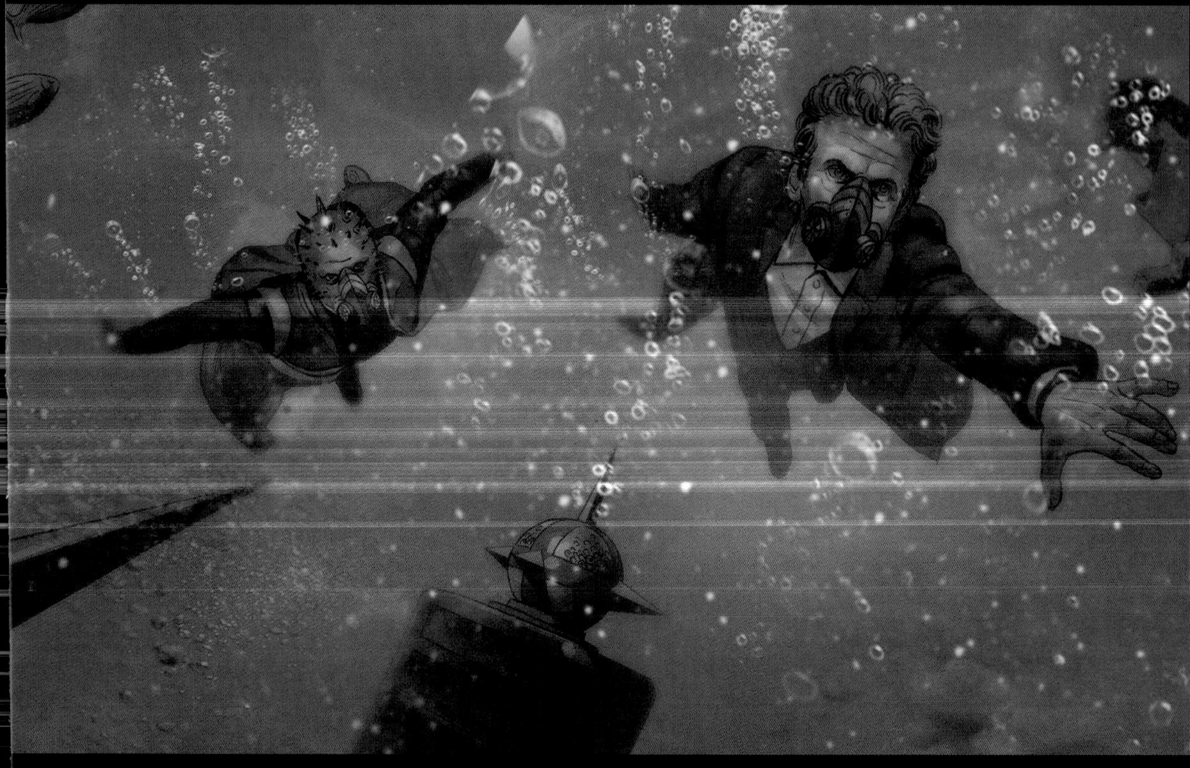

READER'S GUIDE

With so many amazing *Doctor Who* comics collections, it can be difficult know where to start! That's where this handy guide comes in.

THE TWELFTH DOCTOR – ONGOING

| VOL. 1: | VOL. 2: | VOL. 3: | YEAR TWO BEGINS! VOL. 4: | VOL. 5: |
| TERRORFORMER | FRACTURES | HYPERION | SCHOOL OF DEATH | THE TWIST |

THE ELEVENTH DOCTOR – ONGOING

| VOL. 1: | VOL. 2: | VOL. 3: | YEAR TWO BEGINS! VOL. 4: | VOL. 5: |
| AFTER LIFE | SERVE YOU | CONVERSION | THE THEN AND THE NOW | THE ONE |

THE TENTH DOCTOR – ONGOING

| VOL. 1: | VOL. 2: THE WEEPING | VOL. 3: THE | YEAR TWO BEGINS! VOL. 4: | VOL. 5: |
| REVOLUTIONS OF TERROR | ANGELS OF MONS | FOUNTAINS OF FOREVER | THE ENDLESS SONG | ARENA OF FEAR |

THE NINTH DOCTOR – ONGOING

| VOL. 1: WEAPONS OF | VOL. 2: | VOL. 3: | VOL. 4: |
| PAST DESTRUCTION | DOCTORMANIA | OFFICIAL SECRETS | SIN EATERS |

here are currently **four** ongoing *Doctor Who* series, each following a different Doctor.
ach ongoing series is **entirely self-contained**, so you can follow one, two, or all of your favorite Doctors, as you
vish! The ongoings are arranged in season-like **Years,** collected into roughly three books per Year. Feel free to start at
olume 1 of any series, or jump straight to Volume 4, for an equally-accessible new season premiere!
ach book, and every comic, features a **catch-up and character guide** at the beginning, making it easy to jump
n board – and each ongoing has a very different flavor, representative of that Doctor's era on screen.

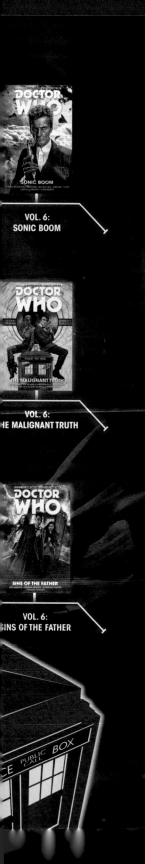

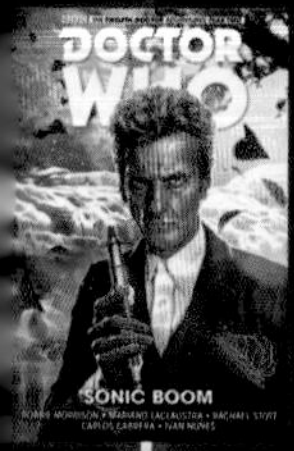
DOCTOR WHO
SONIC BOOM

VOL. 6:
SONIC BOOM

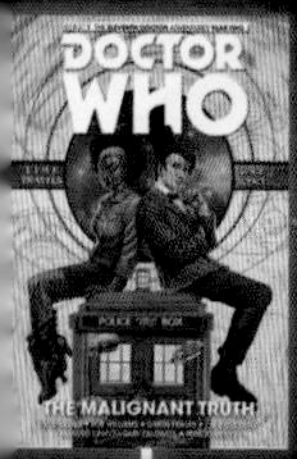
DOCTOR WHO
THE MALIGNANT TRUTH

VOL. 6:
HE MALIGNANT TRUTH

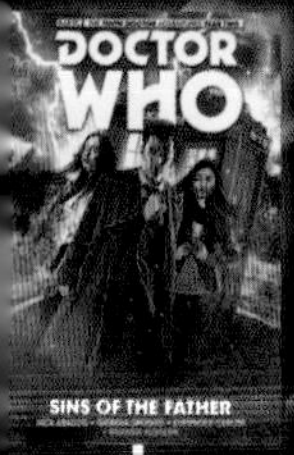
DOCTOR WHO
SINS OF THE FATHER

VOL. 6:
SINS OF THE FATHER

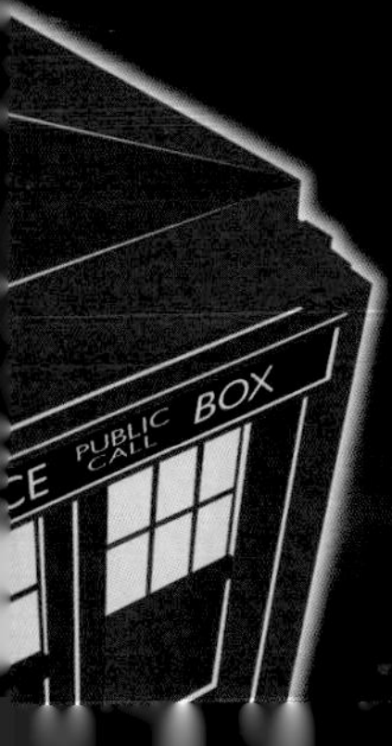
PUBLIC CALL BOX

THIRD DOCTOR

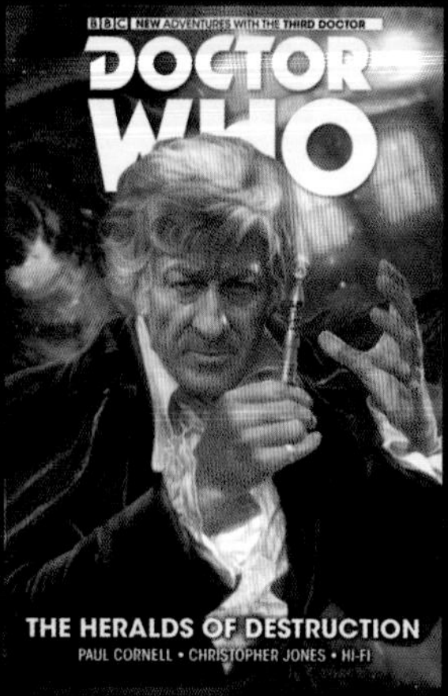
BBC NEW ADVENTURES WITH THE THIRD DOCTOR
DOCTOR WHO
THE HERALDS OF DESTRUCTION
PAUL CORNELL • CHRISTOPHER JONES • HI-FI

As well as the four ongoing series, we have published three major **past Doctor miniseries**, for the Third, Fourth, and Eighth Doctors. These volumes are each a **complete** and **self-contained** story.

There are also two fantastic **crossover event** volumes, starring the Ninth, Tenth, Eleventh, and Twelfth Doctors – the first, *Four Doctors*, sees an impossible team-up, and the second, *Supremacy of the Cybermen*, sees the monstrous cyborgs rule victorious over the universe... unless the Doctors can stop them!

FOURTH DOCTOR

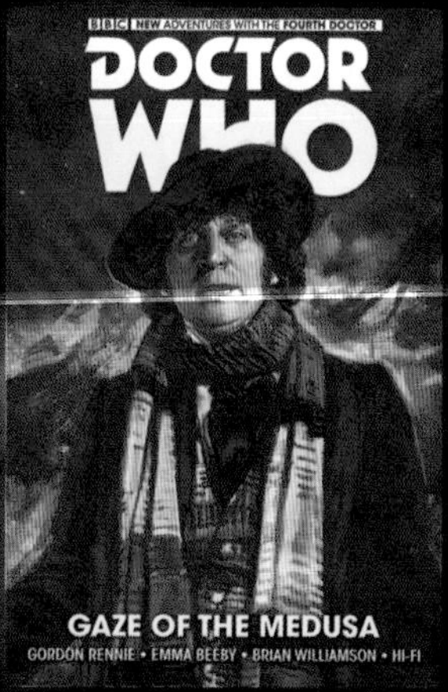
BBC NEW ADVENTURES WITH THE FOURTH DOCTOR
DOCTOR WHO
GAZE OF THE MEDUSA
GORDON RENNIE • EMMA BEEBY • BRIAN WILLIAMSON • HI-FI

FOUR DOCTORS

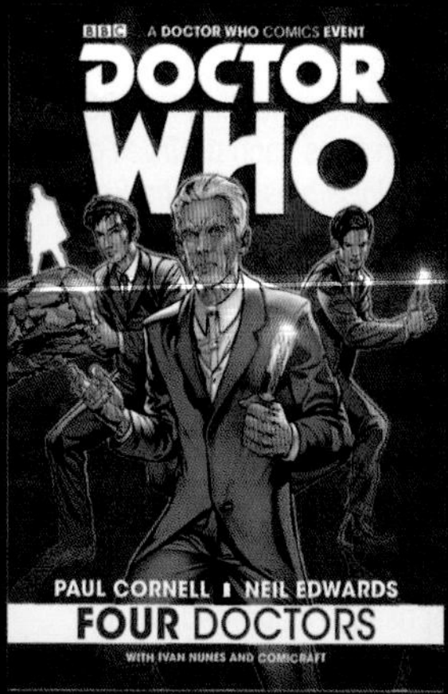
BBC A DOCTOR WHO COMICS EVENT
DOCTOR WHO
PAUL CORNELL NEIL EDWARDS
FOUR DOCTORS
WITH IVAN NUNES AND COMICRAFT

EIGHTH DOCTOR

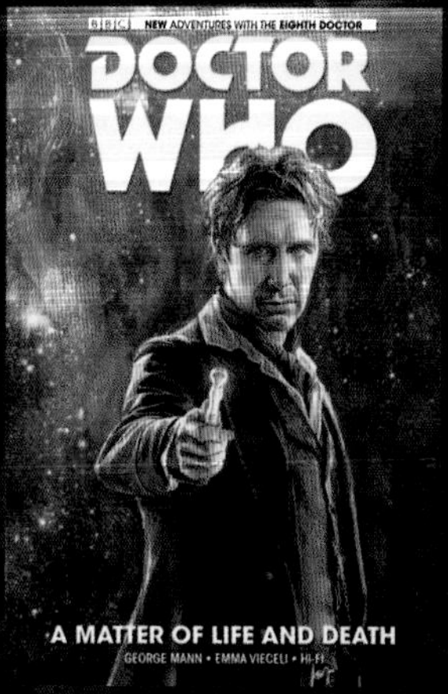
BBC NEW ADVENTURES WITH THE EIGHTH DOCTOR
DOCTOR WHO
A MATTER OF LIFE AND DEATH
GEORGE MANN • EMMA VIECELI • HI-FI

SUPREMACY OF THE CYBERMEN

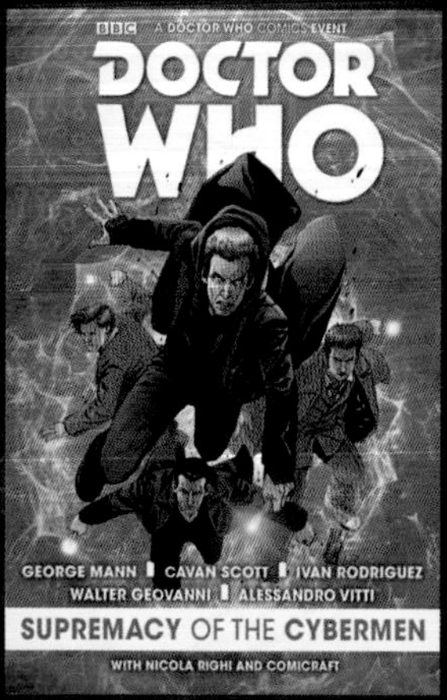
BBC A DOCTOR WHO COMICS EVENT
DOCTOR WHO
GEORGE MANN CAVAN SCOTT IVAN RODRIGUEZ
WALTER GEOVANNI ALESSANDRO VITTI
SUPREMACY OF THE CYBERMEN
WITH NICOLA RIGHI AND COMICRAFT

BIOGRAPHIES

George Mann is the writer behind the *Dark Souls, Warhammer 40,000, Doctor Who: Supremacy of the Cybermen,* and *Doctor Who: The Eighth Doctor* comics, and is the author of *Newbury & Hobbes,* as well as numerous short stories, novellas and an original *Doctor Who* audiobook. He lives near Grantham, UK, with his wife and children.

James Peaty is a British writer and director, whose comic works include *Supergirl, Batman, Green Arrow, Doctor Who: The Tenth Doctor* and *Doctor Who: The Eleventh Doctor.*

Mariano Laclaustra is a creator with a background in the Fine Arts. A freelance artist based in Argentina, he has worked with publishers across Europe and the United States, including for *Dark Horse Presents.* In between drawing and coloring comics, he teaches oil painting.

Warren Pleece is a comic artist and graphic novelist with over 20 years experience – working for 2000AD, DC, Dark Horse, and many more – on titles such as *True Faith, Hellblazer, The Great Unwashed, The Invisibles,* and *The Ballad of Franklin Bonisteel.*

Carlos Cabrera is an up-and-coming colorist with many diverse projects to his name, such as *Invincible Iron Man, Agents of Atlas,* and *Doctor Who.*

Hernán Cabrera is an Argentinian coloring talent who has worked on *Legion, Priest,* and *God is Dead,* among many others.

Hi-Fi, comprised of Brian and Kristy Miller, is a digital color studio founded in 1998. The team has worked on comics, animations, and video games. Most recently, they curated the *Femme Magnifique* anthology, celebrating inspirational women.